SEASONS
with
Storey

SEASONS

with

Storey

A Mother's Memoir

SANDEE
BARRY MILLS

This is a work of non-fiction. Nonetheless, most of the names have been changed, some have not. Sadly many friends/doctors/healers mentioned in this memoir have passed since the inception of this writing. For information on rare disease sites, see addendum.

100% of the proceeds will be donated to www.eaglemount.org, Bozeman, MT. Eagle Mount provides adaptive recreation and sport opportunities for people with disabilities and young people impacted by cancer.

Thank you for scanning here to visit Eagle Mount Bozeman:

Photos by Sandee unless indicated.

Published by: *StoreyLine* Publishing.

ISBN: 979-8-9925760-1-6 (paperback)
ISBN: 979-8-9925760-0-9 (eBook)

To

HAYDEN

*whose free smile got me out of bed every
morning and still makes me laugh.*

&

To every child and family struggling with a rare disease.

*Add to those of us with dyslexia…it's a challenging
and creative road but worth the ride.*

PART 1

2004
1998-2001

Chapter 1

When I slid into bed that night, I realized that it was the first day in four years I hadn't worried *every single second* about my 6-year-old daughter, Storey.

Chisel's muzzle tickled my nose, nudging me from dreams of unheard cries. She placed her paw on the edge of the bed and slipped in a kiss. I scratched her massive, tan chest before I ran my index finger between her forehead wrinkles and down her back. Through blurry eyes I watched heavy snow wiggle down the bedroom window. Miles away, blue-grey clouds hid Mount Ellis. On the deck below, snowflakes dressed our picnic table with wet lace. It was 2004, a typical late spring morning in Bozeman, Montana. I sat on the edge of my bed and dropped my head in my hands. I needed sun.

Our house was surprisingly quiet at 6:50 a.m. I listened for Storey's morning squeal, for her giggle like she's playing with invisible fairy friends dancing above her head. My head hurt from a night of choppy dreams; I craved fifteen more minutes of sleep. It had been years since I slept through the night without a kaleidoscope of bad dreams.

I squinted my dry eyes in the bathroom light. I looked out the window to the back pasture to check on my horses, Dagwood and Angel, and to look for visiting wildlife. The part of my brain where guilt lives lit up when I saw my horses shivering in their crude, unsheltered corral. I pulled my long-sleeved shirt over my right hand, stepped into our cold claw-foot bathtub under the window and wiped the condensation across the glass. On the second wipe, I noticed something else in the corral. I opened my eyes wider, cupped my hands to the window, held my breath, and looked again. What I thought was a fawn morphed into a baby horse walking in the snow next to Angel.

"Oh my God. John, look outside!"

I ran into the kids' room waving my arms and talking too fast. "Hayden, Storey, wake up, Angel had a baby! John! Can you bring the kids downstairs? I'm going outside!"

I cleared two stairs at a time and slipped on my Carhartt jacket before bolting out the door. Angel, our gray quarter horse with white hair and soft eyes, watched me stare at a short, curly black-and-white tail dance across the foal's brown butt. The sun peeked through an opening in the clouds and a beam of light landed on the foal's back. Steam rose from the moist mud under her hooves. When the baby horse turned and looked into my eyes, my heartbeat passed my knowledge of time and space.

Angel walked over to me. Her foal followed. White hair covered three quarters of the foal's face, including her right eye, which was outlined in black. White lightning bolts ran down both sides of her brown neck, large white paint splotches splashed her sides, and four falling white socks dressed her legs. Tears rolled down my face as I ran my fingers through her fuzzy chin hairs, smelling her colostrum breath. My legs and feet grew heavy. The gift before me was to be treasured forever, in my time.

I studied the corral and stared at the afterbirth, imagining Angel giving birth like a wild Montana horse. Angel's entire left side was caked with mud. I was grateful neither horse had become tangled in the rusted, loose barbed wire or died from exposure. I had been suspicious Angel was "in foal." The previous owner failed to mention the possibility.

Months before, I had reduced Angel and Dagwood's hay on warm winter days, not wanting a fat or colicky horse. However, had I known she was in foal during our sale bidding, Angel would be in someone else's corral.

Minutes later I was in the car with our kids heading to their Montessori preschool. I slipped in our week's favorite CD, *Steppenwolf*, and cranked the volume on "Born to Be Wild." We sang and bobbed our heads until I got a headache. Inside the school, I announced the birth of our foal to anyone within earshot. Eager to get back home to play with the little one, I skipped hot yoga and broke the speed limit driving through the spring slush. When I saw our foal, I rested my right hand on my heart and took a breath, then slid my arms across her warm back and down her leg before picking up her deer-sized hooves. She lay on the moist ground next to me, putting herself in a horse's most vulnerable position. I lifted her head into my lap and caressed the silky lightning bolt that decorated her neck. She relaxed like a giant golden retriever; it felt oddly natural.

Months before, we leased a horse named Dagwood. I read the chapter "Imprinting a Foal" from *The Complete Idiot's Guide to Horses*. The chapter resonated with me, even though I had no idea a foal would soon grace my pasture. The chapter emphasized touching, picking up their legs, and introducing it to scary things like plastic bags from day one. I got right to work.

All afternoon friends arrived to see the baby. She walked up to each visitor as though she had known humans for years. Angel stood by like a proud mother passing her newborn around without a care in the world. I called a recommended vet clinic, who sent out a vet and three young technicians.

"Do you know if the mare has had her shots?" the vet asked, kicking off a thick chunk of clay-like mud on his left boot against the back of his right. "Where is the afterbirth? We need to make sure it was completely expelled. Has the foal pooped yet?"

Embarrassed by my amateur horsemanship skills, I led them to the placenta drying in the mud.

"I bought this horse a few months ago, and I was suspicious she might be pregnant," I said, picking mud from Angel's right side. "When I called the woman to whom I handed over a wad of cash,

Spirit hours old.

she casually mentioned she knew this horse wanted to be a mother. Then she admitted she pulled her stallion off Angel twice. She didn't know when Angel had last been vaccinated. But I *can* tell you what the stallion looked like."

"Well, you're one lucky horse owner, a two-for-one. This could have turned out sad for everyone. We're going to give Angel a couple of standard vaccinations, which the foal will receive through nursing. Call us with any questions." The vet grinned like Harrison Ford. Before he was done speaking, a vet tech jammed a needle in each of Angel's muddy hind ends.

"Thank you," I said, letting the foal nibble on my shirt.

"And... aww... you shouldn't let the foal think it's okay to nibble on you like that. She'll create some bad habits," the vet told me.

Embarrassed again, I caught a glance between the vet technicians.

In the van on the way home from school I asked the kids, "What should we call our new little one?"

"How about Lightning, like a dark cloud?" Hayden said.

"Moonbeam?" I asked.

"Ho' 'bout Spirit?" Storey said.

"Yeah, Mom, remember that movie, *Spirit?* We love that movie, and she looks like Spirit's mother with those spots," Hayden said, flapping his fingers.

For a savored second I looked in the rearview mirror, where Storey's clear blue eyes invited possibilities, and Hayden's big toothy grin smiled at passing truck tires.

"Yes, we will call her Spirit. What a great idea, Storey!"

Spirit spun in circles and kicked up her heels next to Angel and Dagwood before trotting over to us. I lifted Storey's hand and opened her fingertips, and we traced the white lightning bolt on Spirit's neck, which felt like velveteen compared to her brown hair. Hayden reached up and the foal's chin hairs tickled the back of his hand. He jumped and his blonde hair bounced.

"Hey, Mom! Are we going to keep her?"

Dear *Storey*,

Dagwood was proud to help you ride. I can still see your giant smile and hear your giggle when you ran your small fingers down his white blaze or when Dad walked next to you when you rode. But Dad and I wanted to own a horse for you to ride after Dagwood's lease was over.

There are a few heavy-hearted memories I can't forget. One is December 2003, when you were 4½. We drove with Kristin and Molly west of town for ten miles to check on a horse for sale. You smiled, your face relaxed, and your eyes sparkled in the car the whole way.

The cold north wind swirled snow above the road; the car felt like it was floating. The closer we got to our destination, the more the wind blew and the sadder I got knowing how much the wind might steal your spirit.

Molly drove the car down a steep gravel driveway toward a woman and a cow dog.

"Hi puppy," you said.

The horse lady leaned into the car and said, "See those horses up on that hill? I'll grab a bucket of grain and be right back."

I squeezed you tight. Kristin and Molly rolled their eyes, wondering how long it would take to round up the skittish herd. I was bummed when the horse owner finally haltered a white horse, because I was hoping the horse for sale was the brown and white paint horse. Kristin and Molly got out, and a gust of wind swirled through the car. You gasped. I lifted you out of the car and the wind hit your face. You sucked air in and held your breath— your scared look.

"Let's go pet the horse," I said.

The horse owner handed Kristin the lead rope.

"She's a sweet quarter horse. Turned twenty this spring. We call her Mouse."

Mouse? I thought. What a perfectly awful name for a beautiful horse. You and I laced our fingers and stroked Mouse's neck, then headed to the car because a burst of cold wind hit our faces. Out the car window you and I watched Kristin and Molly take turns riding Mouse. Mouse remained perfectly calm under a stranger's ride in the wind. When it was my turn to ride, I left you in your car seat and told you I'd be right back. I nervously tightened my legs and Mouse trotted away. A jolt of adrenaline filled my body. Why didn't I wear a helmet? I'm a mother with young kids, I thought. Then I said, "Whoa!" and Mouse came to a dead stop, then turned to look at me as if saying, "Hey lady, you squeezed your legs, what did you expect?"

I knew Mouse was perfect.

When I opened the door and told you that I had just bought you a horse, your lip quivered and you whispered, "I want to ride horse."

My heart dropped. My hands began to shake. By then the wind was worse and the temperature had dropped further. I patted your tears, then mine.

Little Princess Storey, you rarely cried for something you wanted and didn't get. You were different that way. You had an innate understanding of how the world worked. Your cry was an ancestral love of horses and for the freedom you felt when you were on and around horses. Your cry was for your physical limitations. Your cry was my beautiful daughter who never had 2-year-old tantrums or asked for anything but to love and to be loved.

I felt dizzy. I had let you down. I didn't know what to do. The horses were already running up the hill into the wind. You calmed down and smiled when I suggested we ride Kristin's horse, Dunnie, when we dropped her off. But for the rest of the ride home Kristin, Molly and I wiped our eyes with soiled tissues.

I'm so sorry you couldn't ride Mouse that day.

I love you,

Mom

Dear *Mom*,

When you and Kristin lifted me onto Dunnie's back, I closed my eyes and felt his warm body and his heart against mine. The wind was gone. The sun peeked from behind the clouds to kiss my face. Right then I knew I would never forget what it felt like to feel the warmth of a horse. I giggled because I felt so free; so alive. Dunnie spoke to me and said I could ride him whenever I wanted, and he'd be very careful. I thanked him. And then I saw the look you and Kristin gave each other. It was a sigh of relief because you knew I was happy again.

Mom, I'm always happy, even if I cry. But I'm happiest on a horse.

Thanks for bringing horses into my life.

I love you,

Storey

P.S. I'm glad we changed Mouse's name to Angel.

Chapter 2

In 1991, thirteen years before Spirit was born, I studied a confident, dark-haired, blue-eyed man with a splash of meekness walk through the glass doors of Kinko's Copies where I worked. He placed a four-inch binder on the counter. I pushed my co-worker aside. *He is the kind of man I want to marry,* I thought.

"Take your break, I got this," I said to my co-worker.

Reviewing his massive copy project, I assigned myself as his project manager. A few weeks later I used my talents to draw him a picture riddle and checklist, asking him on a date by faxing it to his office. For three days I walked around with a stomachache before he responded. He couldn't go, but at least he had left the box—*sorry, I have a girlfriend*—unchecked.

Persistence paid off two months later when I faxed him another picture riddle. We dated a couple years, and I knew John was the kind of lifelong partner I wanted: brilliant, athletic, didn't drink too much, and he had a healthy relationship with money. I knew arguing about money wouldn't be on the top of our list, like it had been with my parents.

Clearly my female biology was aging. According to my life plan, I purposely delayed serious commitments by dating free-spirited party boys until I was ready to settle down. Being a summer baby myself with fond memories of birthday parties in the sun, I wanted my children to experience the same. Knowing that the women in our family have always been very fertile, I wasn't surprised to conceive right on schedule. Two years into our marriage I was pregnant with Hayden at the age of 34.

When I shared the news of my pregnancy with friends, they felt obligated to relay their successful birthing plans and nightmares, or how I could avoid a C-section by delivering my baby in our living room in a child's plastic swimming pool, with the aid of essential oils and chanting under the care of a midwife without liability insurance. Too much information swirled in my head, and I feared something horrible would happen, or that I'd end up with a C-section. Then I had this dream.

> *I'm standing on our porch, looking east at the hilly pasture behind our house. The sound of rumbling shakes the porch. I look left; a herd of elk runs through the pasture, and a herd of buffalo follows. The buffalo stop abruptly right in front of me. Their dust cloud clears, and in unison they look at me. They form a circle, leaving a graceful opening. In the middle of the circle a rare white buffalo calf appears. It takes a few steps toward me and the buffalo step back, bowing to the calf. I can see and feel the strength of White Buffalo Calf Woman. When the calf's eyes meet mine, I hear: "Don't worry, your baby sent this dream to you letting you know that everything is going to be alright."*

When Hayden decided to stay in his perfectly cozy nest two weeks past his due date, void of any pre-labor pains, red flags went up and the doctors scheduled his induction. For thirty hours under a Pitocin drip trying to soften my cervix "naturally," I blamed myself for blocking the birthing hormone because I gave the fear of childbirth too much energy. So, I called upon the energy of White Buffalo Calf Woman. And I focused on the stuffed white buffalo calf named Miracle, resting on the table across from my delivery bed. My mother had sent me Miracle after hearing about my dream. A few hours later I signed the C-section consent forms after Hayden's heart rate suddenly dropped. A half hour later the doctors lifted Hayden above the blue surgical drape on June 13th, 1996. He smiled at me before he cried.

Two years later, my hands studied my inflated belly. In the quiet morning under the shadows of Mount Ellis, I anticipated the surgical arrival of my second baby. Beyond pre-delivery nerves, I sensed that this baby was special.

I thought of Hayden's arrival two years earlier and my sister Cindy's first-born, Meredith, sixteen years before. Cindy had a sensitive constitution and she successfully birthed four babies, and I thought about all the women in the world who survived childbirth in horrific conditions. *If they can do it, so can I.* But the words "geriatric pregnancy" spinning in my head weren't helpful. I wasn't mentally ready to deliver our new baby any more than I was when Hayden was born.

When I was in my late twenties, I dreamed of playing in the mountains under the Big Sky as long as I could, and deleted thoughts of driving a van with dried McDonald's fries and smashed bananas on the floor and living in a house that smelled like apple juice and diapers.

Then years zipped by, and luckily, I was still on schedule with my plans, and mentally preparing to have my second C-section for my last child at 37.

John and I chose to be surprised by the sex of both our babies. I nudged him awake, taking one last glance at Mount Ellis before heading to Hayden's room.

"Hayden, time to get up, remember you're having an early play date," I said, rubbing his back.

The doctors chose Wednesday, July 1st (1998) to perform their magic—out of their convenience, not mine or my baby's. At the time, a repeat C-section after a previous "failed natural delivery" was standard procedure. Jokingly, I asked the doctor if he could retrieve my baby on July 4th. Ultimately, I wanted my children to enter this world on their watch, but I couldn't control everything, and I wasn't interested in birthing complications.

At seven o'clock I was wheeled into the operating room, unable to feel the lower half of my body and surrounded by big eyes and blue masks. I saw the distress in John's eyes, and he squeezed my hand until a blue curtain went up, blocking his view of the doctor's scalpel. I had been there before, but that time I was under light sedation, so I was mostly conscious. My anxiety grew. All my senses buzzed like an old radio antenna. I attempted to manage my thought patterns, but I couldn't shake my apprehension. I didn't know if the anxiety was solely coming from my brain or if I was picking up on my baby's fear, who was about to jump off a cliff into this confusing world.

I reminded myself that this medical team had successfully performed thousands of C-section deliveries. So, I took a few deep breaths and asked the surgical team for a tummy tuck or an appendectomy since they were already in there. Doctors' voices hovered, then I felt as though my ribs where being punched. I closed my eyes, found my breath again and pictured the white buffalo calf.

What felt like a second and a lifetime later, I was pulled back into my body when I heard the words, "It's a girl!" John wiped his moist cheeks. Over my left shoulder I tracked our daughter in the doctor's arms. A shot of tingles filled my body when I noticed my baby's skin was reddish-blue and not crying. I strained my neck and eyes to read Dr. Feist, our pedestrian's expression.

Our baby seemed fragile, scared, beautiful, and *so* not ready to be here. Dr. Feist massaged her feet, and I heard him whisper, "Come on." I closed my eyes and squeezed John's hand. Time paused, and after what felt like hours, we heard her wail! John followed Dr. Feist to the nursery, and I was sent to recovery. More than two hours passed while the drugs played tricks on me, and I wondered what would happen to Storey and Hayden if I had reached for heaven's portal. Strangely, I knew my baby wasn't any more ready to face the future than I was. The peace, the euphoria I felt after I had Hayden, was out of reach. A somber exhaustion confronted me. I dug deep and wondered what the hell was wrong with me—I had just delivered a planned miracle; a girl who we named, Storey.

A few hours later John introduced me to Storey. A full head of black hair stuck out of her blanket cocoon. John puzzled her into my elbow and time ceased. With her Mills appetite and lower lip, she latched on like a professional. For the next four days Storey slept in a plastic nursery bin next to me, and even though I physically healed quickly, I milked my health insurance for the maximum stay in the hospital after a C-section. In the nursery, Storey and I were loved. The nurses kissed Storey on her forehead before they handed her to me like she was one of their own. I wanted to be that loving, but my hormonal confusion questioned my competence. Certainly, John would never understand my gloominess. *I had just birthed an angel. I had it all.* But back then, women's hormones and their influence on mental health weren't something we knew a lot about.

At home one day, out of the corner of my eye, I noticed a brown tail and a boy's small truck T-shirt and oversized cut-off Levi shorts flash by. Hayden lifted Storey's blanket for a peek and touched her forehead with his left index finger. Wonder crossed his face. Then Chisel sniffed her blanket.

"Chisel, this is our sister," Hayden said. Then they ran off.

Chapter 3

I n the 1950s, my father, Jack, and my mother, Pat, met while working in Yellowstone National Park during their college summers. One summer my father was handed a firearm and a ranger's hat with little training. Eventually my parents settled in Salt Lake City, and for the first thirteen years of my life, our family visited Yellowstone Park each summer and for weeks we restored our small, run-down cabin along Denny Creek outside of West Yellowstone.

Each summer my sister and I whined and complained, knowing our neighborhood friends back home in Salt Lake were playing kick-the-can and riding their bikes to 7-Eleven for candy. Montana was so boring. We watched the Povah Black Angus cows graze and the tall grass change color in the open range next to us, while we piled rotten wood and cleaned mice poop out of old sheds in our back pasture. It took a few summers before my sister and I were struck by the Big Sky Country spell.

We said goodbye to our cabin in 1975 and our family moved from Salt Lake City to Davis, California. Years later I took my parents' advice and headed to Yellowstone to work three of my college summers. After graduating in the spring of 1984 from California State with a Fine Arts degree and confused about my role with newly divorced parents, I returned to Yellowstone for two more summers. My folks were right: working in Yellowstone was an experience and a gift I have kept with me forever.

After my fifth summer in Yellowstone, I headed back to Davis without a plan. But after three weeks, I felt the Big Sky calling.

"Mom, I'm moving to Bozeman," I told her.

"There aren't any jobs, plus you'll hate the winters," she said.

"I have five hundred dollars. I'm going."

"That's not enough, you need a cleaning deposit, first and last month's…" Ignoring her criticism, I walked away.

"Dad, I'm moving to Bozeman," I told my father standing in his driveway the next day.

He helped me pack, and I knew he was secretly envious. He knew Montana well, having spent many summers in the Montana forests working for the United States Forest Service.

In the fall, among evening shadows and songs of crickets and toads, I said goodbye to both my parents (in their separate driveways). We exchanged long hugs and "I love you's" seldom shared. My father knew I wasn't coming back. My mother hoped I would.

The next day, secured with my backpack and my old ten-speed bike, I headed toward the Rocky Mountains in my red Nissan truck. Fifteen hours later, sick from junk food and chain smoking to stay awake, I touched Bozeman's welcome sign. Four years later I bought a house, and seven years later John and I were married.

Before I went to the hospital to deliver Storey, I stuffed flowerpots with annuals to create a kaleidoscope of color slinking down our porch steps. My dad (Grandjack) and his wife Valerie (Grandma Valerie) arrived a week after Storey and I came home. Valerie presented us with a beautiful gift box carrying a baby quilt fresh off her sewing machine. We welcomed their visit; they fed us, Dad made repairs and planted blue spruce and aspen trees in our yard. Their help gave me space to heal and bond with Storey.

After a week of volunteering his assistance, my father grew antsy. He wanted to continue our family tradition of experiencing Yellowstone at an early age. He, Valerie, the kids and I packed his white Suburban and headed towards Gardiner, Montana. We stopped for a break at Canyon Campground, a favorite place near Yankee Jim Canyon where car-sized boulders had tumbled to the valley thousands of years ago. Grandjack tried to educate Hayden on the area's geologic formations. "It's never too soon," Dad always said. Grandma Valerie nervously held the back of Hayden's shirt while he climbed the boulders. Storey and I stayed in the car to nurse. I leaned my head back, closed my eyes and let the sun filter through the clean window to warm my face. In that transient moment I heard Hayden's voice in the distance and felt Storey's warm body against my skin.

Seconds later, the Suburban doors shut. I anticipated the long drive ahead and possible car sickness from Dad's braking style. Miles later, Storey fussed and Dad sighed impatience by clearing his throat. My anxiety grew—the road trip to Yellowstone didn't seem as exciting as it had that morning. Eventually, we made our way around the lake to Old Faithful. I bought a Wilcoxson's mint-chip ice cream cone at the Upper Hamilton Store, where I worked in 1982, to "settle my stomach." The lingering geyser sulfur smell reminded me of running to watch Old Faithful erupt under a full moon with my coworkers.

Before we left Old Faithful, I nursed Storey again, knowing we had more than a hundred miles to drive. I changed Storey's diaper in the back of Dad's Suburban; she had diarrhea. On the drive home I said little. I was worried and physically felt sick. I couldn't wait to get out of that hot car and take a nap with Storey under our bedroom fan. We were almost home when I noticed she felt feverish.

Dad cleared his throat and said, "Want to go into town and pick up some salmon?"

My shoulders sank; I looked at Valerie. "No, I just want to go straight home. We feel sick back here. I don't care what we have for dinner."

Once home I took Storey upstairs and closed the door. I turned on the ceiling fan, shut the shades and cuddled Storey in the crook of my right arm. She cried when I slid off the bed. I gently picked her up and walked downstairs where a simple dinner waited. The table was beautifully set to Valerie's and my father's high standards.

After a long night with Storey, I took her to see Dr. Feist. His nurse said Storey had a temperature slightly over one hundred degrees. Forty-five minutes later, I saw the shadow of Dr. Feist's footsteps under the door of our exam room. I felt fortunate we were able to see him, who came to the hospital on his day off when Storey's birth was scheduled.

"Hello Miss Storey," Dr. Feist said.

I cried.

"Her heart sounds good, but her fever is a concern at her age. I feel we should take a blood sample and run some tests," he said moving his shoulders.

The nurse came in carrying a caddy of supplies. "You're not going to want to see this," she said.

"Yes, I want to be here."

They held Storey down. She screamed. Her entire body turned red.

"Sandee, believe me, you'll want to wait outside the door," the nurse repeated, looking up at me.

Reluctantly I left the room. I felt helpless and ill. The walls floated; I didn't have knees. I slid my body down the wall and dropped my forehead on my crossed arms. A few minutes later the nurse, smelling like antibacterial gel, came out of the room with Storey. I pushed against the wall to stand like I was drunk, and she placed Storey back into my arms.

"The doctor just called the nursery. Storey is going to be admitted for a few days."

"What do you think is wrong? She's only two weeks old," I said, sniffing my running nose and wiping my wet face.

Dr. Feist came back around the corner. "We don't know, but we will look at the blood tests for infections and monitor her fever and wait."

"Wait?"

I used the back of my sleeve to wipe my nose and followed the nurse through the maze of hallways to the nursery. She lifted Storey out of my hands, placed her in a small plastic tub and attached white wires to her tender body. A neonatal nurse recognized me and gave me a hug. I cried. Helplessly, I rested my hand on Storey's back and whispered our song: *"Hush little baby… don't say a word…"* My voice wove through the attached wires and beeping machines. Since the delivery ward was slow, they assigned me a familiar room.

That night I stared at a beam of light reflecting from the hall. *What did I do wrong? Was it the glass of wine I had night before last? Did the long car ride through Yellowstone make her sick? Was it the pain medication I was prescribed after my C-section even though I only took a few? Where did she pick up a virus?* I thought I had protected her at a recent outdoor party by nursing and keeping her away from onlookers and their children's dirty fingers.

For years I wondered.

The blood work was inconclusive, but at least it didn't show something horrific. Dr. Feist concluded Storey had a virus and reassured me I did nothing wrong. After four fitful days and nights, Storey's temperature slowly went away and we were released from the hospital.

The experience reignited my fear of illnesses. I was preoccupied with where Hayden's hands had been and where they were headed. If he got ill, Storey was next. I wasn't ready for another serious illness. I lived on edge and never offered play dates—not a great idea since we lived out of town without neighborhood kids. Yet, when I dropped Hayden off at preschool I was able to turn off my phobia, reminding myself that Hayden and his immunity needed the exposure.

Other mothers' variety of comfort zones have always amazed me. Like mothers who pick up dropped pacifiers from public floors, lick it themselves, and stick it back into their baby's mouth without a thought. Or mothers that let their babies crawl on bacteria-laced airport carpeting while eating. Those mothers, I envied.

Storey began to thrive after a few months of occasional diarrhea. I worried less. But she often cried after breastfeeding. She wasn't happy being fed every two and a half to three hours the way Hayden and my friends' babies had so easily adjusted to the nursing schedule outlined in the trendy book *Babywise*. It didn't work for Storey. When I withdrew my breast, she worked herself into a frenzy; her whole body turned beet red. After several doctor visits they concluded she was just fussy, not colicky. Later I realized I probably wasn't producing enough milk after feeding her through almost two episodes of

Seinfeld—including commercials—because my weight had dropped significantly.

Hayden was so content with observing the world after feeding; always happy with just the minimal amount of everything. With him I thought I was the perfect mom, doing everything right, until I wasn't with Storey. Finally, at five months I offered Storey solid baby food. She gobbled it up like a Mills and she stopped crying.

Like Hayden, she was in the tenth percentile for height and weight, meeting all the normal developmental milestones. At seven months she began to "crab-crawl," scooching across the floor pulling with both arms, sliding her left hip under and pushing off with her right bent leg. This didn't send off alarms in the doctor's office, but I knew bilateral crisscrossing with traditional crawling activates both brain hemispheres and is essential to hardwire new neuro connections.

Chapter 4

Surprisingly to many people, Y2K didn't send the world into chaos on January 1st, 2000. For us, the new year meant Storey was old enough to join Hayden at his Montessori preschool a few mornings a week. She looked forward to school; thrilled to get busy. Hayden was still apprehensive, skeptical after attending more than a year. I loved knowing they were learning, socializing, and being stimulated in ways I was unable to provide. And it also gave me the freedom to exercise and reconnect with real friends, instead of staying home and worrying if Erica was going to get married again in *All My Children*.

Like most siblings, Hayden and Storey were very different. One evening during dinner Hayden spilled his milk for the third night in a row. I hid my laughter because that was my trick to get out of drinking my milk when I was his age. But like puppy training, engagement fuels encouragement. Hayden was funny and very inquisitive—his brain raced, his body reacted, he didn't have time to worry about his immediate environment. Whereas Storey sat politely devouring her dinner. Little did I know that those toddler days of spilled milk, and the frustration of keeping my house picked up, should have been treasured. No one told me the truth—time doesn't crawl when we're raising little versions of ourselves. It zooms by when you turn your head.

Storey was agile and deliberate as she played; it was her personality. She didn't bounce off the walls or spill everything like Hayden. However, on a warm spring day in 2000 at preschool pick-up, Storey's teacher said, "I'm a little worried, Storey seems shaky and is unintentionally spilling her favorite pouring lesson. She didn't used to do that."

I shrugged off her concern as a tired day for Storey. But John and I both noticed she walked slower than most kids her age. We figured it was growing pains, or constant colds, or being smaller than average. By July, when all the grandparents visited, they too commented. I tried to reassure them it was nothing and she would grow out of it. Taking advice from the older generation, who didn't understand unconventional ways of raising kids, wasn't one of my strengths. We noticed Storey wanted to sit more and hang out in our laps when other kids were over. We just thought it was her personality.

By September, we took her to see Dr. Feist again. After his examination, he had *that* look in his eyes and sent a referral to Dr. Black, a pediatric neurologist ninety-nine miles away. He also wrote a prescription to see Sheri, the best pediatric physical therapist in town. The earliest appointment I could get to see Dr. Black was in six weeks. Hopefully that was a sign that he was worth the wait. What we didn't know at the time was that only two pediatric neurologists practiced in the entire state of Montana. Concerned friends suggested we immediately head out of Montana to a large children's hospital or the Mayo Clinic, but John and I agreed to start with Dr. Feist's recommendation.

A week after I made the appointment with Dr. Black, my friends organized a back-to-school mother's weekend away. And I was up for a distraction. Seven of us handed detailed notes to our husbands, packed spa accessories, bottles of our favorite wine, and headed to my in-law's cabin in Big Sky. We turned up the music, slid into our favorite worn-in flannels, served antipasto, clinked wine glasses, and covered our faces with pore-nurturing masks. By the time the Brazilian wax kit and the kitchen scissors came out, we were glasses deep and ready to bare all.

I was grateful for the laughter and for these friendships that had developed because of our children. Toasts continued through the night, and I vowed to myself not to talk too much about my fears seeing Dr. Black. By late evening we were relaxed, waxed and raw. Our lipstick-stained wine glasses decorated the living room, and we settled down in front of the fireplace for chick flicks.

An hour after falling asleep, still drunk and almost hungover, images of Storey smiling and crying swirled in my head. I rolled around for the rest of the night, unable to sleep. I placed five pillows around my body for security, turned on the TV and watched stupid infomercials until I was so disgusted with myself that I tossed the remote across the room. My head pounded after a brief sleep and a heavy blanket of sickening fear came over me. I had visions of pushing Storey around in a wheelchair, driving around in a handicapped van, moving out of our wonderful house. *You idiot. Why the fuck did you drink too much?* In my deepest, darkest moment I pictured Storey's death. I couldn't shake the terror. I prayed for the sun to appear, to cleanse my self-induced nightmare. At the first sign of dawn, I walked outside and looked up at the 11,000-foot peak of Lone Mountain. The girls' weekend wasn't fun anymore. I wanted to go home and hug Storey, and to feel normal.

The next six weeks both flew by and crawled. John and I knew seeing a neurologist was serious. Dr. Black's office was adjacent to the hospital in Helena. I felt nauseated walking into the 1970s institute-style building. Our footsteps echoed across the scratched linoleum floor. On the outside we were a happy, normal family, but one step through the glass doors a doctor might paint us a different picture.

At the appointment I filled out the mounds of paperwork as we patiently waited for over an hour among dirty toys and scattered books. Storey was already scheduled for an EEG (electroencephalogram) to detect seizures, and a brain MRI (magnetic resonance imaging). She was so patient, considering she was famished since we couldn't give her any breakfast before the anesthesia. Hayden's curiosity of everything there was refreshing. The toys I packed were of no interest. We liked having him with us; he made us laugh, a normality we depended on.

Dr. Black caught me off guard when he walked into the exam room and focused on Storey, averting our eyes. There was no putting us at ease; his silent candor made my stomach drop, and Storey felt the stress. She cried having to walk a few steps for the strange man who looked like a science professor. After a few minutes of examination, he said Storey had ataxia. I wrote the word down in a small notebook and we were escorted into a strange, dark room. A nice nurse handed Storey a Dixie cup of anesthesia, but it looked like bubbling Kool-Aid in dry ice. It was chloral hydrate. Even the name made me nervous. I questioned the nurse and the doctor about the liquid.

They both said, "We give this to kids all the time, she'll be fine."

A half hour later, Storey swallowed it. We waited for the medicine to make her sleepy, but her body reacted to the chloral hydrate like she was on a bad acid trip. For more than an hour her arms flailed; she kicked, moaned, and her eyes rolled around. She fought like hell. I felt like we were torturing her. I sang her our favorite hummingbird song, but nothing calmed her down. A different RN, who was dressed like she had just walked out of a scene from *One Flew Over the Cuckoo's Nest,* gave Storey a second cup of chloral hydrate. Storey swallowed without knowing what she was doing. John and I took turns holding her, and finally, she fell asleep.

We wanted the day to end.

Like most people, I hate hospitals, yet I'm fascinated by stories of why people land in a place they most fear. When I was at my wit's end from waiting for the nurses to take Storey for testing, Hayden and I walked down the stark hallway. The door shut behind us, and my throat tightened. There wasn't anything comfortable about this hospital. I craved cozy carpet under my tired feet and walls displaying pictures of healthy, smiling people. I could have done without the alcohol-smelling, weathered-looking man carrying a hospital discharge bag who stared at us with bloodshot eyes.

"What's his problem?" the man asked, looking down at Hayden.

My stomach fell. Hayden and I hugged the opposing wall. Hayden grabbed my leg like he'd seen a ghost. On the fifth doorknob we tried, we finally found our way back to our waiting room. John and Storey were gone. I fell into a chair and Hayden crawled into my lap. I closed my eyes, hummed, and waited. After Storey's MRI, John carried her back into our room for her EEG. She slept unnaturally deep in John's lap, sticky wires protruding from her curly hair.

The EEG revealed no seizure activity, and to our relief everything appeared normal. We took turns holding Storey as her body tried to shake the anesthesia. Her body twitched like she had delirium tremors trying to reenter this world. For more than an hour we waited in the main waiting room for the MRI films to be developed. John and I tried not to stare at the other waiting patients.

Screams echoed from down the hall. A heavyset lady entered; like a strait jacket, her arms were wrapped around an obstreperous boy. She heaved the boy, who looked around ten years old, on the couch and said, "Help! I just can't handle him!" The boy shrieked louder and buried his head upside down in the crook of the couch. It was obvious they didn't have an appointment, and the staff carried on as though this was a common dance.

Another mother waited. Her tall teenaged daughter, who had multiple challenges, sat quietly in her lap. The love emanating from that mother rippled confidence and a knowing to me that I too could endure, if need be. We had nowhere else to go. My curiosity spun; I wanted to know the diagnosis of these special lives. I gave both mothers an apologetic smile for staring while we waited to hear Storey's future.

Another exhausting hour passed. Storey's body continued to flail, to fight off the drug. I glanced every two seconds at the receptionist's plexiglass window that separated the neurological problem patients from the medical staff. At last, our names were called as though we held a number at Baskin-Robbins. In slow motion, we followed Dr. Black down the dark hall. The only sounds we heard were of the large floppy X-ray films that he carried. He slid the films under the light table brackets. I studied the furrow between his eyes trying to read his poker face, and pictured trimming his long, bushy eyebrows. I had watched enough medical programs to know pediatric neurology was one profession where emotional detachment was necessary.

"There is no tumor, that's the first thing to rule out. The films look pretty good, except there's a little cerebellar hypoplasia—an underdeveloped cerebellum. Otherwise, I'd call these MRI films mostly normal," he said with relaxed eyebrows.

Then the doctor pointed out a very tiny spot that looked a little unusual, but he wasn't too worried about the hypoplasia. With a normal EEG reading, we couldn't have asked for a better outcome. John and I let out sighs of relief. John hugged Storey and I squeezed Hayden's sticky hand.

The doctor pulled out a blue pad of paper and checked off about fifteen boxes for blood tests. Thyroid, CBC, and Vitamin D were the only ones I recognized. He noticed our confused faces. "Let's wait for all these blood tests before worrying too much," he said.

And that was that. Even though we didn't get any conclusive information, John and I couldn't get through the clinic's automatic doors fast enough. Outside, I gasped and bent over. Limp in John's arms, Storey threw up right outside the door. Sympathetic to those with emetophobia—fear of vomit—I returned and informed the hospital greeter that their welcome mat was decorated with fresh pink throw-up.

The drive from Helena to Bozeman wasn't enough time for the drug to wear off. I pictured each mile as a cleansing wind blowing away what might have been. The further we drove from there, the better John and I felt. Colorful fall trees passed my car window in a blur, and I thought of my mother, who was concurrently receiving a toxic dose of chemotherapy for stage 4 breast cancer. I thought of Chisel, whose black and tan muzzle would be waiting at the top of the stairs to offer us comfort. I turned around and looked in the back seats at the two beautiful children I had put off having until I was ready for the unknown. Everything seemed perfect. Storey was going to be fine—I just knew it.

"Oh, what a beautiful house," I said, as usual, driving up our steep driveway. Chisel was waiting at the top of the stairs as predicted. John carried Storey's limp body inside. We had thought by the time we walked into our house that Storey would be smiling and strong, but instead she was shaky, delirious, and couldn't sit up. The doctor and his nurse insisted she'd be fine and back to herself in a couple hours.

It had been four.

As she tried to eat oatmeal for dinner, John and I stared at her like we were watching a drunk person sip coffee.

Days passed for her to sober up, but she never returned to her baseline.

Our journey had begun.

Chisel, my first baby, a female bull mastiff.

CHISEL

Most of the time I have freedom to run around our property, sniffing wonderful smells as long I stay off the road. If Mom caught me down there, well...

My favorite time of day is walking up the road with Mom, Hayden, and Storey. I'm the leader of the pack. I love to feel my ears bounce and drink moist smells that only a dog of my stature can appreciate. Mom hands Hayden, and sometimes Storey, my leash, and I'm careful not to pull when that little sweet thing is holding it. Hayden—that rascal—thinks he's in control of the leash, constantly yelling at me to slow down like I'm an ordinary dumb dog. One bunny chase would leave him with a serious road rash, and I'd be in the doghouse for an undisclosed amount of time. So, I tell my bunny brain, *Take it easy Big Gal, you will be rewarded with tasty treats and wrinkle rubs.* Self-control isn't high on my list, but let me tell yaw, there are benefits.

Lately Mom seems weirder, she smells different. I know our walks help her because Storey giggles and Hayden asks a lot of questions. Sometimes when Hayden is in school Mom takes me and Storey on extra walks and I can smell her happiness. Occasionally Mom will say, "Oh, what a beautiful day."

After our walks, Mom lets Storey and me spoon on the floor. I hold very still. I'm happy letting her do that because I can smell a rough road ahead.

I love my family.

Chapter 5

Since the day of the anesthesia, Storey's gait and tremor grew worse, but she still rallied and tried to be her silly self. A week later, John and I headed to the hospital lab with Dr. Black's blue slip lab orders that contained long words we hoped we'd never have to learn. I strained to keep my fingers from Googling the medical terms. John and I were confident Storey's condition was caused by a chemical imbalance or something treatable with a colorful pill.

Anyone who asked me why Storey walked like she had just ridden a horse or why her hands shook, I was transparent. Their concerns solidified my belief. I often ended conversations with, "I just know she is going to be alright."

I grabbed the hospital lab doorknob with my coat sleeve and held it open with my foot. John rolled his eyes.

"Well, better safe than sorry," I said, looking up at him.

The lab was sparse: three chairs and a few wrinkled magazines. A confident nurse, obviously in charge, greeted Storey with a big smile. I handed her Storey's lab orders. She looked at the paper, then down at Storey, and with throaty voice said, "Hi, sweetheart." Then she peered over her readers at John and me with a worrisome look. Four people in lab coats gathered around her, looked at the blue paper and whispered.

"We can only do a couple of these orders today; the rest will take a while, and I'll need to order special tubes. We'll need more than 30cc of blood for all these tests. We'll do what we can today, but this amount of blood is too much for her to give in one day."

"The doctor didn't say anything about the amount of blood or special tubes," I said, looking lost.

Storey sat in John's lap, and I distracted her with a book while they tightened a blue band around her bicep then tapped her forearm for a vein. She whined and wiggled. Her blood stopped flowing after only 5cc.

"Is Pam here? She was the only one who could find a vein in my daughter," I asked upon my return two weeks later.

"Well, eh, unfortunately Pam isn't here."

My stomach dropped. My shoulders rolled forward. I watched two phlebotomists wearing blue gloves gather around Storey. They massaged her innocent skin. Her right arm didn't produce a vein, and her left arm was worse. Then they inspected the top of her right hand.

"We can't find a vein," a phlebotomist yelled to the back room.

Six people in lab coats surrounded us. One gal stuck Storey so fast the audience of white coats marveled. My eyes crossed adding the cubic centimeters of blood flowing into tubes. Distracted by all the attention, I forgot that I had dropped the book blocking Storey's eyes from their work. Her body went heavy, her eyes rolled, she turned white, and her blood trickled to a stop. One technician grabbed her from my arms.

"Mrs. Mills, we are just taking her to the emergency room as a precaution. Follow me."

A different technician held Storey's head lower than her body and they disappeared around the corner.

"Please be careful with the tubes of blood. We don't know what is wrong with her and it will be torture repeating these tests," I pleaded with the remaining phlebotomist, grabbing a tissue on my way out.

In the emergency room a few minutes later, Storey looked better. By the time Dr. Feist arrived, she was alert and smiled at him. He said the reaction was a stress response, not from taking too much blood.

I wished I could have promised Storey this was her last blood draw.

At the time we were unaware it would take six to eight weeks for all the results, and it was routine for the doctor to call only after all the results were available. Patience has never been a top skill of mine. I worked hard to find my patient dance by focusing on special moments; there was Play-Doh, preschool, books, walks, and love to share. I hid my fear and reminded myself to treasure Storey's and Hayden's giggles while they tossed Beanie Babies and lined up Matchbox cars across the living room. My optimism allowed John to focus on his business without worrying if he was going to walk upstairs to a wife plagued by madness.

On the last day of eight weeks, we got the call.

"Hello Mr. and Mrs. Mills, how is Storey doing? I have all the blood test results. Good news overall—all the tests came back within normal range."

"Is that it?" I said.

"Not necessarily. For now, there are no disease markers. Occasionally things like this can be *static*, meaning the condition is just there and could present differently in time."

"That's great news, I guess," John said, breathing into the phone.

"Time will tell, sometimes we need to repeat tests if things aren't getting better because disease markers will then have a heavier load, which means the disease becomes measurable in the blood. Unfortunately, there are some cases where we are unable to make a definitive diagnosis."

"Ever?" My hands and legs shook. I couldn't remember how to breathe.

"Okay… well, we'll take static for now," John said, running his hands through his hair.

"There are other tests like a nerve conduction and an electromyography. If she gets worse, we should run these tests to rule out other neurological conditions. But for right now, let's wait and see how she does in the next few months," the doctor said.

"Dr. Black, Storey is worse! She refuses to walk without help. After the anesthesia she hasn't been the same, and she is still shakier than she was before the anesthesia and testing." My voice cracked through the phone line.

The word "static" was all I wanted to remember. I circled *nerve conduction* on my yellow pad. Questions swirled in my head; the back of it throbbed, my mouth became paralyzed, and I knew it would be impossible to get the doctor back on the phone once I could speak.

"Well, that anesthesia is way out of her system. We need to see what happens in the next few months. Call when you want to do the nerve conduction tests," Dr. Black said.

Over the next few weeks Storey's body remained the same: weak and shaky. She still smiled but had lost some of her spunk. We kept telling ourselves it was temporary.

A month later, trusting the medical field, I called the doctor's office to schedule the tests. A week later we walked through the same

institutional-style halls. New to the gamble of anesthesia and neurological problems, I trusted that the doctors and nurses had Storey's back, even though I questioned the nurse about the liquid in
the Dixie cup. I pleaded with the staff to do something different this
time, but they just made a stronger concoction.

Mothers have an inner sense when it comes to their children, like
when you're dreaming your child is sick and you wake to the sound
of them throwing up. Or you know they will have a fever when you
pick them up from school, even though they were fine in the morning.

My "mother's intuition" had yelled at me, and I had failed to listen. I could have said no to the bubbling liquid they made Storey
drink the second time. I could have taken her away and done more
research. But we were two-and-a-half hours from home, and I still
had faith in Western medicine. I wanted to believe they went out of
their way to "do no harm" to a child. John and I watched Storey gag
and her body shiver sipping the "new and improved" yellow liquid
(1mg of clonidine and 25mg of amitriptyline).

It was brutal. I felt pulled; all this felt like Storey was just another
cute girl with problems who walked through those neurological doors
every day. To our relief, Storey went to sleep faster.

The nerve conduction and electromyography (EMG) consisted
of inserting larger needles into the nerves and muscles of the arms
and legs, to measure nerve conductions and muscle reactions, which
were recorded on a computer printout.

Storey was in a deep sleep. The neurologist conducting the test
allowed me to be with her, and I quickly found out why—Storey
needed to know I was there even though I allowed this person to use
her body like a pincushion. Each time the doctor inserted a needle, he
wiggled it around and then hooked a wire to the needle to measure

its stimulation. Storey moaned and cried with her eyes shut. Every time the doctor inserted a needle into Storey, I could feel it like she was someone's voodoo doll. My brain imagined black-and-white historical photos of experiments done on children. The doctor adjusted the machine knobs and waited for the readings to print. Then he put new needles in new nerves... this went on and on. Nausea rippled through me. Holding Storey's foot was the only thing that saved me. The door out seemed miles away.

The less the doctor found, the more he dug.

"Not many doctors will do this to children," he said, looking up at me.

I gave this experienced, apologetic neurologist with graying temples a look—*then how could you?*

I sang from our favorite book, "Hush Little Baby, Mama's Going to Show You a Hummingbird." Storey and I both relaxed—a little. I raised my voice whenever it looked like she was going to moan and twitch. I sang softly, yet I wanted to scream and yell *STOP!* But the doctor was too deep into the test, and I wasn't going to agree to a do-over.

It was clear that at a large children's hospital, Storey would have had proper anesthesia and perhaps a memory-blocking drug like Versed. Suddenly I understood why my friends suggested we immediately take Storey to a large hospital outside Montana.

"THAT'S ENOUGH, STOP! You're not going to get any more information than you already have!" I told the neurologist.

He looked up at me and turned off the machine. I picked Storey up, who felt like a sleeping sloth in my arms. I ran to John, and his face turned white when he saw me.

"Get us out of here. That was torture," I said.

I cried into Storey's neck running to the car. On the way home I sat in the back seat with my arms around her as she slept off what seemed like another high gone wrong. I was furious at myself for signing the permission slip to that torture chamber without conducting more research.

I knew it was all going to backfire.

I was careful not to talk about it too much. I didn't want the memory to be ingrained with Storey's spirit.

The next few weeks proved what I suspected—the stress and the wrong anesthesia was detrimental to Storey's nervous system. She was more withdrawn. Her whole body shook when she tried to stand against us or a table, and she whispered fewer words. The nerve conduction test only concluded what we already knew—that her reflexes and nerve impulses were slower than average. We didn't know that it was an insignificant diagnostic tool. A few months into her second year of life, her body and spirit had been pushed too far. She never walked again without help.

Not one step.

Storey Anne, my princess,

    I am so sorry for that horrible test. I was torn between what the doctors suggested and my own fears. We hoped for answers. Knowing what I know now, I would have asked more questions. I would have insisted on a real pediatric anesthesiologist to administer short-lived anesthesia through an IV, with the ability to reverse adverse reactions—but I didn't know better. We shouldn't have had to know better.

For weeks after, I whispered to you, "Storey, I'm never, ever going to let any anyone do that test to you ever again, because a promise is a promise."

In the grieving night hours that memory hovers, and then I see your forgiving smile and I'm okay for a while.

I love you to where the hummingbirds fly and back again,

Mom

Dear *Mom*,

Don't ever think about that day again. When you started singing "Hush little baby, don't say a word, Mama's going to show you a hummingbird," my body relaxed, and I found my happy place—I felt my soul swirl and my crown chakra open. Red and orange auras surrounded you and my body, and with a breath I flew up with the hummingbirds. I watched you cry, and your love formed a pink healing aura, and it blocked my pain. Then I went to a new place. Hayden and I were lying on your bed, and you were between us pointing at the hummingbird picture in our favorite book. I felt safe and secure wrapped like a burrito in my pink bath towel. We giggled.

I cried because I felt your pain, not mine. I was light and free. You sang, "When that star has dropped from view, Mama's going to read a book with you."

Mom, your singing echoed in the distance, and with intention as freeing as lying in the grass watching clouds, my spirit flew without effort; I hovered above the table in the doctor's office and concurrently I was in our yard with my hummingbird friends. We zipped around in circles like neighborhood kids running through sprinklers on a warm summer day.

I noticed a little girl pointing at me. "Look Mom, a hummingbird," she said. I flew down and wrapped my tiny talons around her sticky finger, and she smiled at her mom.

My soul pulled away from the little girl when I heard, "ENOUGH, STOP!" Instantly I dropped back into my dense body on the table. My arms and legs throbbed, and you lifted me off the table and ran out.

Part of my spirit stayed with the hummingbirds. I didn't want to be back in my body. It felt chaotic, weak; yet my hummingbird spirit continued to play. I could find freedom with just a thought whenever life or pain was too challenging. But Mom, your love kept me grounded on this earth, with our family.

Mom, thanks for always trying to make me feel better.

I love you,

Storey

Chapter 6

My dive into alternative therapies began after our terrifying experience with the nerve conduction test and our inability to find answers using Western medicine. I knew healing didn't come without a lot of effort and risks; the challenging part was finding a unique combination that would work for Storey and me. I also knew that physical and mental trauma made the spirit and the body vulnerable to "dis-ease." Storey's spirit seemed to drift, and her head would cock to the side. It was my responsibility to bring her back.

To stimulate Storey's neuropathways, Hayden and I taught her how to cross crawl—the way most kids crawl—while Shania Twain played in the background. Storey watched Hayden and I crawl on all fours around the living room. I placed her knees and hands on the floor, then stood over her and physically moved her opposing legs and hands. She giggled.

"Storey, you can do it, follow me!" Hayden cheered.

Within fifteen minutes, Storey was playing follow-the-leader and Chisel was the caboose. To my relief, this became her preferred mode of transportation, and she never returned to the crab-crawl. This new way of crawling stimulated her brain. We encouraged Storey to walk at every opportunity, holding her hands above her like you do with a 1-year-old. John and I got discouraged at times when all she wanted to do was crawl.

Storey continued to go to Montessori preschool with Hayden. She was stimulated and played like an average 2-year-old. All the teachers at school showered the children with patience and love. One teacher often took Storey under her wing and into her cozy lap. I worried Storey might catch every illness that circled, exacerbating her situation. It was a tradeoff. Storey and Hayden thrived in school. They chose their own lessons and books, learned social skills, and built confidence in a nurturing environment.

Before Montessori became mainstream, the Yellowstone region had a higher number of certified Montessori teachers. Many of them were certificated through a school offered within The Church Universal Triumphant (C.U.T.), an unorthodox religious commune forty-five minutes away. When I worked at Kinko's Copies in the late 1980s, I made hundreds of color copies of Mother Mary, ascended masters, Jesus, and their leader Clair Prophet, for C.U.T. customers. This New Age religion was eccentric. However, I found them no more dogmatic and less damaging than religions who, for centuries, allowed their leaders to molest children behind the cloth.

I believe humans arrive in our world with a resonating curiosity for the mystical unknown and a social need to feel love and support by a community. As my exploration grew beyond the practice of Western medicine, I understood why many sought answers to life's mysteries by means of unorthodox religions and non-traditional healing therapies. I, too, was desperate to explore the communal soup of healing options. Who was I to judge?

My first new flavor of alternative healing, besides energy work and reading some metaphysical books, was a diagnostic muscle-testing technique. A dear friend had recommended we visit a couple who tested a person's energy by using applied kinesiology and muscle testing for the body's energy imbalances. And the couple was trained in using Standard Process® supplements and elixirs to help the body return to its natural balance.

I drove Storey and Hayden twenty miles over a snowy mountain pass to the couple's home office. I introduced myself and my kids to the husband-and-wife team who looked more like siblings with matching red hair. We sat on the edge of a dirty couch and waited a few minutes for them to gather their suitcase of delights. Suddenly I wondered what I was doing there, looking at a familiar Kinko's color copy of Jesus on the wall and layers of dust on their white baseboards. Storey sat in my lap and pulled things out of my purse, and Hayden stared at the ceiling fan.

When the couple approached, their energy felt compassionate. I explained what little I knew about Storey's illness. They explained applied kinesiology and muscle testing and how the techniques gave them assessments on what organ(s) and system(s) needed support. Naturally, their words sounded like pseudoscience in layman's terms, but I was already a little familiar with this method of diagnostic testing.

I felt their pull. I wanted it to make sense.

The couple opened their large suitcase of tiny bottles nestled between holes in foam. The lids on the bottles contained organ names and strange abbreviations I didn't understand. The couple faced us, standing side by side. The man stuck out his arm and touched the woman's extended arm and fingers, like in Michelangelo's masterpiece, *The Creation of Adam*. The woman placed a variety of bottles in Storey's hand, then lightly touched Storey on the top of her head, her stomach, and lastly, her feet. Where there was a negative muscle response from Storey's body, the man's arm went completely weak and dropped to his side with a thud (it seemed a little dramatic to me). This indicated the essence of the organ, or an allergen that caused a weakness in Storey. They retested for further negative responses to establish the amount of supplements Storey needed. I liked that this testing method was non-invasive, but they sold the supplements, presumably for profit, which didn't feel right with me.

In twenty minutes, the couple determined Storey needed adrenal support and to be treated for intestinal parasites and a few other things I can't remember. Then they tested Hayden and me. As we left, they gave me a lecture on well water. The overabundance of minerals could bind to Storey's nervous system and cause harm, they said. Naturally, they sold Pure water filters.

"My husband is a groundwater geologist. We have had our water tested and I don't think he would agree with that water theory," I said, looking at my feet.

They began to lose me on the parasites and almost lost me completely with the water lecture. I wanted to believe. I wanted this to work. I had knocked on their door. After all, a good friend had recommended this red-headed couple. In the car I looked at the expensive bag of supplements. I grew weak and felt the collective anguish of thousands of mothers in similar situations.

Every morning for six weeks I woke Hayden and Storey. They sat on the kitchen counter as I mixed the anti-parasite substance (bromelain power, dried pineapple parts) in applesauce. Half asleep in the morning light, they ate it.

The supplements gradually disappeared, and I pictured Storey learning to walk again. I fantasized about taking her to Dr. Feist.

Look, she can walk again, and all I did was give her a few supplements.
I wanted to attest that integrative medicine *and* Western medicine
was essential to healing.

I waited. Storey didn't get better, but she seemed to have stopped
getting worse. We did the muscle testing a couple more times; different supplements were added, some were taken away. Because Storey
tended to hold her head slightly to the right instead of straight, the
couple suggested I take her to see a child chiropractor who special-
ized in helping kids with learning problems, like dyslexia. *Dyslexia?*
I understood my mother's tenacity in carting me around Salt Lake
City in the 1960s to help with my dyslexia.

Intrigued but generally opposed to chiropractors, I immediately
called the number. The chiropractor answered on the second ring,
and fifteen minutes later we walked into his office. I recognized his
face from my gym and without thinking, I laid Storey on his table.
He knew the look of a desperate mother.

"Particular adjustments increase blood flow to the brain and can
cure learning disabilities. Many kids with dyslexia come to me weekly."
His plump lips moved while he massaged Storey's neck.

CRACK.

The hair on my neck stood like acupuncture needles. It shocked
me that a noise like that could come from someone so small.

Everything happened so fast. Storey's eyes bugged out and her
bottom lip turned down. I jerked Storey from the table before she
saw my face. She tucked her face into my chest like a shy 1-year-old.
I set her down against my legs while I scribbled out a check. The chiropractor opened his appointment book and pointed to next week's
schedule—it was wide open. I strained to be polite. Storey attempted
to take two steps toward the door holding my hand, but I grabbed

her and ran. In the car I locked the doors and dropped my wet face in my hands. The steering wheel took a beating.

"Storey, we're going to McDonald's for fries and a 101 Dalmatians doggy toy."

"Yay, cam have some?" she said.

Storey sat up straighter that night at the dinner table and later held out her hand to walk, but we never, ever went back.

Dear Pumpkin Eater *Storey*,

We love Halloween! Remember the surprise pumpkins and gourds that grew in our garden? For therapeutic fun I stuffed your school backpack with gourds, and I held your hands and waist. Light returned to your eyes, and you laughed walking around in the living room. That exercise strengthened your core and connected your feet to the ground.

However, by late 2000 you hesitated to put any weight on your legs and our hearts sank. Some days your spirit lived more outside your body, and other days you were bright and focused. One day I had an idea—if you wore heavy snow boots, your neuro-synapses from your brain to your feet might wake it. We headed to Payless Shoes and made a big mess. You and Hayden were laughing, and both of you climbed the stair railing. You reached for my hand and took a few steps in your new snow boots before you crawled as fast as you could chasing Hayden. Behind shoe boxes, I felt whispers from other mothers. I didn't care what they thought. Unbeknownst to them, I wondered if that was going to be the last time I would see you that active. In their eyes, my kids were out of control; in mine, it was a special day.

I love you,

Mom

Chapter 7

ate that fall, a high school friend suggested we watch the 1992 movie *Lorenzo's Oil*. The movie was based on a true story starring Susan Sarandon and Nick Nolte. John and I sat together on the couch and watched Lorenzo, a healthy, gregarious 4-year-old boy, lose function. It took two years for the doctors to find Lorenzo's disease: Adrenoleukodystrophy—ALD—a rare neurodegenerative disease which saturates the nervous system and adrenal cortex with very long chain fatty acids (not to be confused with Amyotrophic Lateral Sclerosis: ALS or Lou Gehrig's disease). Many rare diseases present with similar symptoms: ataxia, seizures, tremors, loss of muscle function. ADL affects approximately 1 in 45,000 children, mainly boys.

The movie focused on the dedication of the parents, who didn't believe doctors when they said, "There is nothing that can be done. This disease is usually fatal in a few years."

The parents' love for their son spearheaded their journey researching with many other scientists who tested complicated forms of fatty acids to help Lorenzo. Eventually they developed a unique formula of erucic acid and oleic acid, which slowed the progression of Lorenzo's degeneration. But at one point in the movie, the parents looked at each other and admitted that their son's nerves were beyond repair.

Lorenzo had already lost most of his sight, his ability to eat, move, and to communicate. However, he was able to breathe. As sad as this movie was, Lorenzo's parents knew the disease prognosis and still chose to fight with fervor and love.

John was too heartbroken and went to bed halfway through the movie. But I couldn't look away; I felt the love-pull of many mothers who were wrapped in angelic webs of similar fates. For a week, I couldn't concentrate. I wondered if I was made of the same cloth as Lorenzo's mother; if not, I had to find my bulldog courage and the energy to help Storey.

The only time I felt the lightness of life was walking up the road with the kids, watching Chisel's tail bounce or listening to Hayden and Storey's giggles, watching them toss rocks in the creek or the stillness I found in yoga. Those times created space for me to find my valor.

Storey's doctors had no answers and the "wait-and-see" wasn't working for me. My Googling fingers sifted through limited and inadequate information on the diagnostics of rare diseases. What I found were stories and photos of children with horrific diseases—diagnosed and undiagnosed—that were robbing them of their childhoods. Many of the children had beautiful smiles; some looked miserable. I stared deep into their innocent eyes on my lousy computer screen and asked them to send me an epiphany of insight. When I couldn't stand it any longer, I Googled the scary words I had scribbled on a crumpled piece of paper in Dr. Black's office: Batten disease, rare genetic diseases, neuro progressive degenerative diseases in children with ataxia. I kept my obsessive research from John—he didn't want to hear about it anyway. His heart felt sick. Googling before bed isn't something I recommend, unless sleeping well is optional and you can afford to peek through the crack of your child's bedroom door all night and think of all the worst-case scenarios. I found myself falling into a vortex of depression and had to steady myself without antidepressants. It was necessary to be clear enough to notice and appreciate everyday gifts, like Storey's ease of acceptance and how hard she worked at physical therapy to make us proud. And the funny things Hayden said at the dinner table.

I knew the more I educated myself, the "easier" it would be to find acceptance. Research was especially overwhelming with flashbacks of my parent's favorite saying, "Look it up in the encyclopedia," which always triggered immediate anxiety in my dyslexic and ADHD brain. Nevertheless, the more I learned the better I felt. Not only were there dreadful stories, but miraculous ones too. A 1-year-old baby was in the hospital for months, near death, and no one could figure out why she threw up every bit of food until a new intern convinced the doctors to do an intestinal biopsy. She was diagnosed with celiac disease, almost unheard of at the time. There was another story of a child whose seizures stopped after the parents fed their kid a lot of olives (she needed the fat). And we have all heard stories where families pray over their child's sick bed and by the grace of some higher power (if you will), the child is better in the morning. Those stories filled my tank. The sad stories I tucked away, and for a distraction I turned on *Seinfeld* every evening. I laughed. My kids laughed. And John laughed. For twenty minutes we gave ourselves the luxury to laugh.

The *Harry Potter* books had been out for a couple of years, and fortunately, the magic of those books rekindled my interest in reading.

I couldn't remember ever reading a book that thick other than a college textbook, which I probably only read enough for a passing grade. Each night I found myself wanting to get the kids to bed so I could read. For once in my life, I felt like that smart fifth grader.

My rekindled interest in reading directed me back to the metaphysical and spiritual section of bookstores I enjoyed years before. I called myself a "Hay House Publisher Junky."

Hay House was started in 1984 by Louise Hay after she wrote her book, *You Can Heal Your Body and You Can Heal Your Life.* This book was one of the first self-help books I purchased in the mid 1980s from a store that smelled like Nag Champa incense and lavender. I devoured mystical books by the authors Sylvia Browne, Doreen Virtue, Sonia Choquette, Neale Donald Walsch, and the legendary Dr. Wayne Dyer. These books reconnected me to a different world, and to a familiar way of thinking that I had shared with my mother years before. Doreen Virtue's world of angels, indigo and crystal children, and her beautifully illustrated oracle card decks drew me in. Her books explained that special "spiritually-minded old souls" were incarnating into this world to balance humanity.

These books helped me understand why Hayden—who was so wise and happy beyond his years—and why Storey—who, despite what was going on, often said "Mom, I love you,"—chose me to be their mother. It made sense that they were more my teachers than I theirs. My friends of similar thinking agreed and shared the honor of navigating our unique children through the clutches of this mystified world. This tasted better to me than the dogma of religion.

As I explored and learned more alternative possibilities—energy healing, Reiki, massage, prayer circles, craniosacral therapies, laser therapy, positive affirmations, essential oils, Bach Flowers Essence, etc.—I made personal guidelines: to always explore a healing option if I listened to my "mother's intuition," and/or if I heard about a modality three times within a short window. I knew healing was possible with the right combination when integrative medicine was explored. And I knew everyone was unique. I had to investigate to find something to save Storey. I fantasized of shouting Storey's miracle healing to the world from the saddle of our property.

Because of my guidelines, alternative healing modalities came in like a transistor radio. Three people, within a short time, talked about the same chiropractor who incorporated craniosacral work using *light* manipulation without the traditional snap-crackle-pop-scare-the-shit-out-of-me modality. Though skeptical from our last chiropractor experience, I made an appointment. My hands shook carrying Storey into Dr. Bouma's dark, small waiting room. Three people sat in chairs under familiar framed color copies of ascended masters. Two scenarios played out in my mind: he's either poor at managing time, or he's nice enough to see distressed clients who call at the last minute. The room was no different from medical waiting rooms in testing my patience. I was tempted to leave after an hour when Storey grew antsy. But then Dr. Bouma peeked behind the brown curtain like *The Wizard of Oz* and called our name. He looked a little gaunt with deep-set eyes under the poor lighting, and I wondered if he'd scare Storey. But Dr. Bouma took time to listen. He looked into our eyes, was relaxed and present. He was a man of few words except to share a few success stories as he gently touched Storey's head. With better lighting, his scary look morphed into compassion. A sense of nurturing energy filled his treatment room. Time stood still. After a few minutes Storey and I relaxed. With his soft fingertips on acupuncture points, Dr. Bouma sensed Storey's cranial rhythm to find stagnant energy along her nervous system to clear using a light touch. After Storey's third appointment, I carefully set her down on the floor like a mother would with a toddler learning to walk. I held her hands, then let go. She took three steps unassisted—steps her body had been unable to orchestrate for months. My heart released a rush of energy.

I kept fighting.

Over the next two years, we drove twenty-five minutes to see him a few times a month. Our insurance paid for most of the visit, and I brought books and toys with me, knowing he always ran late. Storey looked better after each appointment and usually asked to walk in his office with assistance, but her walking didn't progress from there. Between Storey's other therapies and appointments, I found a craniosacral therapist closer to home. The treatments made her nervous system relax and she always slept better.

Around the time we began seeing Dr. Bouma, I was introduced to Tony, a Reiki healer and essential oil consultant who had qualified under my guidelines.

"Look Mom, pumpkins," Storey said at the same doors we walked through to see Tony, and where I had taken Chi Gong classes months before.

In the treatment room with Tony, I felt right at home. Uncharacteristically, Storey easily engaged with him. He was young and unpretentious, with credentials of energy healing beyond weekend workshops and who looked more like an engineering student. I gave him Storey's spiel while he held his palms open facing her, backed six inches away and slowly moved them up and down. He said Storey's and my healing was part of an ancestral lineage. I understood enough to know that people's energies are congruent and bound by an emotional and energetic blood line.

I, too, felt a warm sensation move around my neck and back. Storey, who was right next to me on the table, looked up at me and we both took a deep breath together and smiled. For an hour Tony moved his hands around our bodies in a fluid motion. I realized since this journey had begun that, despite yoga, I had only been breathing from the top portion of my lungs. I gripped life by my toes and fear had nestled in my nerves. After the session with Tony, he suggested that I visit the co-op. He wanted me to roll lavender oil on Storey's feet before bed and defuse grounding oils of fir, sandalwood, and cedarwood to support her nervous system. Tony's calm, grounded energy was what we both seemed to need. In the car I turned around to see Storey's radiant, smiling face.

In the days that followed, with focused intention like Tony had taught me, I moved my hands over Storey. I pictured pulling and releasing stagnant, negative energy into the light. It felt right. But the healings—craniosacral, oils, prayer, and supplements—weren't making the drastic changes that I wanted.

We kept doing life. Storey and I swam at the hot springs across town while Hayden took swim lessons there. We went to open gym at the gymnastics center. Storey's favorite was the rings—she held tight and dangled. My kids continued with preschool. We kept up with Storey's physical therapy and occasionally we visited Dr. Bouma and stayed positive. We saw Tony a couple more times. Storey was always brighter and had more energy after seeing him. It didn't last, but Storey consistently felt good for a few days, so it was worth it.

Storey went through a period where she pulled at her ears, but doctor visits revealed no ear infections. She cried easily, lost self-confidence, and didn't smile as much as she used to. Other times she surprised us. She looked stronger and happier, and her eyes were clear and focused. Encouragement lifted my momentum. Many mornings she'd wake too early.

"Mooooommmm, moke please." I'd bring her milk and lie next to her.

And the rollercoaster ride continued.

After Thanksgiving I made an appointment with Dr. Feist because we had to admit Storey was getting worse. When she ate, her spoon shook. She always wanted to crawl. She whined when we encouraged her to walk. Her muscle tone had decreased.

Dr. Feist suggested we travel out of Montana to see Dr. Pranzatelli, a movement specialist in Springfield, Illinois. He warned us to be patient receiving a call back from his office because of the holidays. I rolled my eyes; we knew how to wait. Not that we did it well, but we knew how.

John and I worked hard to be present for Christmas 2000 with his entire family in Big Sky. This was Storey's second Christmas there. She was 2½ years old. John's brother David, his wife Kyria, and their two kids flew in from Davis, California (by coincidence they lived a mile from my father and Valerie). John's sister Cindy (not to be confused with my sister, Cindy) and her 18-month-old daughter flew in from Minnesota. And John's parents drove from Green Bay, Wisconsin. Family gatherings around a large river-rock fireplace inside a cozy log cabin, toasting to good health while watching snow fall, was a storybook story.

John's family was aware of our recent challenges. The Christmas two years before in Big Sky, Storey had been a perfect 6-month-old, blue-eyed, dark-haired baby surpassing all normal developmental milestones. That Christmas the joy of was replaced with apprehension and anxiety being around John's family members of doctors and scientists. Instead of just the two of us worrying about Storey, there were a total of seven adults sending sidling looks around the fireplace, watching Storey shake and unable to walk on her own, no one knew what to do.

Storey felt everyone's concern. She was withdrawn and shied from adult engagement. I, too, felt at odds. Being an artistic, right-brained thinker among a left-brained crowd and a strong mother-in-law who remarked how lucky and grateful she was with three healthy kids left me wondering if I was supposed to feel unlucky. And although I felt cautiously optimistic about alternative therapies, I knew that educating the family on my latest non-medical healing modalities of lavender, craniosacral therapy, or Reiki would invite my hopeful bubble to pop.

Naturally, they were all sad and concerned and didn't know what to say or do. We were all traveling down unfamiliar roads. The only thing I knew to do was to stay positive and reassure them and myself that we were going to figure out what was happening to Storey. Holding that kind of energy for a few days was draining and my sensitive stomach reacted. Away from the conversations about George W. Bush, I was happiest playing on the floor with the kids. John's dad did too.

Hey *MOM!*

Remember I loved to sit on the couch with Grandpa? He'd hide a puzzle piece between the couch cushions, and we'd giggle. I always felt his love when I was near him. Then

Hayden, Noa, Kathy, and Alea and I would play Pile on Grandpa, and we'd climb on him even though his knees hurt. He was so silly. The best part was that I didn't feel my cousins' worried eyes. They didn't stare at me.

Christmas in Big Sky was my favorite, I'm sorry you felt stressed there.

I love you,
Storey

Storey,

It warms my heart knowing you were happy there!
Love,
Mom XOXO

Chapter 8

I t was a long three months waiting for Dr. Pranzatelli's neurology department in Springfield, Illinois to call us and schedule our appointment at the end of January 2001. I imagined Storey's name on a piece of paper in someone's desk organizer. My stomach flipped and the back of my head pulsed when the nurse at the other end of the phone explained we needed to be in Springfield in three days. Some people thrive on spontaneous travel. I do not, yet I knew I had to make it work.

"Storey is scheduled to have a Magnetic Resonance Spectroscopy—MRS—which is a step up from an MRI that measures the biochemical changes and cell loss in the brain, followed by a lumbar puncture—spinal tap—to measure her cerebrospinal fluid for infections and abnormalities, and then a blood draw for more testing," the nurse said.

My body froze at the thought of sedation. I had flashbacks. Storey depended on me to be her protector, her advocate, her voice.

"Will Storey have a pediatric anesthesiologist? What kind of anesthesia will she have and how will they administer it? She hasn't been the same since the last time she drank a 'cocktail sedation,'" I said, interrupting the nurse.

"They will use Propofol, a short acting anesthesia administered through an IV. It is very safe. All the kids we see who have neurological problems do well and recover quickly without additional neurological side effects. I understand your concern. Dr. Pranzatelli is one of the best pediatric neurologists in the country."

"Okay, that makes me feel better. I'll read up on Propofol," I said.

"Plan on being here at ten o'clock on January 24th for the appointment. The doctor is very cordial. He will explain everything and address your concerns. At eleven o'clock they will take Storey for a pre-op and her MRS will be at noon. She will be under anesthesia for about an hour and the doctor will give you the results that day. You will be called later when the blood tests are back. We'll see you soon."

Thoughts of flying my entire family across the country during flu season worried me. Anesthesia and learning bad news or not getting a diagnosis worried me.

"John, we need to be in Springfield, Illinois to see Dr. Feist's referral," I told John in his basement office.

"That's good news. I'm relieved be going out of Montana instead of seeing another wack-job alternative person," he said.

I rolled my eyes, but I, too, felt relieved to be going to a respected doctor across the country.

"I'll make flight reservations right now," I said.

John's folks volunteered to drive from Green Bay to join us in Springfield to entertain Hayden during Storey's appointments. Hayden found joy in anything new. And at 4½, he already understood Storey's needs.

Too early in the morning, Hayden enthusiastically asked Storey if she liked planes, flipping his excited hands. John and I both smiled and let out breaths of relief.

"Dad! I mostly like trucks, but I like planes too. *Dad, Mom!* Look at the trucks driving around the planes. Mom!" he said, tugging at my shirt.

After boarding I had plenty of time for my airplane sterilization ritual. Luckily, the flight was uneventful. Storey was tired but not as shaky as I had anticipated. Stress and the lack of sleep usually made her symptoms worse.

At the hotel, the room's essence was heavy and stale. John shared a bed with Hayden, and I shared one with Storey. My monkey mind woke me several times. I reached for Storey and looked at the unfamiliar digital clock—3:33 a.m.—the lonely grieving hour of the night. Street noises and Grandpa's snoring drifted through thin walls. I wanted to see a slit of the sunrise peek through the hotel curtains to clear my thoughts. I wanted to be on the other side of the day, for Storey to be unharmed psychologically and physically. I wanted a treatment for her.

Storey slept until eight o'clock—later than usual. She and I watched *Clifford the Big Red Dog*, distracting her from realizing that John and Hayden were eating breakfast downstairs. Later I explained to her that we were going to see a nice doctor to have some tests done, so she couldn't eat.

"But I womp brokefast." Her bottom lip turned down. We both teared.

In the doctor's office, I pulled out some new toys for her so she wouldn't notice her hunger. John, John's father, and Storey and I sat in the quiet waiting room. We asked John's father, an ear, nose, and throat doctor, to join us for her appointment to have a medical ear with us.

We were called back quickly. A friendly, stocky nurse took Storey's vitals and gave her stickers. Then Dr. Pranzatelli arrived. His demeanor was polite and focused. He looked at me over his readers as he flipped through Storey's stack of medical records.

"Let's take this from the beginning. How was her birth… when did you first…?"

My shoulders dropped. I expected this question. I was glad he wanted to hear from Storey's mother first, but a wall of exhaustion hit me, and I wondered how carefully he had studied her medical file.

"She was a C-section on July 1st, 1998. She had a fever and diarrhea at two weeks… she was fine until around twenty months, when she began to walk—it was as though she had just gotten off a horse. She never really made it to a run like most kids her age. She is happy. We have seen many doctors and tried many alternative therapies," I said.

Then John gave his account, almost repeating what I said. Storey grew whiny and uncomfortable from all of us staring at her. I hugged her and blotted my eyes.

"I'm extremely worried about Storey receiving anesthesia, what will she be given?" I asked the doctor, wondering if he'd give the same answer as the nurse.

"Propofol is very safe for kids with neurological issues, and it will clear out of her system quickly. We administer and control it through an IV. I see what she was given in Montana, which is old school and possibly dangerous. We don't use that here. While under anesthesia, we will take a blood sample to repeat a few tests. Many times, diseases don't show up in blood work in the early stages, because the blood tests aren't sensitive enough. And we'll run some new tests, looking for genetic markers and for storage diseases."

"Okay, let's get this over with," I said.

The doctor left and the nurse returned. Storey knew something was up. She tucked her arm behind me, hiding it from the blood pressure cuff. We were directed to another larger room with a hospital bed, and we waited. A few minutes later, a skinny, gaunt man with glassy eyes came into the room. He introduced himself as a medical aide and immediately reached for Storey. Instantly a shiver of fear shot up and down my body, the kind of fear that I've felt only a few times. I smelled alcohol—not the hand sanitizer alcohol smell, but the rancid alcohol smell that people with alcohol problems smell like. I gagged and wrapped my arms around Storey tighter, turning from his reach.

"I need to take her now," he said.

"I thought we could stay with her until she's asleep. She hates needles, and she doesn't have any veins. She might throw up on you. She needs us to be there."

"No, she will be fine. We need to do everything in the pre-op room. No parents allowed. I need to take her now," he said, reaching his arms out again.

And before I knew it, he lifted her out of my arms like she was a small sack of potatoes and walked away. Storey cried hysterically and reached for us. Her cries echoed down the hall beyond our safety. I had spent a lot of time protecting her from negative people and environmental toxins. My body shook and my knees buckled. John wrapped his arms around me and said Storey would be okay. We walked toward the cafeteria. I reminded myself she wouldn't be scared that long. It was out of my control; I had to trust the process or risk a panic attack, even though I had never had one.

I stared at the weak coffee pouring into my Styrofoam cup, almost forgetting to pay for it before I sat down across from John.

"That guy gave me the heebie-jeebies. Did you smell the stale alcohol on him? My ability to smell better than the average person is a curse." I ran my hands through my messy hair and pulled. "I can't take this mental torture much longer. I sure hope we get some answers."

"Sandee, I didn't smell anything. Everything will be fine," John said, but I knew he was also trying to convince himself. He reached for my hands over the white Formica table. I looked around.

"John, have you ever noticed that many nurses are of somewhat large proportions? I think it's because they put their patients first and themselves second. If you think about it, it's reassuring. Everyone has been mostly nice. I liked Dr. Pranzatelli."

"Wha... what did you just say? I don't know, this is the Midwest," John said.

I gagged on the tasteless coffee and looked at the wall clock—only fifteen minutes had passed. I slumped down in the plastic chair, looked up at the tiny holes in the ceiling and let my eyes play tricks. I couldn't tell if the ceiling was two inches or five feet away. A half hour later we walked back to the special waiting room. Minutes after that, the same medical aide arrived. Our puffy eyes looked in his direction. My feet couldn't find the floor.

"Storey did well. You may come with me to transfer her to the recovery room. This isn't standard procedure," he said.

I liked the man a little better knowing he could have blown us off. We followed him and Storey's rolling bed into the tight elevator. Storey looked peacefully asleep. Her color was good. I held her ankle and her right hand. She tried to smile. The medical aide directed us where to wait until Storey was fully awake. It almost felt worse, seeing her and then being told to wait again. I fiddled with my hair. John tapped his fingers against one another.

"Mills, go to room 333," we heard over the speaker. Storey was bright and smiled when she saw us, not a limp rag doll like I had prepared myself for. She pointed to a sticker on her leg.

"Wook."

"Hi sweetheart, I see fun stickers on your bed, too."

The nurse handed her more stickers. Storey's tremor wasn't any worse.

"Is this normal for her to be so mellow after this kind of procedure?" The nurse asked. Storey's tiny fingers tried to stick a sticker on the back of my hand.

"Yes, unless she is really scared. She looks good. Can we leave now?"

"Let's see if she'll drink some apple juice. Dr. Pranzatelli will be here in a few minutes," the nurse said.

"She will perk up when she has some protein," I told the nurse.

"Storey did well, she shouldn't have any side effects," Dr. Pranzatelli said. "From what I can see on her MRS films, there's significant reduction of her cerebellum compared to her previous MRI last fall, but we'll have to wait for the final radiology report. The spinal tap was clear of any infection or encephalitis. However, we will send out the special blood tests, and it will be weeks for the results. It was great meeting both of you and Storey. She is a beautiful little girl. Sorry you're going through this."

I asked for a hard copy of the new report and carried a large manila envelope with Storey's MRS films down the hall. Once outside, I felt my head pound. I dropped my head back to feel rain on my face. Another stressful hospital visit was behind us. We were back at the start of the waiting game.

At the hotel, Hayden stared at Grandpa snoring. The TV blasted. Grandma sat at the desk scribbling and pushing eraser crumbs off her crossword puzzle.

"Hi, Grandma took me to the zoo. My favorite were the snakes. Mom, remember the snake we found on our road and brought it home?" Hayden said, jumping up and down.

We wanted to tell John's folks a diagnosis. We wanted to wave around a magic pill we had picked up at the hospital pharmacy. Instead, John and I were exhausted. We knew a little more and none of it looked promising.

The next morning, Storey was her smiling self when we said good-bye to Grandma and Grandpa. The doctor was right that she had tolerated the Propofol—she was the same kid. We boarded our flight on time, I sterilized our bubble area, and then we waited and waited. Once seated, I looked out the window and had flashbacks of the 1970 movie *Airport*. The storm clouds grew from white, to gray, to scary. I reminded myself that searching for any kind of medical or alternative answer didn't come without a tremendous amount of effort, including flying through storms. An hour late, we made our Denver connection only because all the flights were delayed. I closed the window flap, wrapped my arms around Storey, and again we sat and sat for three hours on the tarmac. Fortunately, the flight wasn't full. I felt less claustrophobic. Hayden thought it was fun asking John questions about the engine and wings. For two hours Storey pulled my credit cards out of my small coin purse one by one, then reversed the procedure. She was happy if she had something to do and food to eat. We arrived in the Denver airport at midnight before being escorted to a packed bus headed to the closest Motel 6. By the time we slid into the scratchy sheets, it was 1:30 a.m. I worried how the stress of the hospital and traveling was going to affect Storey.

A week after arriving home, Storey came down with an awful flu. She moaned all night, and we didn't know how to make her feel better. I checked her temperature every five minutes. I counted down every three hours to give her another dose of Tylenol, even though the directions said four. The Tylenol made little difference.

Dr. Pranzatelli called the next morning. John and I both listened on the landline.

"Illnesses can be detrimental to her nervous system and fevers will cause more cellular damage," he said. "We will send you a copy of the MRS radiology report and the test results; the spinal fluid was clear and doesn't seem to indicate a parainfectious or paraneoplastic disorder, meaning infection and/or cancer."

"Even though I'd like to, I can't keep her in a bubble," I told him.

"I know it's hard. We didn't repeat the tests: urine metabolic screen, organic acids, lactate and pyruvate, ammonia, lysosomal enzymes, biotinidase screen, lipoprotein electrophoresis, cholesterol, alpha-fetoprotein, and IgA and IgE, all which Dr. Black conducted in October, because we didn't want to stress her body any more than necessary by taking extra blood." He took a breath and continued. "We tested her blood for phytanic acid and biotin, did a paraneoplastic antibody screen, DNA panel for spinal cerebellar atrophies, DNA analysis for Friedreich ataxia, DNA testing for mitochondrial disorder, neuron specific enolase, Vit-E, oligosaccharides, T4 and TSH, EBV panel, and pyruvate dehydrogenase, as well as urine for oligosaccharides and metabolic screen."

"Whoa, slow down, I didn't get much sleep last night. I can't write that fast," I said.

"It will all be in my report. We *do* know she has pancerebellar syndrome—cerebellar atrophy—with a predominance of cerebellar vermis. Signs manifest as truncal titubation and gait ataxia, moderately severe, with little reflexes, a reduction in cerebellar size, hypoplasia, or atrophy. I am concerned that Storey's cerebellar disorder may slowly be progressing—meaning she could have a degenerative disease since her cerebellum has decreased in size in three months. We just don't know which degenerative disease she might have. Dr. Feist will get a copy of my report. I hope she gets over this virus soon. I'm sorry I don't have more information," Dr. Pranzatelli paused.

"Okay, thanks for your help," John said.

"Thanks, but I only understood the word cerebellum and we already know her cerebellum is smaller in size, but *why?*" I asked.

"I'm hoping the remaining blood tests will give us a diagnosis, but I am worried that if the DNA testing comes back negative, we will not find the cause. There are more than a few cases where we are unable to make a diagnosis after exhausting every test. I have a few cases like Storey's and if I come across any additional tests, I will call. But unfortunately, I'm afraid Storey may fall into the undiagnosed category. Keep up with her physical therapy and swimming. It will all help."

"Thank you," I said, and hung up.

I wanted to slam the phone down. John and I chose to let the words *degenerative disease* flow through us. We didn't want to ask for exact details of what that meant. I fell to my knees and buried my face in my hands. *Fuuuccccckkkk!!!* John and I looked at each other the way Lorenzo's parents had in the movie.

My mind never stopped thinking of ways I could help Storey. There was always something else, someone else to try. Something had to work.

Minutes later I heard giggles from upstairs. Storey was awake. She needed me. I looked around the corner of her bedroom door and she smiled. I knew I was the luckiest mom alive.

Storey,

Lifetimes I hold your love, reading books forever in a moment.

You let go, smile, your wings expand, it's torment.

I want something more.

I want messes on the floor,
    where childhood wishes bloom with dreams of miracles.

Instead…

I'm exhausted carrying broken glass and dizzy from the
    roller coaster.

Doctors waving charts, others push crystal carts.

   HELP. WHERE AM I? WHERE ARE YOU?

Together we must expand our love, your wings.

Life is forever resilience in the craze.

Our love sparkles in life's shivering waters, we toss worried
    rocks to the bottom of the maze.

We eat artichokes and ice cream; grow pink flowers,
    name cloud animals that dance in the quilt of blue.

You giggle spinning your swings, and there's nothing better.

   Mom

Chapter 9

M y fight for Storey—researching, listening, Googling—weaved into a normalcy like planning a nutritious meal. In John's fight, he had to succeed in his new business. Mornings he helped with the kids, then headed to his basement office and returned there after the kids went to bed. Our family and Storey's unknown monetary needs depended solely on him. And John depended on me to be Storey's mama bear.

I made sure Storey had every supportive opportunity: swimming, horseback riding, going to school, weekly physical therapy, and home exercises. I watched, studied, and learned how to make Storey's homework fun. Storey's favorite exercise was playing music and bouncing with me on a big exercise ball—which had become part of our living room decor. Ball exercising strengthened her core, and she thought we were just playing.

As usual, I asked Sheri, her physical therapist, a lot of questions during Storey's appointments. She knew of our struggle to find a medical diagnosis and reiterated the number of undiagnosed clients she had helped over the years. She felt our pain and knew I was open to alternative methods. A few months after we saw the red-headed muscle testing couple, Sheri mentioned that a friend of hers, who was a former physical therapist turned energy healer, was coming to town.

We met George and his wife, Susan, in the same building we saw Tony for Reiki. George looked like the actor Bob Odenkirk in *Breaking Bad* and Susan looked like your favorite grade schoolteacher. We followed them to a different treatment room in that building. Hayden sat in my lap and Storey sat in John's. I gave them just a little information about Storey; I didn't want to cloud their sensing. George explained how they worked through clairvoyance, and by calling their healing guides for assistance to run universal light energy down their client's crown chakra. George and Susan stood about ten feet across from us, their legs hip-width apart, arms relaxed, palms open facing us, and their heads and eyes lifted slightly. The first thing they said was that there was an excess amount of energy in the back of Storey's head. I didn't tell them about her shrinking cerebellum.

"Storey has some very large, beautiful wings, and they're a little high," George said.

It didn't surprise me that she had wings. I assumed most young kids had holographic wings, knowing they are still a little connected to spirit.

George and Susan shared success stories of people they had helped, but I didn't care. I was more distracted and worried about Storey's "large, high wings." I already knew she was a kind of angel, an advanced being from an unknown place who struggled to stay grounded in our world. Mostly I prayed that Storey didn't have the power or temptation to use those wings to fly away.

Then Susan asked me if I had lost a boyfriend in high school. I immediately thought of a boyfriend, Troy, who died of cancer while I was in college and how that grief had blindsided me. It was irrelevant to Storey's healing, yet a validation to the healer's talent before me. But I was still too distracted by the image of Storey's wings.

Like Tony, they did a healing on me first. I climbed onto the massage table while the kids played in John's lap. Relaxing was a challenge because I knew John was noting reasons to point out to me later why their work and stories were bogus.

Finally, I relaxed my eyes. George gently moved my head side to side. Then he backed up and Susan joined; their palms faced me. Their chins were raised, and they moved their arms in small circles. Susan said I had a dark cloud over my right shoulder. Then they took deep breaths and released them toward the window like they were blowing out a birthday candle two feet away. They continued to move around my body. Unexpectedly, I felt a tingling ripple through my core. When I sat up, I was dizzy. Then John got on the table—with reservations—and they walked around him breathing and moving their hands. I saw John's closed eyes roll under his eyelids—he wasn't buying any of it.

Storey sat on the table next to me for her healing session. I gave her my yellow notepad and a marker. George and Susan repeated their dance around her. Their eyes glazed like a shaman smudging a sage stick. They performed light craniosacral therapy, and Susan asked me if Storey got headaches, dizziness or was nauseated.

"Most likely," I said. "Ataxia brings dizziness, and Storey often grabs her ears like they are itchy, even though she's never had an ear infection."

I explained that Storey had recently begun tilting her head to the side and staring into space, like she was having an absence seizure, or the way some children with ADHD might slightly tilt their head when reading. Susan said she saw a thick heaviness over Storey's head and down her left side. They worked to "break up" the heaviness and then sent it to the light of the window. Oddly, Susan left the room a few times while working on Storey.

In the end I thanked and hugged George and Susan. John shook their hands and half smiled. Hayden patiently picked up his truck books from the floor and waved goodbye. This session felt like a puzzle piece of hope, but I knew enough about energy patterns to know that for a new physical or mental pattern to integrate permanently, the new pattern needs reinforcing and adjusting more than a few times. One time won't do. There's never a quick fix.

Outside, the sun seemed brighter and I bathed in my lonely hopefulness. I wanted to share my optimism with John, but I knew it was only mine.

Storey looked into my eyes and smiled and let out a deep breath; her eyes twinkled for the first time in many months. I felt regenerated on this ordinary, windy afternoon like I had just taken a happy pill, and I didn't want the feeling to end.

"Yea! I'm excited, I'm happy!" Storey said, giggling and kicking her legs in her car seat. My skin grew goose bumps. I looked at John, who turned and smiled at Storey, but the look on his face was surprised confusion.

"Storey, your happiness warms my heart," I said.

"Mom, remember I'm always happy?" Hayden said.

John didn't say anything or look at me on the way home. I could feel his doubt. But for Storey, he allowed himself to dream.

The next day I felt a shift in Storey's spirit. Her eyes were still bright, she sat straighter, and she talked more. A light halo followed her. And in the lightness my senses opened. On our walk, birds sang more, Chisel's bounce was cuter, Storey's voice clearer. At our turnaround spot I closed my eyes and lifted my head to the sun, feeling a stream of warmth wash over my worry.

"Mom, that's a big worm, where is it going? I'm going to name it Kramer because it's sooo silly," Hayden said.

"Do you think it's happy? I asked.

"Yea... it is," Storey said.

"Can you guys smell the worms?" I said, wishing we didn't have to turn around.

On Sunday we returned to see George and Susan for the last integration before they left town. Susan apologized for leaving the room on our last visit. She explained she had suddenly become physically ill, and that when they got back to their hotel, she realized that she hadn't protected her boundaries and had taken on Storey's dark cloud instead of sending it into the light.

"Hopefully it's all down the toilet now. Thank you for taking it away. I'm sorry you had to go through that," I said.

"Storey still looks better than she did two days ago," George mentioned.

They worked on Storey the same way. Then George worked on the back of my head, and simultaneously Susan worked on the back of Storey's and felt a release of energy from Storey's head slide through mine. It felt like shared love. Again, they mentioned Storey's wings. I was afraid to ask if they thought her wings could fly.

Hayden climbed on the table. They worked on the welt on his forehead that had instantly formed when he slipped and did a faceplant at Costco a week before.

"Keep waving your hands around, it feels good," Hayden said.

We didn't stay long. Storey felt safe and reached out to give Susan a goodbye hug. That night, in the middle of her oatmeal dinner, Storey smiled and said, "I want to go see Susan." And I noticed Storey's spoon shook less.

I craved that John and I could share in the possibilities of energy healing, but I knew I'd risk a melting of the hope I guarded so close to my heart. John and I were put together differently; I accepted that. John went along with George and Susan for one of two reasons: he either had no other suggestions, or he wanted to prove to me that this energy healing stuff was a bunch of malarkey. After dinner, John picked up Storey, Hayden, and his newspaper. I walked upstairs to start the bath water.

Chapter 10

Tony, George and Susan were long gone. I feared the energy work they did on Storey's nervous system wasn't strong enough to sustain the healing pattern. A week later, when Storey developed a fever and cough, it was as though the illness had erased all their work. Her halo had disappeared, her tremors were worse, she grew weaker, and the sparkle in her eyes faded. I was determined to lift Storey back into her lightness—into herself. My friends arrived to help and offered ideas. At that point I found that researching their friendly suggestions became all too consuming. But I kept at it.

At the beginning of March 2001, I received a call from my friend Izzy, who had had life changing experiences working exclusively with a spiritual healer named Tara. He knew I was spiritually open and determined.

I knew that from the beginning, Storey's destiny was as much an enigma as her undiagnosed disease, and that she needed special people to guide her. I figured perhaps working with Tara was part of our journey. It was obvious to me that Storey was still connected to the spiritual realm—frequently gazing into the sky, listening, pointing like ET. She needed my support to keep her connected to spirit and simultaneously grounded in this physical world. And those damn wings...

Tara anticipated my call. I described Storey's past: the doctor visits, alternative healing attempts, and goals. Tara explained how she worked and that it didn't happen overnight.

"First, I dig around in the akashic records, which is an eternal imprint of every thought, word, action, physical and emotional vibration, sound, memory, and soul experience—past, present, and future. Think *Harry Potter* and the books stacked to the sky. Every person has an akashic record. I'll study Storey's to see if she's on track. Remember, though, that souls have free will to change their journey at any time," Tara said.

"Okay, I have heard of akashic records, but it sounds a bit much," I said.

"Good, that will make it easier for me. I'll carefully scan and analyze Storey's energetic layers in her auric field and look for blockages or attachments. It's called a Body-Mind Connection, (BMC). Then, with the help of my spiritual team, we remove blockages and refill the open spaces with positive thought forms and healing light. During each session we usually only work with one layer at a time, allowing the body room to open and time to integrate the healing. At this healing level, the light and thought forms awaken the intelligence of the body to heal energetically and physically, which can ripple through generations of akashic memory. I know it sounds bizarre, but it's quite simple—it just takes a lot of what you call *time*," Tara said in one breath.

"Wow, wow… okay, I'm familiar with some of your language, and can visualize what you said, and I talked to Izzy at length about it. Is Storey ready for this?"

"Well, I'll do my scans on Storey and you this week, then I'll call you back to set up a BMC appointment," she said.

Tara didn't offer a magic bullet. She never said she could heal Storey, and I took this as a good sign. I knew that true healing—medically and spiritually—didn't occur without a lot of effort, tenacity, and courage. Tara's method had window appeal, considering she was in human form and her support team was on the other side. I knew that Tara and Storey, who seemed to live in simultaneous worlds, might make a good fit. I gave Tara the green light even though I was running with blind faith.

We began working with Tara a couple months after Dr. Pranzatelli said Storey's disease seemed to be progressing like a "neurodegenerative disease."

Storey still had some good days; walking while holding our hand, less shaky, and more smiles. And bad days; poor balance, glassy eyes, and whiney. However, no matter how she felt, she always ate even though her hands shook like she had Parkinson's. I used to tell people her disease was like infantile Parkinson's disease. Storey still liked to talk: "Mom, wov you." "Hayden needs hug." "Where Chisel?"

Tara suggested I buy Storey a special healing blanket—a gift to use during our sessions. A soft, blue and white cotton blanket was the perfect choice. Storey smiled as she opened her gift and hugged it immediately. Tara also encouraged me to give Storey raw goat's milk instead of cow's milk. At the time, the raw milk health fad had returned. I put the brakes on raw. The word "raw" meant unpasteurized; it meant that if the wrong bacteria was present, it could seriously harm Storey's already fragile immune system. There are scientific and health reasons why unpasteurized dairy products are illegal to sell in many states. But Tara's suggestion of goat's milk was only half crazy. After some simple research I switched Storey from regular organic cow's milk to ultra-pasteurized goat's milk because it was the closest milk, biochemically, to breast milk. It contains more calcium and minerals, and less allergenic sugars. It's easier to digest, and I knew the transition would be smooth. Storey drank and smiled through the musky goat flavor.

Next on Tara's list of dietary recommendations was to mix powered super-greens into organic applesauce. Her suggestions made my eyes roll, so I did my green food research and headed to our local food co-op. I bought a green mixture of dried leafy green vegetables, wheatgrass, and beets topped with a pinch of dirt. On the large plastic container, it read: *Your liver loves green foods, an energy catalyst aiding cells in the process of creating more fuel and it protects cell damage from the inside out. Your entire body will thank you.*

Prevents cell damage. Storey's MRS noted cell damage—I was sold. The next evening, I mixed one teaspoon of the magic green potion into Storey and Hayden's applesauce. It looked like *Soylent Green* baby barf. Hayden gagged and swallowed. Storey ate it and smiled. I, too, began putting it in my smoothies. I crunched grit between my teeth, plugged my nose, and drank.

Even with the healing benefits of goat's milk and our green regenerating-cell food, Storey seemed to catch every illness, leaving her tired and withdrawn. Her speech slowed, she wasn't her happy self, and she often stared into space like she was having petit mal seizures. During those episodes, I worried she was leaving her body.

Then one day she said, "MOM! quit looking at me." The worse she got, the worse I got. The more I stared, waiting for the next horrible thing to go wrong, the worse she felt. It was a vicious cycle few people, much less me, had the skills to break. In contrast, the more I wore a happy-go-lucky mom-mask, the brighter and lighter she became. So that's the wolf I tried to feed.

At the end of March, we had Storey's first Body-Mind Communication (BMC) appointment with Tara. I didn't care to understand exactly how this all worked. I just wanted to get started.

Storey and I settled down in the living room among her favorite things: baby horse, ladybug, beanie babies, apple juice, cheese sticks, and her new blanket. John pulled up his loose pants, which had become baggy from stress-induced weight loss and stretched out on the couch with his newspaper.

I dialed Tara's phone.

"Hi Sandee, to begin we need to clear the room. Please light a white candle and put out a bowl of saltwater, then tap Storey's and your thymus about five times."

I did as she said.

"Now I want you to journal about how Storey has been—physically, mentally, happy or not, just anything that comes to mind. This isn't a test; I'm not going to read it. My healing helpers and I will connect with Storey on a soul and energetic level while you write. We will study her auric levels beginning with the seventh layer." While I wrote, Tara continued. "Over the next few months in our BMC sessions, we will go deeper exploring the layers and looking for blocks and attachments that may be causing some of her physical challenges. Eventually, we'll peel away to her first layer from the root chakra. Hi, John, I'm glad you're joining us," Tara said with enthusiasm.

I looked at John. The newspaper was folded on his chest, his eyes closed.

"Hi," he said, letting out a breath. His eyes remained closed.

"Hi Storey, this is Tara. Over the last week we have been talking to you, and you have visited me in my dreams. My spiritual support team and your guides are here. You are loved so much by your parents and everyone around. Your spirit is highly evolved, as you and your mother know. You are safe, safe, safe."

Tara went on and on talking to Storey, sometimes out loud and sometimes in silence.

I pictured Tara's healers like doppelgangers perhaps, even Jesus, or like a group of baffled doctors next to one's bed, calling Storey to a party on a cloud where everyone was discussing what needed to be done.

"Storey's body says it doesn't want to be worked on today. She doesn't give us permission; she doesn't feel safe," Tara said about an hour into our call.

My head and heart dropped. I rolled my neck. I wanted the spiritual realm to be on my time clock.

"Did you ask Storey when we can try again? She has been so sick lately," I said.

"We will try in a couple weeks, hopefully she'll feel better by then. Storey might be irritated that we were tapping into her energetically. Give her a chamomile tea and an Epsom salt bath tonight, it will support her nervous system. Call me in a few days and let me know how she is feeling."

"*Ugh,*" I said under my breath. "Okay, thank you, Tara."

We hung up. I felt defeated. John was snoring. I left him there and put Storey in the car, hoping she would take a nap on the way to pick Hayden up from school.

"Sandee, do not move from the parents' waiting rug, you know the rules. I will get Hayden. And, by the way, we are having trouble with him. He doesn't sit still and never completes his assignments," the owner of Hayden's school said to me when I walked in.

My shoulders rolled forward. My throat tightened. I wanted to run from that owner and her stupid rug. Even though the teacher had been on his case most of the day, Hayden ran over to me smiling. I reached for his hand and by the time I buckled him into the car, I lost it.

"Mom, what's wrong?" Hayden asked, looking out the window for trucks.

"I'm just so worried about Storey and your teacher drives me nuts. She's like the mean soup guy in *Seinfeld*," I said. "But Hayden, don't repeat what I just said."

"What? Huh? Mom, look at that truck," he said, pointing.

In the rearview mirror, he was still smiling, wiggling his hands, and kicking his legs. I ran my hands through my ratty hair. *Wow, I have a lot to learn from my little Buddhist monk.*

"Hey, want to go to Dairy Queen?"

"Yeah!" Hayden said.

"Yee," said Storey.

CHISEL

Dairy Queen? Oh, maannn … I heard that! Mom thinks I'm not listening. She forgets that bull mastiffs are one of the smartest dog breeds. You see, I felt the car make the right number of turns. When little Hayden asked me if I wanted a doggy cone, my slobber dribbled in his lap. Sweet Storey giggled. *Chiz wat a cone?* she asked. I behaved because I knew I'd get some luscious licks. Hayden carried my cone to the red tables, and I couldn't help myself—I almost bit his hand off.

Ordering at Dairy Queen.

"Chisseellll … Mom!"

"I'm sorry, Hayden, you can't tease her like that. I think she loves Dairy Queen more than we do."

"Mom, Chisel just ate the chocolate that dropped on my pants," Hayden said.

"That's good, she helps us clean up and we love her for that," I said.

Ice cream dripped down Storey's arm and into my lap, and Chisel licked it clean. Our ice cream fun didn't last long enough for my nerves to settle, so we headed to The Museum of the Rockies to watch the ball machine. Small balls gathered then poured from one level to the next, which dropped a lever and the balls then poured onto another platform, where they dropped again and moved around a maze, and sometimes a red light would turn on. Hayden jumped up and down and flapped his hands hoping to see the red light glow.

"Mom, do yo twink dee light will go on?" Storey whispered.

"I hope so, that would be good luck," I said, gripping her stroller. Even though I didn't have a plan for dinner I couldn't wait to get home to watch *Seinfeld*.

A couple weeks after Storey said no to Tara's first BMC attempt, she looked strong and bright. One day, Storey had so much energy after we picked Hayden up from school that we went to the mall, and she let go of my hand and took a few steps on her own, smiling and laughing while pushing her stroller with Hayden riding in it. She pushed him halfway down the length of the mall. I felt an overwhelming feeling of reserved excitement. *Storey was getting better and better. She walked on her own. Maybe Dr. Black was right, maybe she really does have a static situation. Or maybe the craniosacral manipulation was working, or the Dairy Queen ice cream made her so happy it released so much serotonin and dopamine that her body naturally reduced her cortisol level and created a heavenly environment for cell repair.*

I was so happy to have my Storey back that I called my mom immediately, knowing it would be an uplifting conversation rather than one of questions and condescending undertones.

Chapter 11

During Wayne Dryer's lectures he often said, "We are spiritual beings having a human experience." In my darkest moments when I found myself silently screaming, "*What is happening to Storey, and why?*" Wayne Dryer's quote reminded me to pause, to find a slice of stillness. In those micro-seconds of the present moment, life made sense and everything in its imperfections seemed perfect. However, because of my human ego and impatience, accessing that stillness and the knowing that arrived with it was almost impossible.

My warrior archetype was impatient with Tara, whose world of time wasn't where I lived. I wanted to get on with our work. For two weeks I called and bugged her several times to set up an appointment for our second attempt for Storey's first BMC.

When we finally connected, she read me more of Storey's akashic records.

"A couple hundred years ago, you and Storey were together in a tribe in the Yellowstone region. Storey was a very powerful young girl, like a shaman, who could predict weather patterns and talk to the animals, especially the buffalo," Tara said.

"She and I have a special bond with the buffalo," I said, convincing myself.

"The shaman in the tribe was very jealous and resentful of the person Storey was at that time. He made a deal with the white people, and they kidnapped Storey and kept her in a hole in the ground and used her to ask when the buffalo were going to come back or when it was going to rain. You were like her mother, and you looked for her for months and months. You were suspicious the shaman had something to do with her disappearance. She was mourned by the tribe for a long time."

"Man, why are we going through this again?" I asked, almost unable to form words. I felt my heart break, even if the story wasn't true.

"Storey has been prosecuted in many of her lives because of her healing powers. She's a very old soul. She has ascended through past lives with a desire to help people, like Mother Teresa.

"The experiences of all our past lives are carried vibrationally in our subconscious and cell memory forever. To some this may explain child prodigies. Storey is a spiritual prodigy, if you will. She doesn't feel safe here as a human because she didn't invite enough of her soul, her spirit, to support her body in this life," Tara explained.

"What you're saying resonates with me. But how many lifetimes do we have to go through the same shit?" I asked again.

"It depends on your free will choices," Tara said, taking a deep breath. "Our BMC work will help to integrate her spirit and body and to support her healing and functioning in the human world. I don't have the power to say our work will heal her completely; that is ultimately up to her. All this is part of her kismet."

Tara's narrative of Storey's past lives didn't surprise me. Although Tara shared more of Storey's past lives, our life together in Yellowstone was the only one I remembered. Just *knowing* we were together in Yellowstone felt a little healing. Was Storey's cell memory triggered when

Grandjack drove us through Yellowstone when she was 2 weeks old and began to get sick? I didn't know, but it felt more than coincidental.

All this sounded crazy. I knew this wasn't new thinking—there have been books written about akashic records and of one's soul journey. Since I was very young, I'd always felt those deep ancestral roots of past lifetimes. As fascinating and intriguing as Tara's report was, I had just one thing in mind: to understand what was happening to Storey *now* and how we were going to save her so she could live a long, healthy long life with us—forever and a day.

I laughed then cried when I pictured being escorted to the psych ward after telling my family: "*I think Storey's problem might be ancestral cell memory from past lives.*"

On our second attempt at Storey's BMC, I set up the living room as Tara instructed. I lit white candles next to a crystal bowl of Epsom salts and journaled before we began. This time John stayed in the basement, at his desk. Storey was fighting a new cold yet looked alert and happy. Through an inner dialogue of Storey's soul, she said yes to Tara's work. Tara then called on her spiritual reinforcements. I pictured angels floating around my living room holding magic wands with loving intentions.

In the beginning Tara explained that the procedure of a BMC was like peeling onion layers that needed attention, some having blocks or stagnant energy. Tara and her healers examined Storey one layer at a time, sweeping away sluggish energy and replacing the space with light and love.

For three hours Tara and her team scanned, investigated, and dissected Storey's seventh layer. Then her healers focused on Storey's heart

and throat chakras, scanning for congestion. With confused acceptance I went with it all, not wanting to jinx the process. Of course,
I blamed myself that Storey had any energy blocks at such a young
age. Then I remembered the intelligence of the soul. Tara said many
things as though she spoke a different language during our session,
and I couldn't keep up.

My head felt like a toy top spinning from listening, interpreting,
and keeping Storey busy on the floor. I was glad John wasn't in the
room. His looks would have made me feel like a total loser.

Tara ended the sessions with a series of sentences that she called
"positive thought forms." I was to write the sentences on cards and
read the words to Storey every night for a particular amount of time.
The "positive thought forms" would fill the space where Tara and her
team had removed energy blocks.

Every night I repeated these words to Storey while she was wrapped
in her special blanket, or until enough time had passed to solidify the
thought forms and light that filled the stagnant area of that energy layer.

- Card #1 read to Storey 8-10 times in a row, twice a day
  for 15 days straight:

  Grounds in a plan of action in subconscious of self.
  Positive corrective infusion order is restored. Life is
  better than normal and magical things start to appear.

- Card #2: read to Storey 6 times in a row twice a day for
  9 days:

  Conduit of light, qualities of positive corrective infu-
  sion-spontaneous combustion can only occur when

your essence and understanding is grounded. You are protected and looked after. Be the communicator of possibilities.

- Card #3 read to Storey 8-10 times in a row twice a day for 9 days:

  Inspirational center, qualities of positive corrective infusion is all there is and always has been if you believe. Being truly loved by the soul is an honor to be whole.

Chapter 12

*I feel tiny diamonds slip through my fingers. I must find some-
thing, anything—the right bowl or a magic towel to grab
and catch the shiny minerals. Or I must call upon someone
else's healing hands to save the diamonds. But I can't find
the right person or the right thing. I scream. No one hears
me. The stones continue to pour through my fingers. I can't
stop them. I know if I can't catch them, my world will end.
    …Storey's world will end.*

Soon after my diamond dream and the session with Tara, Dr.
Pranzatelli called with the results of the remaining DNA blood
tests. My body froze.

"Hi, Mrs. Mills." Dr. Pranzatelli cleared his throat. "The DNA
results were all normal. There wasn't a marker for any of the genetic
conditions that we can test for at this time."

"Does that mean we still don't have a name for what's happening
to Storey?" I asked.

"I still suspect it's a degenerative disease of unknown origin. All I
can tell you is that we know Storey has a low cell count in her cerebellum, her carnitine levels are low, and her neuro-specific enolase
are a tad high," he explained.

"Shit, okay, what does all that mean?"

"Low carnitine can cause weakness, and her high neuro-specific enolase can be caused by a genetic problem or because of her cell loss. These are just noted, they don't give us a diagnosis. We can repeat some of these tests in a few months. I'm so sorry, I know this is very frustrating," he said.

The conversation was short. For once I had run out of questions. I was frustrated, mad, sad, and fried. I thanked the doctor. My body felt like I was wearing ankle weights walking downstairs to tell John.

"That was Dr. Pranzatelli on the phone. He told me the rest of Storey's blood work was negative and that it's a possibility Storey won't ever be given a proper diagnosis. We may never know why Storey is losing function," I said, choking.

"Sandee, why didn't you come and get me?" John took a deep breath. "I wanted to talk to him."

"I don't know, I'm sorry, he sounded like he was in a rush to tell me bad news. You know how it is. What would you ask him?"

"I don't know, Sandee, geez." John turned his back and started punching the keys on his computer.

I tripped on the first step walking up the stairs. Storey was undiagnosed and John was mad at me.

The next day Dr. Feist called. He consistently made me feel better. In the beginning of this fight, it never occurred to us that it was possible for Storey to be undiagnosed. Why couldn't our situation be like a hospital show, where a diagnosis only took fifteen minutes?

After the phone calls, I had no choice but to continue to tackle this demon on my own using whatever insane means I could find, whether it came from this world or not. Having Tara and her supportive team made me feel better, but I knew it was too crazy to be a solution. I'd been wrong about almost everything and I was losing confidence.

I was anxious about the next BMC session. Morning and night Storey and I stuck to the card reading rules, then one day out of the blue Storey said, "I want to call Tara."

Storey's strength and mood continued to wax and wane. Sometimes she asked to stand up in the Costco cart while I held her tight. I took advantage of every one of her standing opportunities.

One of her favorite pastimes was cutting up old magazines into little pieces. She remained focused and smart, spending hours looking closely at books and reading people's energy. In the car one day she said, "Mom, no, no, that garbage isn't supposed to be there." In my rearview mirror I saw her bottom lip turn down. At 3 years old, she knew garbage on the side of the road was wrong.

Like many, I wished I had the ability to stop time and to speed it up. Two weeks after our first BMC session we had our second. I prayed for Tara's exhausting sessions to be behind us. I pictured Tara and Storey conversing through spiritual soul dialogue, like two avatars in midflight, completely oblivious to humans' addiction to time. My future self said, *I want these sessions over and Storey better now! Goddamnit!* But I knew that wasn't realistic unless a beam of light streamed down from a different dimension into Storey's crown chakra and simultaneously healed her. Then we'd dance and sing. And I'd be one of those mothers who wrote a book about a miracle.

Our second BMC session was more exhausting. We were on the phone for more than four hours. Storey was very patient as they dug around her etheric field and explored places I'd never heard about, like her twelfth chakra. They also worked on her fifth layer, removing the negative thought forms in that area.

The new cards were of equal length, and they were grueling. I had to make a game out of it. I put little stickers of animals on the cards and Storey held them while I read. Sometimes I sang them to her, I danced for her, I bent my body into yoga pretzels saying the words. The stupid words swirled in my head as I slept.

The BMC sessions connected me to the spirit world, a world where I knew Storey lived most of the time. I felt it. Consistently she looked toward the heavens, reaching with one hand, like she yearned to return. When she gazed up, she glowed and her wings grew, and she returned to me with less of herself. I prayed to whomever oversaw the Flying-Wing-Pixie-Dust distribution to stop sprinkling Storey.

Chapter 13

M y patience thinned after months of working with Tara. She
said that using her healing model we still had layers to peel. I
felt lost. I couldn't completely rely on her or on Western medicine.

I pictured Storey's healing coming from many places, like the
beginning of an assimilation of carefully examined puzzle pieces,
and it was my job to look in the corners of our world for the missing pieces. My mama bear approach grew stronger.

It was late May 2001 when the sun gifted us with more perfect
days, and I found myself knocking on room 101 at a local AAA-
approved motel in town. Weeks before, a mother approached me at
Storey's preschool. She had an instinct that I might be interested in
a weekend workshop for mystical women directed by a group that
I'll call: The Sisterhood of Hope. The Sisters were offering to energetically activate one's DNA. I had heard about that kind of work
years ago. I wondered if it could help me with my bad spelling, or if
it might activate the DNA from my mother's side giving me the ability to read as fast as she did. Since I had recently heard about DNA
activation more than twice in a short amount of time, it fit into my
healing guidelines.

"The Sisters will active your DNA. Then, like a ripple of good juju it may 'activate' Storey's DNA. They have helped me on my spiritual journey," the mother told me.

The saying *Heal the Mom, Heal the Child* swirled in my brain. Again with blind faith, my friend introduced me to the Sisters, who looked as though they belonged behind a table at a farmer's market selling warm chocolate chip cookies rather than in a random motel room holding sage sticks and crystals. Surprisingly, their old motel room felt cozy and warm. Their silk cloths hid the desk and TV, and clear crystals were arranged in patterns on colorful material.

I was nervous and didn't know what to expect, but maybe a sage wash and prayers were what *I* needed. In layman's terms they explained that their work stimulated the spine with loving, healing light to wake up its natural intelligence, and to open doors of the akashic field, to strengthen the immune system, and to aid unconscious patterns. It may also repair damaged DNA, and possibly bring some clarity to one's journey. If $222 can do all that, I was in.

The Sisters didn't make any promises or try to sell me products. They began to wave lit sage sticks around the room and my standing body. Pictures of me from perhaps a different life appeared in my mind while sage smoke floated to the ceiling. They held healing rods of exquisite crystals and touched my neck, pausing between my vertebrae. I felt a burning throughout my spine, which morphed into a welcome tingle. My eyes remained closed, and I felt like I was sitting in my grandmother's lap wrapped in a love blanket. In that moment, my entire world was perfect. What must have only been a few minutes felt like a powerful dream that went on for hours, and I didn't want to wake up.

I opened my eyes and felt a wave of oxygen rush to my head. My body's senses were fresh. I could feel my cells communicate with the rest of my body, integrating and embracing what had just happened. I rested in a green vinyl chair and sipped herbal tea for half an hour and watched the Sisters perform the same healing on the next gal.

After the activations were complete, I asked one of the Sisters, through quiet tears, if she might be able to help Storey.

"What we just did on your body will help Storey's body too," she said. "You will carry the light and transfer some of the light and healing to her body through intentions and love. But yes, we can do more. I'm sensing she has a negative energy hanging around her that's physically hurting her body. Can you bring her here?"

"Thank you."

With trepidation and elation, I called John and was relieved that he didn't ask any questions. It seemed ironic that the Sister felt the same way that Tara did about a negative energy even though they didn't know each other. Tara's work was taking a lot of time. But this Sister wasn't charging me anything and just wanted to see Storey for a few minutes. I felt optimistic. The Sisters' healing seemed too simple and Tara's, too complicated. Maybe most healers assumed negative energies were creating harm or that it could just be a spiritual to-go diagnosis. I didn't know. I didn't care. I just wanted the dark *whatever* near Storey to be gone.

Twenty minutes later I lifted Storey out of her car seat from John's car. I prayed for whatever the Sisters could do for Storey to be sustainable, and that we wouldn't have to continue with Tara's long sessions.

"Sandee, I hope you know what you're doing," John said, sighing.

My body tensed. "There is always hope and that's what I'm relying on," I said to him, smiling at Hayden in the back seat.

Storey and I entered the hotel room. The Sister who did my DNA asked me to leave Storey with them. This caught me off guard, but

Storey wasn't scared, she wasn't crying. She was happy and smiling like she knew the Sisters well. I stepped outside for few minutes and leaned against the hotel window. I trusted them and assumed they would just wave lit sage and crystals and repeat mantras while asking this supposedly negative thing to go away, but I must admit it felt a little like the 1973 movie *The Exorcist.*

I paced outside the motel room and lifted my head to the sun, took a deep breath and closed my eyes. Ten minutes later the door opened. The Sister lifted Storey back into my arms. She was beaming and smiling, the way she did when she felt good. I reached for her and cried on her shoulder.

The Sister rubbed my back and said, "With the help of many people I think Storey is going to be okay—at least for now. We sent the negative energy away. It was like an energy sucker feeding on Storey's energy."

I wiped my tears with the back of my hand. "It's that simple? She sure looks happy. I'm excited to see if she feels stronger and better from now on. Thank you."

"You never truly know; everyone is here for different reasons." The Sister hugged Storey and me and said goodbye. Storey smiled.

On that sunny spring day, I didn't want to go home. I wanted to let whatever happened to us to integrate longer.

"Storey, do you want to go to the river and throw rocks?"

She giggled a squeaky, "yeah!"

On the edge of the Gallatin River, I gathered handfuls of small stones and piled them next to her. One at a time she grabbed a rock between her weak fingers and tossed. Sometimes the rocks made it to the water. The sparkle of the spring sun reflected in Storey's clear eyes. I imagined our cells communicating and healing like a forever hug. I felt a glimmer of promise. A breeze breathed through our hair, and I wished I had the ability to carry and retrieve the intensity of this bliss whenever I needed to remind myself that life, in its present dance, *was* always perfect. However, I knew how all this worked—living in fragments of time was always a tease of what could be.

I still had to go the grocery store, and there were clothes to wash and bills to pay. At the store I looked down at Storey sitting in the sticky grocery cart. We looked at each other and cracked up for no reason. I kissed her forehead and tossed some oatmeal in the cart.

"Hi, Hayden. Give me a hug. We just came from the store and from seeing some ladies who hopefully helped Storey's body heal. Here, can you carry this bag of groceries for me? I bought you string cheese."

"I don't know, Mom. I only have no hands." Hayden said, opening his palms.

When we got to the top of the stairs, John smiled at Storey.

"Hi sweetheart," he said, reaching for her.

Then he looked at me and asked what was for dinner.

Chapter 14

We waited for tests, doctors, naps, Tara, a healing, and for Dairy Queen to reopen in the spring. Waiting reminded me to practice patience in my rigid time-box. Storey was enthusiastic about her home exercises when I made them fun. Sometimes I'd notice her pulling up against the couch to stand. She was bright and strong when the spring winds blew away lingering viruses. On days when Storey's teachers reported her strengths, ignoring her defeats, I saw possibilities.

Hayden took swimming lessons every Friday night and Storey and I played in the water with her plastic floating dinosaurs. If other kids were in the pool, she gently extended her hand and offered her toys with a smile. Mothers with rambunctious kids looked amazed. Storey was free and happy in the water, and no one could tell she couldn't walk or run. No one looked at her or me differently. On perfect days, I lifted her to the edge of the pool and she bent her knees and jumped into my arms.

Hayden was Storey's cheerleader. Their favorite afternoon activity was standing next to each other on their kiddy step, holding onto our antique washstand in the living room and listening to the CD player. Storey gripped each corner with everything she could and to the beat of Fleetwood Mac's "Rumors." She and Hayden wiggled their butts and giggled until Hayden took out the CD, sniffed it, looked at Storey then returned the CD to the player and giggled.

Spring meant we took more walks up the road. Chisel had no objections.

"Let's walk to see the horses, or let's walk farther and see if Tanner comes to greet us," Hayden often said.

I'd lift Storey out of the baby jogger, and we'd wave a carrot in the air. If we were lucky, Classy, the shy paint horse up the street, walked to us from across the field and gently nibbled the carrot from Storey's hand. Then Classy would rest her nose against Storey's chest. I'd weave Storey's fingers into mine to caress Classy's warm face. Hayden jumped until I lifted him to pet Classy. I'd drink in one more breath of Classy's alfalfa scent before we left.

If we had extra time, we walked farther up the road. Storey sat in my lap and Chisel leaned against us. Hayden gathered pebbles and placed them next to Storey for her to toss. In the simple act of walking up a road, time was a gift.

On Hayden's 5th birthday, June 13th, 2001, we woke to the sound of tree branches snapping under eight inches of heavy snow. For the fun of it I told Hayden that God brought him snow for his birthday.

He asked, "Who's God?"

"The indigenous peoples, who were here long before us, might call God 'The Creator.' Some people think God is a person in the sky handing time-outs to bad people and miracles to good. People pray to God when they don't know what else to do. We don't know if *He* exists. But who else gives us those beautiful sunsets?" I was still talking when Hayden ran off.

Summer was always official when both sets of grandparents arrived in time for Hayden and Storey's annual barbeque-birthday-bash that involved a Dairy Queen cake.

Large 3's decorated Storey's birthday cards, and it marked one year since our journey had begun. Grief and helplessness decorated the faces of Storey's grandparents when they saw her for the first time in months. I smiled and wished I could have shared the lengths I'd taken so they knew I wasn't wallowing in denial. Fortunately, my mother, who visited at the end of summers, understood and lent—mostly—a soft ear.

In our area, summer solstice began the countdown of cherished evenings and sidling darkness. We ate outside. Hayden and Storey bathed in their kiddy pool and Chisel rolled in the soft grass under Mother Nature's palette.

One evening, Storey was playing in her baby walker eating her five chocolate chips one by one while I was weeding my flower garden. I looked at her and said "Storey, look at those colors. This is my church. Aren't we lucky to live here?"

Suddenly her entire body went limp, and her face slammed onto the tray of her walker and into the chocolate chips. By the time I picked her up we were both hysterical.

"Fuuucckk! Storey, what just happened?"

I held her as tight as I could and under the golden light, we folded into a crying ball. I looked up and begged for this to be a single freak incident.

Weeks later, without warning, she collapsed again. It was as though her spirit jumped out of her body and a second later jumped back in. The next day I called Dr. Feist and asked for a recommendation for a different pediatric neurologist in Montana. My fear of losing her was unbearable, I couldn't help but hover.

"Mom, quit looking at me!" Storey said one day.

I kissed her forehead, wiped my tears, told her I was sorry, then looked away and ran my fingers through Chisel's wrinkles. I reminded myself that I must live moment by moment because that was all I had.

Dear *Mom,*

Did you know that my favorite time was spring when the sun warmed my face and gave me strength? And you'd spread newspapers all over the kitchen floor and set mugs of beautiful colors and a basket of boiled eggs next to me. I got sooooo excited because I spent hours playing with the colors and eggs. The eggs peeked above the colored water like full moons.

Together we'd watch tulips and daffodils push through the snow, and sometimes when deer ate the tulips you'd say, "Shit." Then we'd laugh. You kept Chisel inside because you knew how much Hayden and I loved watching the cute faces of the deer. Mom! Did you know I secretly named a few of the deer?

In spring at school, we played outside longer and my teacher, Helen, helped me walk on the melting snow. I loved her so much. I also loved Tara. She lightened my spirit and took away a dark tornado swirling around me.

In the heat of the summer Hayden and I watched the wasps and bees drink from our blue kiddy pool. Sometimes Chisel stood in the pool with us, and we poured water over her back.

Mom, it breaks my heart how much you looked at me and worried. I'm glad you trained for a half marathon for your 40th birthday because I knew when you ran, the world made a little more sense. And we all know how grumpy you are when you haven't exercised. But Dad's worrying eyes were worse than yours, so I'd smile at him a lot and he'd smile back.

The summer I turned 3, I knew you wished I could run around freely and make messes like my friends. My body felt off and foggy, like my soul was floating. Sometimes I'd have a surge of energy in my brain and I'd go to a strange place where I couldn't feel your love. It was scary, but I knew where you were.

I loved to walk up the street calling, "Clllaaassyyy," to our horsey friend. Her smell made us feel better. Farther up the street we wondered if we'd see our yellow lab friend, Tanner, and his wiggly-giggly tail. Mom, did you know when I was around animals, especially Chisel, I felt my soul come down into my body and life was good again? My body changed, but my soul has always been the same.

Thanks for being a good mom.

I love you,

Storey

Chapter 15

All along I had doubts about Tara, wondering if she was scamming me, but unlike scammers who promised you the moon for "just a little" more money, she didn't make promises. In addition to the work Tara and her healers did for us, she ran a consulting business to help executives make decisions from a spiritual perspective by investigating if a place or person had good or bad juju.

Her mystical ways were not for everyone. Yet she felt like a friend, and when I called crying on the phone about Storey's "drop" episodes, she suggested I add a different modality to Storey's healing. She shared her personal psychic surgeon named Babs. Her stories about Babs went on, and I felt restless and intrigued. She had spoken to Babs about us and felt Babs might be able to help. While on the phone with Tara I glanced over at Storey picking up a ball from her ball toy, then she dropped it into a hole and watched it come out the bottom. I stared fearing she'd hit her face on the plastic toy during a "drop" that came out of nowhere. The constant frightening feeling in my gut and nerves was grueling.

Years before, I had read an article about the psychic surgeon "John of God" from Brazil who, with his bare hands, performed miracles for hundreds of people since the 1970s. Even George and

Susan, and a friend of my mother's, had mentioned taking Storey to Brazil. But I knew there was no way in hell John or I were going wear white clothes and pilgrimage in Brazil to stand in lines for hours, maybe days, to see "John of God." But taking two flights to see Babs was doable.

I trusted Tara. I wanted to trust Tara. I knew she cared about Storey. Casually, as if sipping green tea, Tara continued to talk about Babs.

"Babs sits in dark meditation for a day and falls into a trance-like state before she performs psychic surgery. If the body is willing, and wants to get rid of something foreign, like a blood clot or tumor, the body opens under Babs's fingers and she's able to remove what isn't serving the body. When she's done, the skin instantaneously closes back together and leaves no scar. It's a developed talent that a born healer or shaman can do by transforming the body's energy."

Had I never heard of this kind of healing I would have dropped the phone and never talked to Tara again. But I had, and I asked questions. Everything about Tara was so bizarre that nothing surprised me—not even the lengths I considered to help my fading daughter.

Since I vowed to follow my guidelines, to investigate and research something if I heard it from three different sources, I contemplated taking Storey to see Babs if John agreed. And yes, as fucking crazy as it sounded, I wasn't ignorant to the pseudoscience train of trickery, preying on dumbfounded and desperate people, like me. Tara said she was scheduled to see Babs herself and invited us to join. Tara made it clear I could choose my donation amount to pay Babs. I liked that she wasn't asking for my life savings or for me to sacrifice my dog. *Why would someone go through all this trouble if it wasn't for the money, even if it was fake?* I asked myself. Maybe Babs really did have a talent and wanted to help. The more we spoke, the less it felt like Tara and Babs were in cahoots. It felt more like Tara was referring me to her favorite hair stylist.

The next morning, I was a nervous wreck after a restless night contemplating my conversation with John about this outlandish idea.

Finally, I held Storey on my left hip as a prop, and said, "I talked to Tara yesterday. She has a personal psychic surgeon named Babs in Seattle. She's meeting her next week and feels she could help Storey with her 'drops.'" Storey looked up at John with a smile. John didn't say a word. I stirred Storey's oatmeal and continued to explain what a psychic surgeon was. John said nothing.

Later that morning John came back upstairs and said, "Well, at least you and Storey can finally meet Tara."

My stomach dropped. He kissed Storey on the forehead and walked downstairs.

Chapter 16

E very Halloween we drove to town. A week into Daylight Savings, the evening was dark by 5:00 p.m., but felt like 7:00. As usual, I ran late dressing Hayden as a tiger and Storey as a penguin. John and I pushed Storey up and down the street in her kiddy stroller. John picked her up at most houses and carried her to the front doors, or Hayden pointed to Storey from the front porches of houses.

"Trick or treat! Can I have an extra piece of candy for my sister? She can't walk," Hayden asked. He shook with excitement then ran down and dropped candy into Storey's bag. I was relieved the night was over by the time we got home. I wanted to get Storey to bed so I could stay awake all night wondering if we were going to make our 6 a.m., flight.

"Hayden, you can only eat one piece, okay? Aww, okay, two pieces of candy. But I need to check your candy bag first," I said, noticing John's eyes roll. I loved Halloween but I hated having the candy in the house, because I had no self-control.

We got the kids to bed after a quick bath and I packed. If John was going somewhere for two nights, it would take him five minutes to pack. It took me hours, especially with Storey's needs.

CHISEL

Mom smelled nervous and ran around all evening. I heard the words: "Doctors, no walking, Tara." I followed Mom into her room, and I smelled her black bag and Storey's backpack on the big bed. Then I remembered it's the smell of Mom going somewhere without me. If Dad and Hayden and I stayed home, I knew they wouldn't be gone long.

That night the smell of sweet pumpkin floated through the kitchen. Sometimes Mom puts that smell into my bowl after I throw up and sometimes, I think about throwing up just so I will get some pumpkin.

As usual, I parked myself under the table to catch Hayden's mess. I'm proud to say my catching record is 90 percent, thanks to my bull mastiff underbite. A piece of hotdog landed on my tongue. Hayden laughed, then Storey laughed. Then the bits kept coming. Mom kept running around saying "shit" at the clock.

Hayden and Storey looked silly when they put clothes over their heads and turned into stuffed animals. Hayden swung an orange bucket around his wrist and kept hitting me in the head, which I did not appreciate.

"Hayden! Careful, we need to go," Mom said from the hall.

I wanted to eat pumpkin and since I already felt sick from the hot dog pieces I thought of a time when I *was* sick. My drool increased until Hayden yelled, "MOM, Chisel just frew-up."

Man, oh man, I felt better. Mom scooped the mess before I could eat it. "Chisel, are you okay?"

She ran her hand across the top of my head and down my left ear. I showed her the whites of my eyes, wondering when that pumpkin would be served. Instead, she told Dad to warm up the car. When she cupped my muzzle and kissed my wrinkles, I realized I wasn't invited. But I was relieved to be away from the hazards of the orange bucket. I laid on the top of the stairs and rested my head on my right paw. And waited. Minutes later I heard Hayden.

"Chisel, I got a ton of candy, but you can't have any."

"It's late, everyone to bed," I heard Mom say. "Storey and I have to catch a really early flight."

I woke after a couple dreams of hunting for voles, to a yucky smell. I heard footsteps and running water.

"Hayden, you and Chisel threw up on the same day," Mom said from the bathroom.

I wondered if Hayden was going to get my pumpkin.

Around 1:00 a.m., when I was just falling asleep, I woke to the sound of someone gagging. My stomach dropped. "John, one of the kids just puked. Wake up!"

We ran into the kids' room. Hayden half smiled; throw-up dripped from his pajamas onto Storey's bottom bunk. "How much candy did you eat?" I asked. He and I both started to cry. What felt like fifteen minutes later, at 3:50 a.m., the alarm blasted me from choppy dreams of missing our flight.

"Storey, it's time to get on a big airplane to see Tara in Seattle. We won't be there very long, and it'll be fun," I said, nervously convincing myself, *I got this.*

"Okay," she whispered.

Izzy, who had recommended Tara, was five people ahead of us in line at the Delta check in. My body relaxed when I realized his seat was next to ours. Storey stayed busy the entire flight handing Izzy small toys from her bags then returning them. Between the flights I pushed Storey to the restroom. I didn't have the strength to hold her up in one of the small stalls bending against our luggage without touching everything. Storey cracked up when I lined the changing table with about ten seat covers. The airport buzzed with stimulation; I knew this made Storey exhausted. She took in everything. She worried about people. "Mom, who's that?" She sent strangers love, looking up at them, and whispering, "I love you." Unfortunately, few heard her love whispers. Even though it tired her out, she aways gave more of herself.

I wondered how many people running through the airport in heels, clogs, freshly polished Oxfords and running shoes had slowed down enough to appreciate their ability to run and walk without much effort. We all cheer when a baby learns to walk. A month later we expect it and don't ever think about it again… until we must.

I was relieved when I noticed the town car driver that John had reserved for us, holding a MILLS sign. I wrapped the one seatbelt around Storey and myself and braced to arrive safely without a car seat. Raindrops ran down the foggy windows and I asked the driver when the sun last appeared.

"Well, honestly, I don't remember. You have a very beautiful daughter," he said.

"Thank you, I sure do."

I carried Storey into the hotel lobby and eased her feet down to the floor tiles. "Just a minute, Princess, I'll have the stroller open in a second."

She wrapped her arms around my left leg and tried to balance. When I bent over again my backpack dropped over my shoulder, missing Storey's head. Her sippy cup rolled across the floor. I let out a breath and wondered what the hell I was doing there. Then I looked around the lobby for the image I had made up in my mind of what I envisioned Tara would look like: high cheek bones, long dark hair, wearing colorful, flowing clothes.

The elevator ride to the seventh floor made me feel ill. I started to sweat and began to feel nauseated, and I wondered if Storey felt the same. In the hall I glimpsed the backside of a lady with short, curly hair wearing sweatpants and a purple fanny pack. And somehow, I knew. Tara looked nothing like I wanted. But I reminded myself that our bodies are only containers for our spirits. *Who was I to judge?*

The hotel room was musty. I flung open the drapes and turned on the fan. Storey and I watched the ducks swim in a pond below the window. Our session with Babs was in two hours.

Our room phone rang. "Hi Sandee, Tara here—I'm in room 717. I hope you traveled well. Storey needs to be well fed and rested. Maybe order some oatmeal from room service then meet us in my room at three o'clock."

"Okay. We're ready, I think. Storey slept well on the second flight. I hope she feels safe with Babs."

"Babs is very gentle, and I shared Storey's history," Tara said.

I hung up the phone and took a breath.

Out of the blue Storey said, "I want to see Tara."

Three o'clock came quickly. I cupped Storey's face in my hands and kissed her soft right cheek and said, "We are going to meet Tara and her nice friend now."

Storey smiled and reached for a hug. Tara opened the door before we knocked. The hotel room was luminous. Candles fluttered on colorful cloths that draped the hotel furniture. Tara's hug was warm and unconditional. Storey and I sat on the bed looking at Tara, who pointed to a picture in Storey's favorite book. Babs sat stoically in a chair next to the bed. A subtle gold and pink sunset-like aura surrounded her. It was the first time I could easily see an aura.

"I want to take off my shirt," Storey said minutes later.

Tara, Babs, and I looked at each other. Unlike some kids, Storey never took her clothes off. Tara said it was a good sign that Storey felt secure and relaxed.

Babs carefully ran her fingers up and down Storey's bare back, then stopped on a spot. I studied Babs's hand. I wanted to remember every detail, every movement. A light purple aura glowed around Babs's hand. Just a few inches from my eyes, Babs's fingertips made their way under Storey's skin. Storey wiggled like she had an itch. I looked at Babs's face; her eyes were closed, and she made a little hum noise. Her hand stopped. Storey arched her back a little then looked up and smiled. Tara stood next to Babs holding a glass of water. Babs dropped a piece of bloody, stringy body tissue into the glass, and it sank. Tara wiped a drop of blood off Storey's back.

"That's all for today," Babs said. She returned to the chair like it was a throne.

I looked at Storey's back—it was a little red, nothing else. Everything had happened so slowly and so quickly. "Why do you put it in a glass of water?" I asked.

"So you can see what just happened," Tara said, helping me put Storey's shirt back on.

Did Babs pull chicken guts out of her sleeve? Neither she nor Tara wore long sleeves. I tried to make sense of what just happened. Questioning my sanity and desperation, I played the movie over and over in my mind. *Why would Tara fly to Seattle, rent a hotel room, talk her friend into coming, and between them split my two-hundred-and-fifty-dollar donation?*

"I hope this helps, but I'm not promising anything," Babs said.

"Okay, thank you very much."

Storey reached out and hugged them both. I walked out of the room and peered around the hallway for a line of desperate people waiting to be cured by Babs. It was empty.

I knew there were a select few who could perform shamanic miracles and psychic surgeries. I also believed there were more people with snake-oil quackery, but at that point it didn't matter. We were done and Storey was fine.

Storey and I looked down from our hotel window to see the ducks. I couldn't stop thinking about what had happened. Storey watched *Clifford the Big Red Dog*. I called my mother, who I knew wouldn't criticize me—at least not this time. She told me something I heard only on special occasions.

"Sandee, I'm so proud of you. Most people wouldn't take this wild risk. You've been preparing for this fight your whole life." For once

I really listened, and she continued. "You learned how to fight for yourself, and now you're fighting for Storey."

My mother was both quick to judge and quick to praise. The latter was easily forgotten. This time, her validation for never giving up made me feel good.

Then I called John, still doubting if what I had seen was real. I shared what I witnessed.

"Storey is fine, and she wasn't afraid."

"Well, I don't know what to think about everything. But I'm glad you got to meet Tara. Hayden wants to say hi," he said.

Storey and I fell asleep watching cartoons. When she woke in the early evening she said, "Mom, I want to go home."

I cried. Our flight wasn't until eight o'clock the next evening.

Delta's customer service said, "I have a flight at 7:45 a.m., it's nine hundred dollars."

"I'll take it."

We visited the ducks before dinner. Storey squealed watching the mallards paddle in circles. At dinner Tara noticed my skepticism at the day's events. Between bites of salmon, she shared personal stories of Babs removing cysts, small tumors, and blood clots. I said very little. As engrossing as her stories were, I was over it and I just wanted to go home.

John and I never spoke about the visit again. I suspect John supported the trip to Seattle so I'd realize Tara and her healing methods were a hoax. To this day I still wonder if what I saw was what I thought I saw. I'll never truly know.

And it doesn't matter.

Chapter 17

In early December 2001, Storey was 3½ and Hayden 5½ years old. John woke us at four o'clock in the morning to catch an eye-burning flight to Davis for an early Christmas. Hayden was thrilled. I was not.

I woke with a massive headache from dreams of running through the airport nude and screaming because I couldn't find Storey. Our kids' bags bounced against aisle seats, and I noticed silent wishes from travelers hoping our seats weren't near theirs. Right before the flight took off, Hayden stood in his seat and announced, "my penis hurts." Laughter rippled through the rows and the energy in the plane lightened.

Before entering Grandjack and Valerie's house, all the grandkids were given the same lecture: "Do not touch anything!" Their house had morphed from '70s gold carpet and grass cloth wallpaper to a fragile and bright Native American motif. Dad and Valerie lived in the same house my sister and I lived in during our high school years when our parents were still married. John and I slept under the yellow ceiling light I had picked out in 1975. My waterbed was long gone.

Hayden ran around with the excitement of travel and Storey crawled after him as fast as she could. Their short-lived fascination with the Navajo drums was diverted to the perfectly wrapped Christmas packages and Valerie's homemade candy cane cookies dangling from the limbs of their symmetrical Douglas fir Christmas tree.

My campaign to keep Storey away from neurotoxins didn't register with my dad, who, after we had an altercation, reluctantly stopped spraying Raid on ants trailing on the wood floors where Storey crawled. Pictures of frightened bugs on the Raid's label was enough to scare anyone. My dad's profession was an aerial application specialist for the USDA Forest Service, studying and applying herbicides and insecticides to diseased forests. Therefore, he knew a lot more than I did about the can's contents. He told me it was harmless if I washed her hands, but I thought otherwise. He probably assumed I was just being my usual hypochondriac self.

Nevertheless, I was nervous to tell him and Valerie about Storey's "drops," and I worried Storey would have one in their company. I feared they would lecture us about taking her to the Mayo Clinic despite what I knew about what stress did to her fragile nervous system. After interviewing people about the Mayo Clinic, I learned that they would repeat every test, including the nerve conduction, and other invasive procedures. And I—we—refused to put her through that. All doctors and neurologists had told us there were few options because they concluded that it was a neurogenerative disease or progressive degenerative disease (depending on how you want to phrase it).

Both Dad and I were both obstinate and didn't hesitate to say our truth, however, he and Valerie were kind enough not to ask why strong essential oil fragrances of sandalwood and lavender drifted from the room where Storey slept.

My mother, who we often addressed by her name, Pat, lived thirty minutes from my dad. And she wanted to help Storey. It wasn't unusual for her to have a spiritual guide or medical intuitive at her fingertips. I was anxious and wondered if her psychic friend Sidra would be able to tell us anything about Storey's "drop" episodes. Two days after we arrived in Davis, on a gray, rainy day, I strapped Storey into her car seat and with a shot of adrenaline I merged into heavy traffic on our way to visit my mom.

"Hi, Storey. Are you having fun? Look at all these cars. We should be at Grandma Pat's house in twenty minutes," I said, looking at her in the review mirror.

"Yeah, I'm excited." She smiled and took a bite of an apple slice.

When we pulled up to Mom's house, the door flew open. I knew what that meant.

"Sandee, you're late! We need to be across town in fifteen minutes," she said, waving a map above her head.

She and I had a different relationship with time. I rolled my eyes and handed her the keys. Mom loved traffic. She loved swearing at people in traffic. She loved maps and took great pride in always knowing where she was and belittled people who didn't instantly know a town's coordinates.

The rain slowed to a drizzle; Storey and I drew smiley faces on the foggy windows. Mom parked. A dark-haired lady with big brown eyes and casual clothing opened her door and greeted us with a smile.

"Come in and get out of the rain. I hope the sun peeks out today, but it sure doesn't look like it. Storey, you are beautiful. Sandee, you can sit here," Sidra said, pointing to a purple velvet chair.

I nestled Storey into my lap while scanning Sidra's dark office of crystal clusters and plants. I grinned at my mother when she took out her yellow notepad.

"Storey's an angel. You know that light surrounds her, but I first want to talk about you, Sandee," Sidra said, looking in my eyes.

Here we go. She's going to tell me that I need to be a better mother.

"Sandee, I see you moving next year."

What? Does that mean Storey is getting worse and we must move? I don't want to move! I love my house, the hill, and our dirt road.

Noticing my unhappy expression, Sidra continued. "It could mean a spiritual move, traveling, starting a career and/or helping others. In your third eye, your sixth chakra, I see a symbol. I've only seen this once before."

Sidra drew the shape on a small white piece of paper. She showed me a circle inside an upside-down small triangle inside a larger flattened triangle.

"It means you could change the world someday if you chose. We all have free will."

Wow! That took me by surprise. *I don't have that kind of energy. Does she tell that to everyone? Or should I feel special?*

"Spirit tells me in your search to help Storey, you must not give up until you feel the time has come. Always trust your feelings and intuition and speak your truth, and if you have doubts, trust that it's a better decision. In time you and Storey will help other people. Try to make quiet time with yourself through meditation and walks. It's very important for you to take care of yourself while taking care of Storey," Sidra continued, holding Storey's hand. "Even though your husband is a skeptic, he brings a good balance to your spiritual life. He loves both of you with the whole world."

Mom handed me a tissue.

Sidra began running her hands in Storey's auric field, the way George and Susan had. "I feel Storey will recover, but not for some time. She appears to have a disconnect in three spots above her left ear. Storey is extremely sensitive and is probably reading people when she has what you call 'drops'. It's like she is overstimulated and leaves her body all at once," Sidra continued. "I see a number seven, but I don't know what it means. Seven months, seven years?"

My body felt like a weight had dropped in my lap, imagining another seven years before Storey got better.

"Spirit says that's all the healing Storey can handle for today," Sidra said, lowering her hands.

My mother's big eyes grew. She held up her yellow pad for me to see. A giant 7 filled a yellow page. *SHE WILL RECOVER* was all I cared about. It was almost too much information for me to process.

"Sidra, can you tell me anything about my son Hayden? He appears to have ADHD. He can't sit still and jumps in place and repeats the same question. He drives his teachers batty."

"Hayden is an open vessel, very bright, bored with routine and the mundane. He wants to know how things work. Perhaps you should have things around that he can take apart, or things to build with."

"Really? All he does with Legos is pile them on the coffee table and then push them off," I said, laughing.

Sidra held a small tuning fork. "I don't feel he has what society and schools call ADHD, but he will be given that label. Hayden should be in a school that encourages individuality with intellect and freedom of expression. Listen to what he has to say. He's wise, he is listening when most people think he isn't."

I carefully processed what I was hearing while flipping Storey's soft hair around my index finger.

"Your children are of a higher spirit than most people in this world. I know you already sense that," she said.

And with that I stopped listening. We stood and Sidra wrapped her warm arms around us. "I want Storey to have this," she said, handing my Storey the tuning fork.

My body had numbed. I whispered, "thank you" and handed Sidra a hundred-dollar bill. We walked outside into the dark December rain.

After I dropped Mom off, I had a stressful drive back to Dad's. Sidra's words repeated in my head. I looked at Storey in the rearview mirror. She had fallen asleep, then suddenly woke and gasped for air. I tried to remain focused on the heavy night traffic. A dark chill filled the car. She wasn't eating anything, but it sounded like someone was choking her. I couldn't see where to pull over on the slick, dark freeway. In as much of a soothing voice I could summon, I repeated, "Storey, it's going to be okay. You're okay, just breathe."

My stomach twisted. Once Storey stopped crying and smiled, it abruptly happened again. *Fuck!* I still couldn't pull over. She recovered a few minutes later. I didn't tell anyone at my dad's what had happened. I knew it wouldn't help Storey if all of us sat around staring at her. Fortunately, it never happened again—at least not like that.

Two days before our California Christmas ended, Storey, Hayden and I met my sister and a couple of her kids at the new IMAX theater in Sacramento. The theater wasn't full, but I quickly realized what IMAX meant when we sat on the shoulders of people skydiving. My eyes rolled in the back of my head. I covered Storey's eyes, knowing that if I was feeling this ill, she was feeling worse. I knew bright flashing lights could cause seizures in people with neurological conditions; I worried about Storey and held on tight. When the featured movie began, I calmed down a little. Even though Storey and I left the theater a quarter of the way into the movie, my intuition was right. That evening Storey had several "drops," and she looked like she had run a marathon. Persistent guilt and worry followed me like a golden retriever. I was glad we would be home soon and back to the mundane, maybe the predictable.

Relieved to be on the tarmac in Bozeman without travel disruption, I let out a deep breath. Storey was in John's lap. As the plane taxied to the gate, Storey projectile vomited all over him and the back of the seat in front of him. John's seatmate, wearing Wranglers and holding a worn cowboy hat, was trapped between dripping kid barf and freedom. He hugged the window. I didn't know whether to laugh or cry. I wiped the mess with the first thing I could grab—her blankie. I felt badly for Storey and hoped the cowboy wasn't an emetophobic like me.

The trip was very hard on Storey. And because it was hard on her, it was hard on us (except, of course, Hayden). Soon after we got home, Storey said that she just wanted to brush her teeth and go to bed. What tired 2½-year-old asks to go to bed? Her "drops" increased. It took her almost two weeks to be back to herself.

Sidra's words, "she will recover," played enough times in my head that I began to believe them. I didn't tell John everything Sidra said about Storey. All he cared about was that I still had some hope.

My goal for the rest of the holiday season was to notice little moments: celebrating Storey's ability to stand on a stool against the kitchen sink and "wash dishes," and to crawl, or say "Mom, I love you. Mom, let's make Play-Doh." I treasured the ease of Storey's and Hayden's happiness.

Weeks after our trip we received a phone call from a different pediatric neurologist at the University Medical Center in San Francisco. This doctor was a friend of a friend of John's father. My husband had mailed Storey's medical file to this doctor before we flew to Davis.

"Hi Mr. and Mrs. Mills, this is Dr. Vandelay."

"Thanks for reviewing Storey's medical file without an appointment," John said.

"I carefully examined your daughter's medical chart, and I strongly feel she has received a thorough workup for her condition. I'm sorry to say, fifty percent of the time there is no specific way to find out what is causing this kind of condition," the doctor said.

"We've done so much, and each time she gets anesthesia or testing she seems to get worse," I said.

"At this point I feel one could do more harm from the physical and mental stress of testing and digging around the body when there is a degenerative neurological condition." There was a pause on the phone. "In conditions like your daughter's, most of the outcomes aren't good. I'm sorry. There are many rare diseases we know nothing about, and even fewer treatments."

Photo by Grandjack.

"Thanks for checking." I quietly hung up the phone like there was a monster in my room.

John had taken the initiative to contact this respected neurologist. After hanging up, he broke down and cried harder than I had ever seen. This confirmed my gut feeling about the stress of taking Storey to the Mayo Clinic. At least, I hoped, John might feel better about having exhausted the medical field while I still searched the ends of the earth for a miracle.

A few weeks before, during our Christmas, I made time stop when we heard innocent giggles from the Christmas tree area at my dad's house. Hayden and Storey laughed from children's red rocking chairs while Grandjack's camera shutter opened and closed.

There are some things in life that can't be taken from us unless we allow it.

Dear *Mom*,

Remember our cozy altar under the sloped ceiling in our bedroom? At dinner Hayden and I would ask, "Can we do candle tonight?" Hayden sat next to you on the floor and I'd sit in your lap in front of the altar. Our white stuffed buffalo, crystals, pinecones, feathers, and pictures of nature's beauty rested on it. You lit tea lights in special candle holders. Hayden and I held our candles and whispered grateful things.

"I'm thankful for cars and trucks," Hayden often said.

"I am thankful for my body and being here," I said, giggling. Mom, you often thanked the White Buffalo Calf Woman for showing us how to find strength and for

the eagles on our hill reminding us of our power. Sometimes we wrote hopes and dreams on pieces of paper and
tucked them under crystals. We repeated mantras. My
favorite was:

Metta Meditation:
May all beings be happy and peaceful.
May all beings be free from suffering.
May all beings live with love and compassion.
May all beings fully awaken and be free.

And you always said, "I will the energy to harmonize
and balance our being. I thank all the resources I need to
do my work on Earth. May light and love surround and
protect us… so be it."

After that we blew out our candles and returned them
to the altar. The nights that we visited the altar, I slept
peacefully.

Thank you for doing candle with us.

I love you,

Storey

Dear *Sweetness, Princess,*

I looked deep into your bright blue eyes for insight, for
clues drifting within your soul. A year and a half passed
without answers. It felt like a lifetime of malfunctioning
rollercoaster breaks, the ride endless, yet the ride took

me to places I didn't know were real and to love I never knew existed.

Storey, one day you looked at a kids' human anatomy book and you pointed to a child's cerebellum and said, "That's my heart." Shivers rolled up my spine, and I wondered if you knew your cerebellum was shrinking because you were giving everyone a part of your heart—a piece of your soul.

You and Hayden gave me purpose, offering life's truth of hope and worry, and I fell to my knees screaming outside so loud your dad froze. You and Hayden changed how I saw the world and my heart opened. Life offered our family normalcy. Then a friendly guinea pig we called The Pig arrived. While I made dinner, The Pig sat in your lap, and you belly-laughed feeding him carrots. Months later he died in my arms from heat stroke because I accidently left him on our porch on a beautiful fall day. We missed The Pig, even Chisel.

After all the testing you stopped walking on your own. With passionate optimism I stayed on the ride. But your wings continued to grow. Then we watched the Twin Towers fall and sobbed.

I love you forever more,

Mom

CHISEL

There's so much activity around our house, I think it has something to do with little Storey. I know she doesn't feel well. I try to comfort her. Mom unfolds a quilt by my bed like we're on a picnic, and Storey lies down on her side, and I lie against her body to keep her warm. Then, you see, Storey wraps her arm around my chest and giggles. Mom calls it, "Spooning with Storey." I dare not move. I can feel Storey's heartbeat and smell her sweetness. I love her so much. I wish I could lick away the changes I smell in her body.

The house territory I claimed years ago is dwindling, but I don't mind sharing my space with Storey. Recently Mom arrived with a tall thing that Storey stands in, then a big

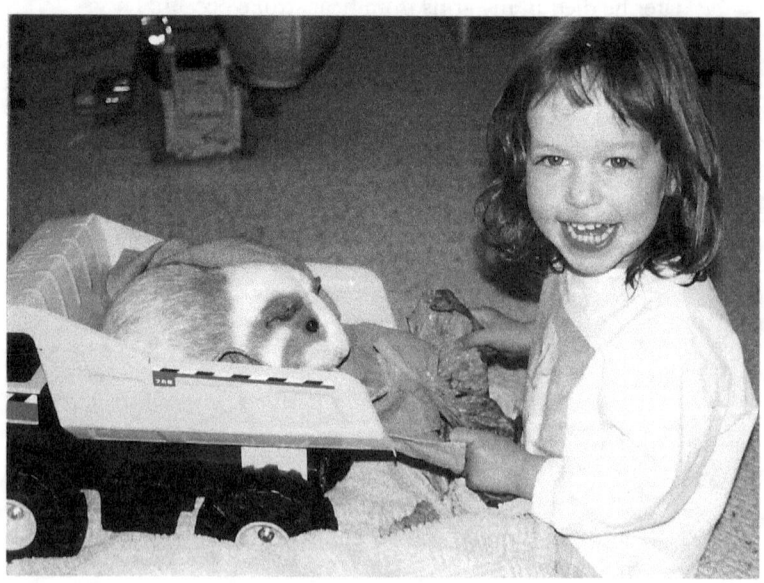

Storey loved The Pig.

plastic tub holding dessert-smelling furballs who squeal every time the refrigerator door opens. Those furballs are lucky I'm well fed. I know if I did anything more than sniff them Mom would make my head spin.

One day a horse arrived, and I caught Mom smelling them. Then when no one was paying attention to me, fat and happy with myself, I dove into those steaming horse apples. When Mom was upstairs, it happened. I up chucked the red apples back on the white carpet. Mom wasn't too mad at me it happened by the door when Dad was in the room.

PART 2

2002-2005

Chapter 18

Americans shuffled into 2002 with solemn smiles. The nation grieved for the lives that had tumbled to our nation's floor after 9/11, and we grieved as Storey tumbled to ours.

January brought incessant east winds, sneaky viruses, and fear that hid in the folds of short, dark days. Like many, I reached for the new year's freshness.

On winter afternoons after the snowplow rolled down our driveway and we saw animal shadows in the low light, the kids and I made a snowsuit sandwich on our blue plastic sled.

"Wheeee, here we go," we said in unison. Chisel barked at our feet. I dug my left heel in the snow and turned right to avoid bobsledding into our road. Hayden helped me pull Storey up the driveway while she sat backwards, holding the sides of the sled. I was happy that it engaged her core muscles without her knowing.

John and Hayden often skied on weekends. I treasured my alone time with Storey—we designed Play-Doh creatures, read books, and shared "I love you's." Outside in stiller moments we stuck out our tongues to the sky and caught fat snowflakes. I fantasized about Storey catching a specially made snowflake sent to her from the heavens to heal her body.

John's parents arrived in Big Sky with ski friends. For a week Grandma Joan stayed at our house while Grandpa John skied with his friends. She alphabetized my spice drawer, washed windows, and by ten o'clock in the morning inquired about dinner plans. When Grandma Joan's friends came, Grandpa John stayed with us. He fixed things and played on the floor with the kids. And in March my niece, Meredith, traded her college spring break in Mexico to help me. I was grateful my kids were growing up with extended family. It was a welcome diversion from our constant worry.

That spring we continued our sessions with Tara. My frustration and impatience grew with Storey's lack of sustainable progress. For a few days to a week after our sessions, Storey was stronger, perkier, and happier. It fueled my hope. But when her progress fizzled, I grew cranky.

Storey and I had invested an exorbitant amount of time and energy with Tara—long phone calls, card reading, waiting. Tara reminded me that we were still peeling the energy layers, like an onion, to expose the dark energy causing her problems. Storey and I had come so far, so I stuck with our commitment even though Tara's methods became more outlandish. There was always something more that needed to be done, she explained.

My demons embarrassed me. Every time I talked to Tara I thought about John's rightful skepticism. John and I rarely talked about our Tara sessions or other things I had tried for Storey. And none of those things were discussed with either side of our families, except my mother. In their eyes Western medicine was the only option, and I didn't want to expose my soft white underbelly.

Most days, searching for something that might help Storey made me feel like I was hanging from a door with Sulley, Mike, and Boo in the movie *Monsters, Inc.*, during the rollercoaster door chase scene searching for Boo's door to safety, to her door home. I had already chosen many promising yet esoteric doors. Still, I was determined to find the door that would take us back to the way Storey was at her Montessori preschool, walking and pouring from one small cup to another without shaking.

I wasn't giving up. I didn't care what people said or thought.

When I was stressed, Storey felt my pain and it caused her body to have more "drops." One moment she was playing and a second later she'd fall. A few times she fell out of her potty and hit her head on the floor. My reflexes to her falls sharpened; often I caught her before she fell. In truth, I knew her "drops" were seizures, but I chose to stay in denial and hoped that Tara's words— "Storey's nervous system is self-organizing; we need time and patience"—were enough for the time being. Nonetheless, my patience with Tara's healing methods began to fade. And denial was beginning to feel less safe.

To survive I constantly reminded myself to stay present, even though my emotions scored an A in catastrophizing. I knew that *true* presence, even for just minutes, could transform horrific moments and give rise to a knowing that everything was as it should be. I worked hard to experience slivers of my knowing moments that Storey's journey was mostly out of my control. On good days, our world made sense.

My second best to knowing was to live with as much normalcy as I could. We visited the museum to watch the ball machine, ate ice cream, read books. We watched *Clifford the Big Red Dog* and went to Friday afternoon swim lessons. I wanted Hayden to learn how to swim and I lacked the coaching skills needed. I'm naturally athletic at most solo sports, but toss me overboard and I'm down the river.

Growing up, my sister and I took swimming lessons at my friend Katie's house. My inability to swim beyond a dog paddle was the result of the teacher's archaic teaching method. She hit the back of our heads with an empty bleach bottle that was tied to the end of a stick when we came up for air at the wrong time. After that we spent our junior high school summers competing for the darkest tans and the skinniest bodies by cooling off at the edge of Katie's pool sipping Tab soda and lathering our bodies with iodine-laced baby oil.

Storey's smile showed me how free she felt in the pool. One afternoon there was a mother with her two toddlers who were not listening and instead splashed water in her face. They kept looking at Storey's plastic dinosaur toys. One child told their mother that he wanted Storey's dinosaur. Storey heard the boy; we moved closer to them and Storey handed him her dinosaur. "Here," she said, smiling. The boy was surprised. We swam away.

Storey's body had a hard time regulating body temperature. Periodically I had to remind myself that even though I loved extreme heat, it was not good for her. If she got too hot or we stayed in the warm pool too long, it zapped her strength for the rest of the day and sometimes part of the next. Because the hot spring pools weren't chlorinated, we showered off after swimming. I held Storey, who felt like a thirty-pound wet pasta noodle, while Hayden carefully rinsed to avoid the rotten-egg smelling water from hitting his face.

In the beginning, swimming exhausted Storey, but after a few weeks she had more confidence and became stronger from squeezing her arms around the cheap plastic doughnut by kicking her legs as hard as she could all the way across the pool. For an hour on Friday afternoons, I got to be just a mother with regular kids having fun in the water.

On Saturday mornings John got the kids up and ready for "open gym." For five dollars kids could run and bounce all over the place. It was a dream for parents and kids on cold snowy days. I fantasized about Storey inheriting my gymnastic ability. Surely hanging from the bars, crawling around, and walking on the long trampoline holding our hands helped her strength and balance. Maybe even rewiring her brain! Storey's favorite activity was bouncing on a giant green ball. She'd lie down and stretch out on the ball while I held her ankles and carefully rolled her around. Or she sat and I held her waist and we bounced. One Saturday morning I noticed the green ball was still on the storage shelf and since it was "open gym" I walked over, took the ball off the shelf, lifted Storey onto it, and we bounced.

A minute later, an employee who looked twentyish, with blood-shot eyes and premature thinning hair, approached. "Hey lady, you should have asked before getting the green ball down. You didn't have permission to take it off the rack. Gym rules."

To me he sounded like the teacher in the Peanuts comic. My eyes glazed over and my head spun with anger. Defiantly, with heat running through me, I continued to bounce Storey. *This jerk has no clue that I just want my daughter to feel free and smile continuously for forty-five minutes.*

"Hayden, come over here," I semi-yelled. "We are leaving."

That under-paid employee sent me folding into myself and running for the door. It was then that I realized how heartbroken and vulnerable I really was. Normally I'd never return to a place like that after getting chewed out. But I wasn't going to deny Storey a few minutes

of freedom or my right to feel like a normal mother, so I showed up
the next Saturday and we never saw that kid again.

One spring day Zuzana and her daughter Sara arrived at preschool
the same time we did. By then I was hypersensitive to children's
developmental milestones. Sara was nine months older than Storey. It shocked me to see Sara stumble like Storey; I hadn't noticed it
before. I couldn't help myself.

"Zuzana, what is going on? Sara and Storey are walking alike."

"Sara started to have seizures, around three years old. We visited
the neurologist in Helena," Zuzana said with her Slavic accent. "They
ran a lot of tests with blood samples and but we still don't have a def-
inite diagnosis."

My shoulders rolled forward, I reached for Storey, maybe unconsciously trying to protect her from Sara's fate.

"Wow, I can't believe it. We went to the same doctor. I didn't really
like him. I don't know, I felt like we weren't getting anywhere with that
doctor and Storey was worse after that awful, bubbling anesthesia."

"We had a 24hr EEG without anesthesia," Zuzana said. "But it
was inconclusive."

"I'm so sorry."

I wiped my tears on Storey's shirt. I scrambled to say the right
words. Words I craved to hear but couldn't find. Sara's story felt visceral, like I was in a bad dream looking in a mirror watching Zuzana
hold Sara's shaky hand while they walked downstairs so she wouldn't
fall. I wanted to know more about Sara and the diseases that doctor
had tested for, but it felt too intrusive following Zuzana, who I didn't

know, to her car to ask questions. I reminded myself that not everyone feels comfortable telling the world their story, as I do.

On the way to spin class I wondered if the lead solder on the old copper pipes at their preschool was leaching into the drinking water (in the U.S. lead soldering was used until it was finally banned in 1986). Or had the outdated underground fuel tanks from the gas station next door leaked into the water pipes? Was the preschool possessed, toxic, or had mold?

At least Storey wasn't having seizures.

My mind exploded. I felt ill for our beautiful daughters who sat next to each other in circle time. Later, Zuzana and I occasionally ran into each other and shared experiences. But looking in a mirror was too painful. We saw it in each other's eyes. At first, sharing similar stories with Zuzana made me feel better because I didn't feel so alone, but then I had another little girl to worry about. I think Zuzana felt the same. Months after Zuzana and I conversed about our daughters, Sara transferred to a different school. Later our paths crossed again when we headed down the same road parents fear more than anything.

It's a lonely road when something starts happening to your child. Good friends offer their hand and heart, and you're grateful, but silently your paths split. I didn't want anyone to feel sorry for me or for Storey. I didn't want anyone, including my family, to know how painful it was to watch Storey decline. Too often I heard, "I can't imagine what you're going through." Those words felt like a worn-out T-shirt no one can decide what to do with. Few of us are taught compassionate communication and writing skills; and even fewer are taught what to say, or what not to say, to a struggling mother. We don't want to believe that what is happening to someone could also happen to us.

I daydreamed of witty *Seinfeld* comebacks for statements I found of little use. I knew people meant well and wanted to help, yet I couldn't tell anyone what I needed because all I needed was for Storey to get better. And since I wasn't Seinfeld, the only comeback that gave me a little nudge of forbearance was: "I don't want you to imagine what I'm going through; that way only one of us has to experience it." Every morning I drew my mama bear card and pasted a smile on my face. It was the only option I had for my mental health.

Storey, Hayden, and I continued our nightly ritual of lighting candles and giving thanks. Our ritual ended with a prayer: "Dear God, Creator, Mother Goddess, The Universe, White Buffalo Calf Woman, all our guides and angels or to whomever is giving out miracles, we are open to receiving. Send down your healing light and help Storey's physical body and keep her with us." Then I'd kiss my beautiful children good night and wondered what lessons I signed up to learn on this journey of aligning my stars with chaos. However, I knew that in the end everyone has their own story to work through and to share—or not.

Why else are we here?

> My Little *Storey*,
>
> Every night I can't wait to hear your pixie giggle and see your smile in the nightlight when I whisper:
>
> Your angels are sending you white, yellow, purple, and pink healing light into your crown chakra.
>
> The lights flow, dance, and fill all your cells with healing, repairing energy and with love.

Then you stand up on your own and walk over to your favorite giant tree waiting for just you. You give it a big bear hug and you say:

"Thank you tree, thank you everyone. Thank you animals and the angels and stars for healing me, I love you."

Then you run away to go eat popsicles.

After this wish, we giggle with our sleepy eyes, and I kiss you goodnight and we turn off the light.

I love you to the light and home again,

Mom

Mom,

Listening to your meditation was my favorite part of going to bed. The other part was that I could feel the energy from those thoughts help my body.

I love you too Mommy,

Storey

Chapter 19

In the United States, close to 50 percent of marriages end in divorce, and the rates climb up to 90 percent for couples raising a sick and/ or a special needs child. Surveys indicate the main causes for divorce is equal commitment from both parents and financial stress (even though it costs more to split up).

In the beginning of Storey's decline, I listened to a segment on National Public Radio about a study which measured the amount of stress on couples who had a child with Down syndrome. The researchers concluded that, on average, after a year or two the parents had adjusted to their new normal and were no more stressed than couples raising a child without Down syndrome. This felt optimistic and encouraging, even though no one could tell us what our future looked like. I knew if other parents could adjust to their new normal, so could I. But parents raising a special needs child knew that moments of everyday stress—a cat's infection, backing into the cleaning lady's car, the dishwasher crashing mid-cycle—made the ground where we walked feel like quicksand.

I grew up with parents who argued about money what felt like every night—Mom spent too much; she turned up the thermostat too high. I heard screams down the hall that Mom's budget didn't cover rising food prices or my dyslexic therapy and gymnastic lessons. My mother was a full-time teacher but made just enough money for her work clothes and bee-hive hairdos. I was beyond grateful that John and my marriage's battleground wasn't about money.

John remembers his parents fighting just once. He had little experience with emotional battles or running interference. Compared to mine, John's early life was smooth sailing: he made good choices, he earned good grades with little effort, and he was fiercely independent—an entrepreneur at a young age. "Johnny was easy to raise," his mother mentioned many times.

My life's toolbox was formed from personal battles. My father, who was also dyslexic, taught me how to develop coping skills by being very organized, and my mother taught me how to stand up for myself. In the mid-1960s, when I was in third grade and no one could figure out why I couldn't read, my mother told a psychologist to go to hell after he told her the reason I couldn't read was because I was "retarded" and should be put in an institution. After that, Mom took me to tutors, doctors, and therapists until I succeeded. And in college I worked at a pizza joint, and while my coworkers played Pac-Man in the corner I talked a man down who held me at gunpoint demanding all the cash in the register.

John's entrepreneurship and hard work paid off—the sicker Storey got, the more successful he became. But we weren't immune to triggering each other. We traded the money arguments for stupid ones, like why we shouldn't buy Costco-size containers of olive oil, or where we should/shouldn't park. Most of the time, because he was left-brained and I was right-brained, it often felt like we were speaking different languages but saying the same thing.

During the peak of Storey's illness, once a week we waited in squeaky vinyl chairs at a counselor's office. I bounced my crossed legs and John sat with his hands facing each other, fingertips spread, touching the opposing fingers: tap, tap…tap. John looked at the bigger picture. I reacted in the moment. We talked with the counselor about our offbeat, finger-pointing marriage dance: "That's not what I meant. You don't listen; I never said that. You said…"

"Sandee, you have a snippy way of speaking, just like your mother. I can figure out where to park on my own," John reminded me.

At counseling, after our initial bitching was on the table, we talked about our important stresses—Hayden's inability to focus and the overwhelming strain of Storey's mysterious disease.

After ten sessions we stopped going. Our problems were too big for the counselor, who was counting down his days to retirement. We wanted homework, productive strategies that matched our dynamics and personalities. John usually left feeling better, but I left feeling worse. In stressful situations I didn't have the energy to filter my delivery when talking to John, but I tried.

To this day the only thing I remember the counselor saying was, "When Hayden is about nine years old, he will talk non-stop." The counselor was right. Hayden's ADHD stimulated his unstoppable inquisitive mind. In a way he became our healer when we were present enough to notice. Hayden and Storey's being reminded us that we could experience the dessert and puppy breath of life if we allowed ourselves to just be here.

Storey and I danced to the rhythm of her alternative home exercises, physical therapies, reading Tara's long thought form cards, swimming lessons, and horseback riding therapy.

My head spun with constant research of healing and medical treatment possibilities. My patience thinned. I pushed both of us too much. During meditations I was reminded: *Least is most; Storey needs love, patience, and time.* Storey felt my urgency, which stressed her out and increased her "drops." Sometimes she'd hit her face on the table. I got good at saving her falls but the horror of it never waned.

It didn't take me long to realize Storey did better with a consistent schedule of a good diet, exercise, regular naps, and bedtimes. However, that was hard to maintain between Hayden's violin lessons, her appointments, and their constant colds. She woke up two to five times a night, sometimes crying from night terrors and bad dreams.

"Mom, I don't want to go back into that hole." She usually went back to sleep after snuggles. I usually didn't. John and Hayden slept through it all.

The constant redness of Storey's eyes was a sign that her energy was depleted. I vacillated between whether Tara's sessions were helping or draining her. Images of Storey's healing occupied my every thought. Many days she was happy and energetic, and in my mind I saw her walking, then a "drop" would zap me back into our reality. And then a healing opportunity would show up, like the day Dr. Pranzatelli called and said there were studies from the National Institute of Health (NIH) that studied positive neurological outcomes from a gluten-free diet because it reduced overall inflammation in the body.

Suddenly the rollercoaster headed toward the sun. This got my attention because it was the first piece of an encouraging neuroscientific study. Dr. Pranzatelli suggested we try the diet for six months.

Storey ate anything I put on her plate; a gluten-free diet would be easy. I called NIH. The gal on the phone suggested I fly out to Boston to learn about the diet. That was absurd to me. I convinced her to send me some information, and I'd figure the diet out myself. Storey ate buckwheat noodles and rice crackers with gusto.

John's work took him on two-week international trips. When he traveled, I feared the three of us would get the stomach flu all at once, or Storey would get way worse, or I'd have a nervous breakdown. My mother arrived a few days after John left, wearing her post-chemotherapy wig. She was helpful; she read to the kids and helped with dinner. It was a lot of work for her during a mini vacation from her breast cancer treatments and her second career of writing real estate contracts. Since my mother had taught me how to be stubborn, her visits triggered our lifelong headbutting. I was grateful for her help, but by the time she left we were both relieved.

Chapter 20

F or my next slice of insight, I visited SueEllen, a respected local psychic/tarot card reader. I met her at a small workshop during my pregnancy with Hayden and before my white buffalo dream. I trusted her. Anyone who has sought advice from someone who can supposedly look into your future knows to be concerned about what they will say, as opposed to what they don't. I reminded myself that "psychics" usually tell you what you want to hear and what you already know.

SueEllen began, "You have a bright son; he has an interesting way of thinking. You feel very misunderstood and you have a hard time explaining yourself. I feel your frustration."

SueEllen had the grace of a kindergarten teacher. She arranged a few tarot cards in a geometric pattern from her worn deck. I knew tarot cards were used as a vehicle into the spiritual world, and that I had free will to choose what I wanted from the session and what I wanted to discard.

I had arrived at SueEllen's door with photos of Storey and my million-dollar question: "Can you see or sense what is causing Storey's health problem and what more I should do?" I knew the answers weren't in the cards.

"Storey's, what you call "drops" are mini seizures and she has an acute hypersensitive nervous system. She feels everything," SueEllen said, tapping the cards. "Storey is a very elevated spirit, a Bodhisattva who is healing others while advancing her spirit at an excessive rate. Therefore, her physical body is paying the price," SueEllen said.

I nodded.

"Storey's spirit is hot. Her nervous system can't adjust fast enough. You need to continue to do all you can to support both her spiritual self and her physical self."

I understood what SueEllen was saying; I felt her words in my solar plexus.

"Horseback riding would empower Storey's spirit and strengthen her body," she said.

When SueEllen mentioned horses, my body tingled. *I was doing something right.*

"Storey just started riding horses with Eagle Mount's equine therapy program," I told her.

"I see horses being healing and very important in your life and Storey's life." Without blinking, SueEllen continued. "I see you writing a book someday."

Since I had watched *Lorenzo's Oil,* I had had an image of a book I had written. A book about how I healed Storey and how we all lived happily ever after.

At the end of the session SueEllen suggested I read *The Reconnection* by Dr. Eric Pearl or attend one of his workshops. I felt overwhelmed by these suggestions because it meant stepping out of my comfort zone, leaving my family to fly across the country to take a healing seminar on raw faith. And worse, I'd have to explain it to John.

SueEllen hugged me goodbye. My curiosity got the best of me. I had just enough time to run into Barnes & Noble before picking up the kids. *The Reconnection* glowed like a magic ticket on the passenger's seat. *If I could learn how to move energy, perform energy healing the way Dr. Pearl teaches in the book, and I continue with everything else—I could heal Storey.*

That night I couldn't wait to get the kids to bed. I had been familiar with energy healing since high school when my mother had taken me to see an 80-year-old energy healer who told me I had healing hands. How hard could reconnection be anyway? The book's jacket said anyone could learn.

But the book made me nervous. I slipped it under my mattress while I made dinner. I didn't want John to see another bizarre book published by Hay House. I knew he anticipated my next move.

After dinner I ran upstairs and opened the handle to the hot water. It made a whooshing sound in our cold antique clawfoot bathtub. Hayden walked on his toes behind me.

"Mom, is the bath ready? I want to take a bath with Storey and pour water with cups."

"Almost. Get ready, but don't get in until I'm back with Storey."

I ran downstairs. As usual Storey was smiling, sitting next to John on the couch while he read the paper. I picked her up and carried her to the bottom of the stairs. She carefully crawled up. I gripped the back of her shirt.

"Storey, you can do it. Want to play with the cups and those things that look like pills, that turn into animals?" I said.

I lifted the kids in the shallow bath water, thinking about the book.

"I'll be right back. Hayden, watch Storey."

I ran to the bottom of the stairs and grabbed a basket of clean clothes. I heard giggling in unison and smiled, then silence... then giggling again. I skipped a couple of stairs running up.

"What are you guys giggli—ugh, what are you doing? Hayden! Why is the floor wet?"

His guilty eyes bulged and he froze, holding two plastic cups full of water. He was just about to pour a cup of water over the back of the tub. Instead, Storey poured hers. Water ran down the wall, under the tub, and arrived at my bare feet.

"Hayden! Don't teach Storey to do that."

They were having so much fun making a mess I hid my grin. Storey was being a kid playing in the tub with her brother. I spread towels on the floor and sat on the toilet lid to watch them laugh and play until the water cooled. I wrapped Storey like a little burrito in her monogrammed pink towel. I thought about the book while savoring every detail of Storey's bright, angelic, giggling face framed in pink.

"Hayden, I'll read *I Know an Old Lady* if you hurry up and climb into bed."

The giggles settled, we relaxed and looked at an old lady who ate terrible things.

Once they were asleep and the laundry was folded, I crawled into bed and cracked open Dr. Pearl's book and sniffed it. I was never a habitual reader before Storey's illness—while growing up, we weren't allowed to be inside on a nice day—but I craved any literature that might help her.

Dr. Pearl's book began with him talking about his mother's near-death experience while he was being born. This fascinated me. Not the dying, but what she saw between worlds. I liked his earthy, organic skepticism, and I was eager to use the tools he explained in his book.

Chisel was my first volunteer.

CHISEL

I like to nap in warm spots, like at the top of the stairs next to a heat vent. I keep one ear and one eye slightly open in case there is something I need to take care of, like a potato chip hitting the floor. Have I told you that Mom loves chips? Sometimes Mom kicks pieces of food close to my nose and I swipe it up like a chameleon.

One day I was minding my business when I noticed Mom walking around the kitchen, talking to herself and moving her hands like she was playing with a slinky. I lifted my head slightly, hoping she was about to drop a chip, but I was startled when a book hit the floor. Mom looked weird and her eyes went glassy. There was a new smell in the room. Then she said, "I did it, Chisel, I did it." I didn't know what she did. All I knew was that she didn't drop any food—I can tell you that. Then she kneeled next to me and with one finger she ran it between the wrinkles of my eyes, up my forehead, and down my back. Love at its finest.

Then she held out her palms over my body without scratching me and began moving them around like she was window washing. She looked relaxed; her eyes slightly opened like the way I sleep. Her hands were still inches above my body. I didn't know what to do so I just lifted my tail and let it clunk on the floor a couple times. It felt like she was rubbing my belly, but her hands weren't touching me. Sweet goodness. Then she waved her hands over the bottoms of my feet, which soothed my crooked toes.

I licked her hand. "Chisel, do you like that? I'm going to try this on Storey and see if it helps her," she said.

I gave Mom my happy wag and rested my head next to the vent. She sniffed my ears then walked to the snack drawer.

After practicing and rereading parts of the book, I decided I'd join Dr. Pearl's weekend workshop in San Francisco in a few months, on my birthday in July. Everything fell into place. As a pre-workshop requirement I called Donna, a certified grid practitioner, who could connect my body's meridian lines to the grid lines of the planet, the way Dr. Pearl had done when he discovered this work. This sounded almost normal in his book. My sister offered to pick me up at the airport and take me to Donna's house. From there, Cindy would take me to our mother's office and Mom would drive to San Francisco. During my workshop my mother would visit her sisters. Best of all, John was off the hook for my birthday.

This felt like a door I was meant to walk through. *If Dr. Pearl could do this kind of healing, why couldn't I? Who was he anyway?*

Chapter 21

The spring full moon bathed Mount Ellis in light like the Star of Bethlehem. At 3 o'clock in the morning I visualized the moonlight entering my chakras, cleansing me of mental and physical things that didn't serve me: my obsessions, not doing enough, bad genetics. And I pictured the moon traveling across the sky, shining into Storey's bedroom, sending healing light into her damaged cells and recycling them back into the earth.

As much as we tried, Storey, who turned 4 the summer of 2002, couldn't walk without us holding her hands, and never tried on her own. Some days she gave 110 percent and could pull to standing. Other days she had little strength, nothing left to give. Her leg muscles had shrunk, and she hyperextended her knees. When she stood or walked with help, she looked like Frankenstein. Sheri, her physical therapist, and I constantly reminded Storey to bend her knees. She tried to straighten them, but she couldn't help it, her brain had forgotten. She used to be so agile, so unafraid of climbing out of her crib, so used to moving her body with ease. On the days when she had energy, she almost looked like she was getting better. Her eyes were clear and bright. During those times, I searched my brain for clues to duplicate what made her feel energetic. On days when she was lethargic and "dropped," I'd analyze the cause, and remember what one healer told me: "Pray for a miracle."

For leg support Storey wore knee braces and Ankle-Foot-Orthosis (AFOs). At this point I tried two different craniosacral therapists (we had stopped going to Dr. Bouma—too far, too long to wait). One too intense for Storey to process, the second craniosacral therapist was calm and just right. We stuck with her.

I added Network Chiropractic Care for a while. The room held many tables, and the chiropractor bounced from table to table making soft adjustments in a connective healing fashion. But in addition to all of Storey's other therapies, going there several times a week for a couple months was exhausting. I came to my senses and stopped taking Storey, realizing it was too much time with little return. John was happy that we quit.

It was a balancing act deciding what was helpful, even a tiny bit. Figuring out how much Storey's nervous system could take running from doctor to healer, took a lot out of me.

I remember how exhausted I had been when my mother carted me from tutor to tutor and back to doctors trying to figure out why I read below average. Like my mother, I couldn't help myself; I couldn't sit and watch Storey lose function. My mom never gave up. For the first time my mother's tracks felt familiar. I understood her pain. I understood her "why."

Sometimes when John and I had grabbed the last knot of hope, Storey surprised us. I'd catch her crawling backwards down the stairs, or I'd watch her from around the corner and find her standing against the chair. Many times she opened the hall closet, pulled out Hayden's violin, unzipped the case, held the violin and bow correctly, and pretended to play.

When Storey stood for a second or smiled a certain way, everything was perfect. When she looked exhausted and defeated, I dug deep and reminded myself that everything was still perfect. Everything was always perfect—it had to be.

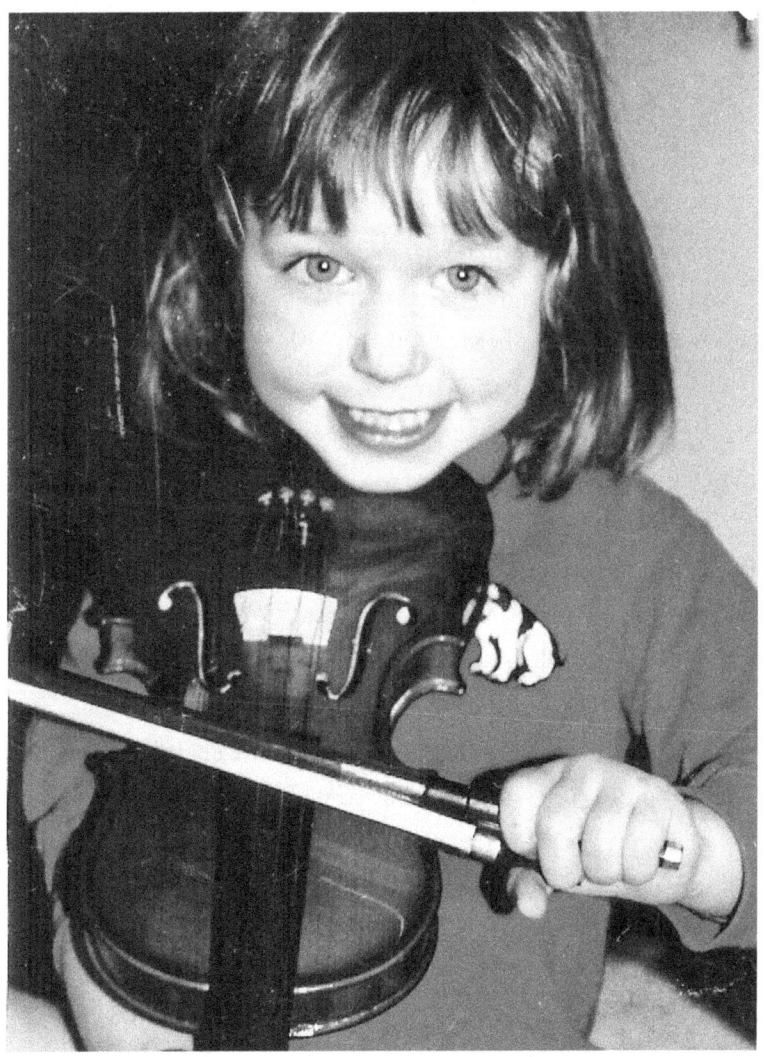

After Storey pulled the violin out of the closet.

Chapter 22

John rolled his eyes when I handed him a list of instructions for the weekend. A weekend of serenity and selfish choices was a dream on Mother's Day. My car headed south to Yellowstone National Park. It felt like I was driving back to my park summer job in the 1980s after a weekend in Bozeman for personal supplies and a night of watching MTV at The Alpine Lodge.

When I touched my cheek where kisses landed minutes before, it snapped me back to my real life where two little people depended on me to be my best. Crosby, Stills, Nash & Young—the official Yellowstone Park employee music in my days there—blasted out the car windows with my terrible voice.

My first stop was Meditation Point, a white chapel smaller than a tiny home overlooking the Yellowstone River with a window framing Emigrant Peak. My first visit there had been October of 1986 on my way to begin a new life in Bozeman. I had no job, no prospects, one friend and just enough money for one month's rent.

I climbed the narrow trail to the chapel, just missing a huddle of baby garter snakes emerging from their den. Fascinated by snakes most of my life, I stopped and studied their movements. Instantly I remembered a dream I had the night before of snakes emerging from Hayden and Storey's toy box. *What did that mean?*

The chapel door was sticky. I imagined a dead person or a ghost on the other side. But inside nothing had changed. Flies decorated the windowsills, eight unoccupied chairs stood like soldiers. Crinkled pages of the guest book flapped in the breeze. I felt like an intruder flipping through pages, looking for my past entries. Energy rushed through my cells when I raised my head and saw Emigrant Peak. Storey's beautiful face came into focus. A breeze wiggled through the cracks of the doorframe and the hair on the back of my head felt like a fairies' playground. I heard: *You're doing what needs to be done.*

My next stop was our traditional pee spot: Canyon Campground near Tom Miner rapids. As if someone else were driving the car, it stopped next to a big boulder. I glanced in the rearview mirror and like a horror dream, the car seats were empty. Then I remembered.

I felt so viscerally alone and empty. When I handed the list to John an hour before, I didn't realize I was relinquishing all control, like I was handing my car keys to someone less drunk. But I needed this, I needed to recharge. I needed to fuel my patience tank so I could be the kind of overachiever mom who had enough warrior energy to fight for Storey and Hayden. Their holographic faces appeared. I reached my right arm into the backseat, but they disappeared.

As I headed down Highway 89 toward Gardner, for a few minutes my time in the park replayed like a reel-to-reel movie of Hacky sack and smoking cigarettes with co-workers during a work break. I felt homesick for my days of instant friends and little responsibility. Inside the Conoco gas station in Gardner, I thought, *What if John doesn't follow Storey's detailed instructions? What if she gets worse before I get home? What if Chisel gets out and eats a rotten deer carcass? STOP*

IT, everything will be fine. I convinced myself. Nauseated from the burnt-bread smell inside the Subway–Conoco convenience store, I slapped a six pack of Coors, a bag of peanuts, and a roll of chocolate Hostess doughnuts on the counter.

Outside, the gas fumes filled my nostrils like sweet perfume, and the noise of metal nozzles banging against the back of the steel gas pumps brought up another slideshow of me pumping gas for YPSS (Yellowstone Park Service Stations), changing oil for confused tourists, nursing hangovers with coworkers, playing softball, and hiking alone. I looked around for familiar faces, but no one around knew me. No one cared.

Yellowstone's allure felt ancestral. I visualized Storey and me living in the same indigenous tribe two hundred years ago. *Perhaps Storey was captured by white men, and I was her mother, trying to save her. Or was she my mother, or sister? Was Hayden our father? This sacred ground has always fed our roots, maybe that is why my extended family longs for this place.*

Like millions of visitors before, I defaulted to Artist Point to view the Upper Falls of the Yellowstone River. Snow and ice clung to the volcanic cliffs. I sat alone on the very rock my mother and father had sat when their photo was taken fifty years before, and then mine in childhood. The same rock where we photographed Storey at 2 weeks old, and again when she was 2 years.

At Fishing Bridge my memories seduced me into turning left. I saw the rustic log cabin where I had lived for a total of fourteen months over four summers. The dusty, orange ruffled curtains appeared behind a torn screen. I remembered my squeaky twin bed often occupied by two, and where part of an arrowhead had emerged from under the broken front steps on my third summer living there.

Next, I navigated south to our family's sacred spot, a long sand-bar between Yellowstone Lake and a pool of water paralleling the road between Pumice Point and West Thumb. Before Storey turned two, we had started a tradition of visiting Yellowstone on Mother's Day weekend, driving to this sacred sandbar if the snowy roads allowed. Hayden and Storey had tossed hand-sized conglomerate volcanic rocks into the lake. At the time we were unaware that life is broken into moments like crushed obsidian.

Mother's Day at Pumice Point YNP, Storey walking
and picking up a rock, before everything started.

Excited to see the pullout empty, I grabbed my journal and coat and walked to the exact spot where we photographed Storey pre-senting a rock to the lake as though it were an injured baby bird, and Hayden following through with a toss from his left hand like a baseball player.

My Mother's Day weekend away was unusually warm. The sand warmed my seat, and I rested against a large piece of driftwood and gazed across the still lake. The colors in the distance changed before my eyes like they had years before. The sound of a few remaining ice chunks crunched together. Warm volcanic sand containing tiny obsidian chips filtered through my hands creating miniature tailings. My heart ached for my present family. John needed to have a weekend without me telling him what to do for Storey. But the heaviness in my heart tried to overpower my craving for solitude. I was tired from Storey waking several times a night, sometimes screaming tears from night terrors, or waking too early, asking, "Mom, some molk, pleezzz."

I'd bolt out of bed and whisper, "You're safe, safe in this life, safe in this body, safe with Mommy and Daddy, you're here with us now." She'd fall back asleep. I had a harder time.

Children's voices and slamming car doors startled me. I stood and smiled at the children running to the sandbar. This spot must be shared. I took one last glance at the horizon and walked away.

At West Thumb Geyser Basin, I stepped on the marbled paper-thin ice and listened to it shatter. As if meditating, I looked deep into the bluebell-colored pools and contemplated what had gone wrong in Storey's body. *Maybe the handmade pottery bowl I used to make the kids French toast had leached lead. Maybe it was her body's response to immunizations, or the stress between John and me, or like Tara said— a cellular memory from a past life in Yellowstone which created a bio-chemical change in her mitochondria. Maybe...* I took a deep breath. My thoughts and the boiling dark blue water erupted in front of me, and I stepped back from the burning hole.

Around the west side of Yellowstone Lake I drove to Old Faithful Geyser Basin, taking my time to stop at points of interest I had always overlooked. More memories surfaced as the smell of steaming sulfur thickened. I walked through the geyser basin hoping to see Riverside Geyer erupt.

The sound of squeaky boards under my feet reminded me of the year before, when I pushed Storey around the basin at six o'clock in the morning when neither of us could sleep. The sleepless night was the result of the furnace in the Old Faithful Inn turning on and off every five minutes, and the nauseating whiffs of fermented chew that previous occupants must have spilled on the carpet next to where I slept. *Karma for being a former member of the Chicks-Who-Chew-Club?*

Storey and I stopped at a bubbling pot. A buffalo bull stood before us. He turned his head slowly and looked into our eyes. We froze. A streak of ancestral wisdom ran up and down my spine and I heard the words: *She's going to be alright.* The three of us connected on a primordial level as though White Buffalo Calf Woman stood before us. I kneeled next to Storey and looked in her eyes. She smiled as though she were home.

A couple miles later I found myself sitting on a log bench with a single scoop of Wilcoxson's mint-chip ice cream and licked slowly. ("Never bite an ice cream cone," Mom always said. "It won't last.") I watched tourists from the same parking lot I had changed Storey four years before when I had realized she was sick with fever and diarrhea. In retrospect, I wondered if that had been the beginning.

My primitive room at the Old Faithful Inn had a one full-size bed, a thin, orange bedspread, one pillow (good thing I brought two extra), and a sink. Two lights lit the room, neither next to the bed. The toilet was down the hall. When I went back to the car to get my dinner of beer and peanuts, I grabbed my headlamp. Before bed I watched people below pointing up to the historic clock hanging on the famous basalt fireplace.

In West Yellowstone the next day, I drove past the historic Eagle Store, built in 1908, where years before, my father bought my sister and me milkshakes at the soda fountain as a reward for completing our chores at our cabin. We used to sit on the bar stools savoring each sip and listening to the cooling soda fountain sounds while our dad shopped for Pendleton blankets. A cool milkshake had tempted me driving past the store, but without someone to share it, I continued north. Memories of the park drifted and once again Storey's needs and challenges occupied my mind the rest of the way home. I thought about my upcoming 41st birthday at the end of July when I would attend Dr. Pearl's weekend workshop.

Chapter 23

M om, can we get a cat? We need one to catch our mice, like in the cartoon *Tom and Jerry*," Hayden said.

"Hayden, I've never had a cat and I don't really like them. I don't even know how to have a cat."

Hayden persisted, and because our house was built on pasture-land, I caved and took him to our local shelter. Our Humane Society had just adopted a no-kill policy—which I was happy about—but it meant that the shelter was grossly overrun, underfunded, and under-staffed. It was housed at the end of an old trailer park. Upon entering, a wall of urine smell hit us. We covered our noses with our shirt collars and opened the cat room door. Cats were in stacked cages; cats crawled the walls; cats coughed; and cats with goopy eyes meowed at our feet. I grabbed Hayden's hand.

"Don't touch any of these cats. I'm sure they're all nice, but they look filthy and sick. I don't want to get attached to any of these sad faces. Let's look in the cat cage outside."

We walked past the caged barking and jumping dogs. Outside were two large cat kennels full of pleading cats. A volunteer said the outside cats were the sicker ones and in need of fresh air.

"Hayden, sit on the edge of that chair and don't touch any of the cats. Let's see who climbs in your lap," I said, pointing to a ripped cloth chair and making a mental note to change his clothes when we got home.

Cats walked between our feet, meowing and rubbing their cheeks against the bottoms of our jeans. Soon a skinny, gray and white cat with goopy eyes jumped in Hayden's lap, curled up, and froze. Hayden wiped his own snotty nose with his sleeve, then stroked the cat with the back of his hand.

"What about this one, Mom? He's cute, isn't he?"

"I don't know, he looks too sick. It's too sad in here; we need to go," I said.

"You said let's see who sits in my lap first! I think we should get this one."

The cat sneezed in Hayden's lap. I cringed.

"Hayden, let's go, I can't breathe. We'll talk to Dad about a cat. He doesn't even know we are looking, plus I don't know how Chisel will feel about a cat on her turf."

"I'll tell Chisel we need one to catch mice, she'll understand," Hayden said, jumping up and down.

"Let's come back in a few days. If that cat is still here and climbs in your lap again, then it's meant to be," I said, smiling at Hayden.

Hayden smiled back. In the car I covered him with antibacterial gel. A week later, Big Dark Cloud—the same cat—followed Hayden and Storey around and jumped in their laps the second they sat. A few weeks later Dark Cloud's health improved, and he left us little gifts on the doormat. A few weeks later a black can, Licorice showed up at our house and adopted us. But when Hayden cuddled with the cats, little white spots developed on his face.

Storey with Dark Cloud, he always snuggled with her.

Weeks later I found the book: *Awakening Intuition* by Dr. Schulz. She was a neuropsychiatrist and neuroscientist who was not afraid to weave her intuitive talents with medical models. The 400-page book intimidated me with its tiny type on thin pages. I persevered through detailed and fascinating pages of her clients' stories. She gave examples of how and why emotions cause imbalances in our minds and spirits, therefore creating "dis-eases" in our physical body.

Upon completing her book, I Googled Dr. Schulz and found her appointment tag. Of course, I made an appointment. It was affordable. In her email she clearly explained how she would look at a name and birthdate, then scan the emotional setting around the client to access the reactive symptoms within the body. She would then explore possible solutions of redirecting the emotional patterns to help the physical body heal.

I sort of understood how a medical intuitive can study a person's energy field from a distance. Years ago, I had read Caroline Myss's books: *Anatomy of the Spirit* and *Why People Don't Heal and How They Can.* She wrote how an intuitive begins by grounding themselves in a semi-altered state focusing on their client.

I felt good about our appointment; however, I created a little more stress worrying what Dr. Schulz *would* tell me. But I was confident and hopeful that she could sense Storey's psychological weakness, if any, and the effects it had on her physically. Or perhaps Dr. Schulz could give me information into the mystery of Storey's genetics, and with that information I would go to Storey's neurologist. I worried how my emotional stress had influenced Storey's overall health. In Dr. Schulz's book she explained how families could have emotional and physical repercussions because of the emotional state of one family member—mostly the mother. So, I worried she would discover my faults and see how my stresses had affected Storey and Hayden.

Overall, I worried I wasn't doing enough. Maybe I wasn't even loving them enough? But I was willing to take the chance to hear any nuggets of advice Dr. Schulz had that I could use to possibly help Storey. More importantly, John and I knew that Hayden and Storey felt our love and that we would do anything for them.

Anything.

Chapter 24

waited weeks for a new patient appointment to see Dr. Marc, a neuropathic physician who was recommended by one of my favorite elder friends. In his waiting room was a pamphlet on Reconnective Healing. I relaxed, knowing that if Dr. Marc was a Reconnective healer, he would understand all the crazy healing modalities I had sought.

Dr. Marc entered and shook my hand. His baroque voice was comforting as he explained his approach of treating the individual and not just the disease. It was apparent that he was intelligent and that he based his practice on research and science. On one wall was a poster of Albert Einstein smiling while riding a bike; on an opposing wall hung a chart which appeared to me like a complicated topo map tagged with unfamiliar medical terms.

He explained that there were five energy systems in all of us: biochemical, energetic, physical, emotional, and spiritual. His approach was to balance the first four systems, and then it was up to the individual to explore their spiritual system. I gave him the details of Storey's rare story: the early illness, doctor visits, ataxia at 2 years old, the MRI showing cerebellum size reduction, energy healings, Tara sessions, and all the other crazy alternative methods I had tried. As expected, Dr. Marc's first concern was vaccinations. He saw me roll my eyes and he could tell I didn't want to go down that guilty road. He spoke to me in layman's terms as much as he could translate coming from a quantum physics education with an eidetic memory. His naturopathic methods felt warm, non-threatening, and less clinical. He wore regular clothes, and I hoped his confidence would work in our favor.

He explained how everyday allergens can throw off one or all of one's systems. "Think of your immune system as a bucket—you can put things into your bucket and it's not a problem until it overflows. Some things make your bucket overflow faster, like stress, eating junk food, or poor gut bacteria. And when it overflows your systems rebel. That's how an autoimmune disease and/or allergies develop," he said with confidence.

"Okay, that makes sense," I said, shifting Storey to the other side of my lap.

"I begin by desensitizing general allergies using an energetic method that originated forty years ago." He walked to a cabinet and pulled out a briefcase like the muscle testing people had used. "Simply put, I shine a laser programmed for desensitizing organs while you're holding the allergen in your body's field. The laser helps to clear and reprogram your energetic body to accept the allergen instead of your body thinking it is foreign," he said.

"Sounds good to me. When can you get started? Wouldn't it be nice if Storey's problem was just horrible allergies?"

"We can do that soon. I'd also like to balance Storey's fatty acids, do a mercury detoxification from heavy metals, and stimulate Storey's cerebellum with a low-level laser," he said.

Traditional testing for allergies is complicated. Research shows that fifty to sixty percent of skin scraping results in false positives.

A month before we saw Dr. Marc, I took Storey to a dermatologist for a persistent skin rash and the doctor said, "I don't know, here's a sample cream."

Dr. Marc began testing Storey for allergies by placing tiny tubes of allergens near her organs—cat dander, dairy, pollen, and others. Then he held her ankles to feel for higher muscle pulsive responses. Storey tested positive to eggs, yeast, dairy, dust mites, and a few more. The good news was that she tested negative for heavy metals, possibly ruling out mercury from her vaccinations. Dr. Marc made me feel better about our holistic approach and I knew that slowly treating her for allergens could only help. In addition to Storey's gluten-free diet, he recommended I remove eggs and dairy. She drank goat's milk anyway, but I wasn't 100 percent strict. After being treated by Dr. Marc's laser, she peacefully slept through the night and woke at seven o'clock. I, too, had a good night's sleep.

Over the next few weeks, we continued with allergy desensitizing and we noticed improvements: her nose ran less, she felt better, she had more energy. We also added one tablespoon of fish oil to her goat's milk to balance her fatty acids, and she drank it without protest. Even though I didn't blame her condition on immunizations, it often crossed my mind (until 2001, thimerosal, which contains mercury, was used as a preservative in some childhood immunizations) because of mercury. It also worried me how much tuna she ate for lunch at daycare. I agreed to retest her for possible heavy metal toxins using hair analysis. When the test came back showing normal levels of mercury, I dropped my immunization guilt.

Because it was easy and noninvasive to allergy test and desensitize Storey, I took Hayden to see Dr. Marc about his continuous thick, green snot that, after years, became part of him. I had already withheld dairy, like many mothers had suggested, but it gave him little relief. I knew he was semi-allergic to our cat Dark Cloud, but his sinus problem was pre–Dark Cloud. By then I had fallen in love with this mouse catcher, and Storey also loved it when Dark Cloud curled in her lap.

Chapter 25

One morning, I woke early, did three loads of laundry, cleaned the house, and got the kids buckled in the car with extra time to stop at our favorite bakery before heading to open gymnastics. Driving there I noticed a young sign spinner twirling the words *Hot Tub Warehouse Sale.* I thought of those spinning words during the kids' gymnastics, and on the way home my car pulled a hard right into the hot tub store parking lot. I carried Storey and Hayden skipped ahead. The smell of indoor pools drifted through the door when we walked in, and I accidently made eye contact with a salesman whose blue polo shirt stretched around his belly. I diverted my eyes and walked over to a hot tub, wondering how I was going to make a clean break. Storey and Hayden leaned over the edge and splashed in the water.

"Hi, ma'am, what beautiful children you have. Your kids are enjoying the water."

"I don't know what happened. My car had a mind of its own and drove into your parking lot. It would be fun to have one. But aren't hot tubs for rich people?" I asked.

The salesman's shirt moved when he chuckled. "We have gently used hot tubs. They are very reasonable."

"Gross, used hot tubs? What are the reasons people return hot tubs?"

"They trade them in like cars," he said.

Hayden splashed water on my face. My head spun as I justified a hot tub for Storey's home water therapy and before I knew it, I was signing on the dotted line.

Every night after dinner either Hayden or Storey asked, "can we do hot tub tonight, pleeeaaase?" The answer was always yes. The kids loved it, Storey found freedom in her legs, and I was able to relax. Hot tubbing became part of our nightly routine.

Monday through Friday I took the kids to their respective schools next to each another. I picked Storey up after lunch, brought her home for a nap, and she and I picked Hayden up at the end of his kindergarten day. By spring I needed to plan their fall schedule since Hayden was officially graduating from Montessori kindergarten. That summer they turned 6 and 4 respectively. Hayden needed to be challenged and stimulated; he was clever, even though he bounced off the walls and appeared to never listen. He kept one step ahead of his teachers, repeating their words verbatim what they told him the week before. Because he was a boy, and boys mature later than girls, I knew that another year before first grade would aid in his development. Therefore, John and I felt a Montessori education was still the best place for Hayden.

I was still trying to get Storey accepted in Hayden's school for the fall. Hayden's teachers were aware of her challenges, and they knew I was doing my best to get her back on her feet. But by the end of spring, Storey's aided walk had grown weaker, she was shakier, and her "drops" occurred more often.

"Storey needs to be able to walk by herself if she is to be accepted at our school," said the owner of Hayden's school.

I was flabbergasted. I couldn't think, and by some miracle I didn't tell her to fuck off.

"I'm trying to get her to walk again. You've been watching over the fence how hard I'm trying," I said with a controlled tongue.

Later, I called another reputable non-profit Montessori school for 4 to 6-year-olds. I feared they too might discriminate. I teared up when the director of the school, Victoria, said, "I am familiar with Storey and I'm sure we could work something out. I would love to meet you and your kids."

We toured the school. Storey smiled and pointed to all the lessons stacked on organized shelves.

"Victoria, this is a beautiful school, I've known about it for years. The drive across town will be worth it. How will you help Storey since she can't walk on her own?"

"There is a Gallatin-Madison County Special Education Cooperative which provides services for kids who live in rural school districts. Since you live outside the city limits, Storey will be eligible for their services. I'll call them and give them a heads up," Victoria said, holding Storey's hand.

"I didn't know any of this and none of her past teachers mentioned their services."

"Here's their number. You should call them and they can explain more. In the meantime, I'll post a job opening for a school aide for Storey, and if you'd like you may help with the interviews," Victoria said, handing me a sticky note.

"Thank you. I'm excited for both my kids. I know Hayden will thrive here since it's a different school. He won't even know he's repeating kindergarten."

Storey reached out and hugged Victoria goodbye. I checked my pocket for a tissue. I took a breath before starting the car. New to navigating my way around a special needs child, I felt held and supported for the first time since the beginning of Storey's decline. It never occurred to me that I wouldn't have to figure everything out alone; much less that we would need this kind of service.

The next day I dialed the Gallatin-Madison Special Education Cooperative (Co-op) and spoke with Ron, the director and school psychologist. My shoulders relaxed. His compassion danced through the phone line; I liked him immediately. Ron reiterated that Storey was entitled to receive support and services right away.

"The Co-op will provide an aide, testing, and therapies at the preschool you choose because you live outside city limits," Ron said.

Two weeks later John and I pushed Storey in her baby-jogger to LaMotte school down the street to meet Ron. Storey looked at Ron and smiled the entire time he explained our entitlements. She was in good hands. At the end of our meeting, and after all our meetings over the years, Ron always said, "Please don't hesitate to call me with any questions. We are here for you." His words always made us feel better. And Storey loved him.

For the first time since the beginning of Storey's decline, I didn't feel completely lost.

Dear *Mom*,

   We loved that hot tub, didn't we? My body felt free kicking the toys toward the jets and back again, and again, until I was tired from the exercise and the heat. My favorite part was sitting in your lap. I felt so loved. My least favorite part of hot tubbing was getting out. Hayden had to jump out first and yell upstairs for Dad to lift me out because you were afraid I'd slip through your wet hug. But I knew you'd never let me go.

I love you,

Storey

Dear *Storey*,

It was a very special time together. Water is powerful.

I love you forever,

Mom

Chapter 26

That first summer when Storey turned 2, and our journey began, a few people advised us to get out of Montana. In the back of our minds John and I wondered if taking a trip to the Mayo Clinic was going to be our next step. I asked therapists, parents, and doctors about the Mayo Clinic and the more I learned, the more I was confused. It was the 21st century after all, where medical breakthroughs were common. I heard of a few miracles that occurred at the Mayo Clinic, but I didn't know of any personally. I needed to protect Storey's sensitive nervous system from neurotoxic anesthesia, the stress of travel, and being poked and prodded. I didn't want her to slip from our world caused by the stress of testing.

And I needed to protect John's and my psyche from medical professionals telling us, "We don't know. Most likely we have narrowed Storey's illness down to a non-treatable degenerative disease."

We had made up our minds: we would not allow a muscle biopsy or another nerve conduction test, even if there was a slight chance of naming Storey's neurodegenerative disease because it wasn't worth the stress of speeding up Storey's decline. I fought every day to keep Storey with us. John and I often remembered the words from the fourth neurologist in San Francisco, who told us: "In the search for a diagnosis, one risks a greater chance of harm."

We needed a local neurologist who I liked. I couldn't forget the words of Dr. Schulz, the neuroscientist, who told me that Storey's "drops" could be seizures. I researched and found a female pediatric neurologist, our fifth, 140 miles away. I liked her profile picture, her credentials, and that she was connected to one of the largest hospitals in Montana. I mailed Storey's two-inch-thick medical file to her office before our appointment. Meanwhile, Storey's "drops" had seemed to be getting better. *Maybe the gluten-free diet was helping.*

Anticipating another dead end, I was relieved that Dr. Grabe's office felt warm and less clinical. Perhaps it was a place we might hear, *"She's going to be fine."* We introduced ourselves to Dr. Grabe. She looked relaxed and made good eye contact.

"We wanted a new local neurologist, and you were recommended by a friend," I said. "Storey hit all the listed developmental milestones her first 2 years of life. She does have periods where she seems to blank out for a second and lose muscle strength, and then she'd be fine. We call them 'drops.' We were thinking of taking her to the Mayo Clinic," I said, helping Storey flip through alphabet cards.

"I'm honored you want to work with me, and as you know, Storey's medical work-up is very thorough. I have read it carefully and at this moment I cannot think of any new blood tests. Because of what you describe as 'drops,' I would like to schedule an EEG. I'll put the orders in today," Dr. Grabe said, watching Storey.

"I'm very concerned about anesthesia during her EEG," I said. "During her first MRI and EEG, she was given bubbling pink witches' brew to knock her out. John, do you remember what it was called?" I said, looking over at him.

"Probably chloral hydrate," Dr. Grabe said.

"Yeah, that's it. She was way worse after that. It took her a month to feel better, and she never reached her baseline after that medicine. I won't authorize a mystery oral concoction of anesthesia again. But Storey did well with Propofol when we took her to see a specialist in Springfield, Illinois."

"Well, I'd like to do an awake EEG, so we won't have to worry about anesthesia. It will take about an hour and we'll see the results immediately. And if what you call 'drops' are seizures, we'll come up with a good treatment. When you get home, call this number to make an appointment right away," the doctor said.

I reached over and rubbed Storey's back. If Storey had seizures, I knew treatment was complicated, but at least it was something medical that would help.

In the parking lot the air felt calm. The valley had begun to warm up for the summer. I was anxious to get home and see Hayden and Grandjack, who had just arrived for the kids' birthdays and to go flyfishing.

The next day I made an appointment for Storey's EEG for the beginning of September. We'd have to wait all summer.

We saw Dr. Marc a few weeks later, just after Storey's 4th birthday. I knew he wouldn't judge my craziness for consulting Dr. Schulz. I shared everything she had said. He was familiar with her neuroscientific research and of Dr. Perlmutter's, and he thought consulting him could be beneficial.

"I will send Dr. Perlmutter a letter. In the meantime, be patient—we will continue to balance Storey with antioxidants, vitamins and Omega-3s."

My patience bucket was running low. At least Storey's "drops" seemed less frequent. With Dr. Marc and Dr. Grabe, and perhaps Dr. Perlmutter, I felt hopeful that Storey had systematic support.

I found myself at Barnes & Noble purchasing Dr. Perlmutter's book, *Brain Recovery*. He was a nationally known neuroscientist whose primary research was brain repair and support through a ketogenic diet, gut health, and brain supplemental nutrition. Like many popular researchers, his approach had been questioned.

I read the book *Brain Recovery* in record time and called his health center in Florida. They scheduled a three-way phone consultation with him, Dr. Marc, and me for September 20th, a two month wait.

Chapter 27

Waiting… waiting… hurry up to wait. I put Storey down for a nap without reading her a book so I could quickly pop in my favorite power yoga DVD by Bryan Kest. As much as I adored Bryan's long, dark, curly hair and seductive eyes—which traveled through dimensions to my living room judging my every move—the yoga gods had been nagging me to expand my yoga practice.

A year before I found Bryan's DVDs, I had read an article in the *Yoga Journal* about an eccentric, short man from India who danced around in a grossly tight speedo, balancing what looked like a Hostess chocolate doughnut on the top of his head, walking between yoga mats ordering students to stay in a 105-degree room with 40 percent humidity for 90 minutes. Bikram Yoga sounded wacko, but I was intrigued as to why so many people would pack like sardines into a very hot room to suffer.

In July 2002, the Bozeman Bikram studio opened in the same building where I took Storey for physical therapy. I noticed a few yoga students leave the building with a yoga glow. I wanted to feel the way they looked. I read the posted class schedule and mentally committed myself to a nine o'clock class the following Monday. The night before class, I dreamed I was topless in a Bikram studio, with wall-to-wall orange shag carpeting. On Monday at 8:45 a.m., my legs felt weak walking upstairs to my new adventure. Behind a clean counter, a tall, handsome, bald man with clear blue eyes offered his hand.

"I'm Chris. Welcome to our studio. Do you know much about Bikram yoga?"

I worried that Chris had a secret talent of seeing my thoughts. I flipped to my default mode and began to talk—too much.

"Well, I read an article, blah… blah… then I had a dream… of orange carpet…"

"Funny about your dream, Bikram suggests that yoga studios paint the walls orange. It's a sign you're in the right place," Chris said, he blue eye sparkled in the morning sun.

I grinned and paid for the class. In the hot room only one student lay motionless. I picked a spot ten feet away from her, unrolled my yoga mat then placed Storey's *Blue's Clues* beach towel on top. Unknowingly, I was right under the blowing heater. Minutes later Chris entered.

"Welcome my friends. Stand with legs together. Gaze at yourself in the mirror. Only drink water when it's party time, after eagle pose. I'll let you know when that is. Never leave the room unless it's an emergency. Follow my instructions and have fun," Chris said.

I've got this. I love the heat. I'm naturally flexible. No problem. Bryan Kest, I'm tossing your DVDs in the trash. We interlocked our fingers and placed them under our chins. My body was trying to figure out how to sweat. I don't sweat easily. My body tingled in protest. Sweat beaded down my back. As instructed, I exhaled like I was fogging a mirror and dropped my head back, guided by my fists. The official water break was minutes later, yet it felt like an hour. Dry heat continued to blow down on me. My head felt like it was going to explode. My breathing intensified.

"Sandee, focus on your breath. Sweat is your friend. No need to wipe. Follow my words."

Chris brought me back. For once, I wanted to be remembered as an A student, a teacher's pet. And just when I wondered how many yoga instructors had been indoctrinated by Bikram, Chris said, "Don't look so sad, it's only yoga."

The only other student and I chuckled. The energy in the room lifted and I knew I would survive and leave with that yoga glow I craved. During the *Savasana*—the last pose—I immediately fell asleep under the fan and woke twenty minutes later, alone in the warm room. Even though my head was pounding, I felt more relaxed than I had since Storey started getting sick. Chris encouraged me to come back. And I did. Again. And again.

Bikram yoga, now called Traditional 26/2 Hot Yoga, is hard. Over the years I witnessed people run, puke, cry, and faint, but mostly smile and glow. Historically it has been therapeutic for hundreds of thousands. Like most fads, hot yoga changed a little with time, including the name. But for over twenty-two years hot yoga has saved me from my dark doors: it taught me to persevere, to find solutions and strength under the stress I carried worrying about Storey and life's lessons. And it taught me how to breathe when I felt panicky. Between each bead of sweat, hot yoga reminded me that all I have in this life are moments between breaths, to listen to my intuition, and to be grateful that I unrolled my mat that first Monday morning.

Weeks after walking out of my first yoga class, I noticed a flyer of a beautiful woman advertising spiritual support. Elaine was offering spiritual and intuitive counseling. I remembered seeing her picture in the building where I took Storey to see Tony, and George and Susan.

A full hot yoga class, in Savasana—resting pose.

I touched the poster and took a deep breath. Elaine had credentials—two master's degrees pertaining to the human spirit. And she developed spiritual and intuitive abilities through extensive yoga and years of sitting in meditation, not from weekend workshops.

Over the next week I couldn't get Elaine's picture out of my mind. Even though I had sought the help of several spiritual counselors, the feeling I got looking at Elaine's photo felt special.

Storey rode on my left hip into Elaine's office two weeks later. I felt like we were walking into a feng shui healing oasis. Vibrant crystals of all sizes and colors were artfully placed. I wanted to run my fingers over each one, but I knew better. Storey sat in my lap and opened her innocent hand to receive a small quartz crystal Elaine offered her. Words spilled over my quivering lip as I relayed our story.

Minutes later I felt a wave of fluid love. For a spiritual lady, she was different. She listened and didn't interrupt. She focused into our eyes. She didn't waste my time bragging about clients she had helped.

It was obvious she had learned to ground herself on earth as well as in her clients' stories. Finally, I shut up and Elaine gave me information I both wanted and didn't want to hear, all the while combing mine and Storey's auric fields using her delicate fingers.

"The love between you and Storey is impermeable; it runs through lifetimes. As you know, Storey is a highly evolved spirit. She is a master and doing important work on the other side while she is in this physical world. She has been your teacher before and continues to be your teacher now." Elaine continued, "I can feel that your energetic systems are tightly interwoven. Storey chose to be with you in this challenging life to exhilarate her spiritual evolvement."

"Your words resonate; like I already know this," I said.

"It feels like her spirit is almost too hot for her body, and this affects her physically. I don't see a negative energy around her like others have told you. This is because I see the love and the devotion in the spirit world. The two of you have an agreement: you are helping each other expand your spiritual selves. When you see her, what you describe as a 'drop,' it's as though her spirit is being pulled completely out of her body. I feel like that will get better in a few months. Storey is dedicated more to the spiritual world than the physical. I'm sorry."

"Geez, that's all good, but I just want her to be a regular little human," I said.

"I see her with the Divine Mother, assisting evolved souls to incarnate into challenging lives. Storey's job is divinely significant and aids in her forever spiritual evolvement. And of course, she also adores John and Hayden," Elaine said, smiling.

Elaine's words spun my world. I pictured Storey standing next to Mother God, coaching and guiding souls before taking the "jump," maybe waving up as they disappear. I stopped taking notes. Elaine's words sounded familiar, as though memories of our agreement appeared before me, like the way I could see Storey's spirit leave her body when she experienced those "drops." Selfishly, all I really wanted on our human level was Storey here, in her body, in our life with us now. Elaine told me what I already felt in my heart, but still, it was unbelievable.

In my nonlinear reality, Storey was beyond perfect. Of course she was helping people in the physical world and the spiritual simultaneously. I knew it was my job to support her body, mind, and spirit so she could continue. The honor of being chosen as her mother intensified. But was I truly worthy?

My eyes burned and Storey looked up at me, smiling when I wiped my wet face. "Elaine, will you tell Storey's guides to fire her from her job of helping the new spirits incarnate so she can be more in her body here?" I asked.

"I'm afraid you're doing too much, seeking the help of too many people, and it's stressing her nervous system," Elaine said, tilting her head. "Focus on your self-care and your marriage. This will help Storey in the long run. I also recommend using Bach Flower essences, like Rescue Remedy. These essences are a subtle homeopathy that work on the emotional level. You can purchase them at the health food store downtown. Essential oils and external negative things, like the news, feel too hot for Storey's delicate nervous system."

Elaine continued, suggesting I follow with Dr. Marc's dietary suggestions, but asked that he back off on the intensity of his laser because of her sensitivity. Then Elaine surprised me.

"I know you like to go to Yellowstone, but the energy of the land is also too hot for her. Just visiting for a day might set her back." She continued, "Storey knows how much you love her; my heart is full just being around the two of you. Sandee, you have been given an incomprehensible job supporting Storey's work. In time you will understand."

The tissue in my hand was soaked. In my heart I knew Elaine spoke the truth. I had felt this truth the day Storey was born.

Elaine wrapped her arms around us and said, "Remember, Storey is in good hands and she's happy."

"Thank you," I said.

Storey giggled and opened her palm to Elaine. She picked up her crystal and placed it in a jar of salt. The sound of my Dansko clogs on the hardwood floor usually made me feel purposeful and in charge, but after our session the clacking down the quiet hall felt obnoxious. I wanted to soak in everything Elaine said, to file it safely in my mind, word for word. I knew I needed to stay on course driven by Storey's love and sense of honor.

Storey and I sat on the grass outside the building and watched a mother mallard and her ducklings swim in a tiny eddy. The mother was attentive and kept her children safe. I wanted to stay in the space of a different world, where Storey thrived. I flinched from the sound of a car horn and remembered I needed to go to the store before heading home.

Chapter 28

On my 42nd birthday, two weeks after seeing Elaine, I boarded a 6:10 a.m., flight for Sacramento to attend Dr. Pearl's (not to be confused with Dr. Pranzatelli or Dr. Perlmutter—their real names) Reconnection Healing weekend workshop in San Francisco. I was a nervous wreck. *What have I done? What if John forgets to give Storey her medicine and supplements? What if the kids get sick while I'm gone? What if Donna, one of the required grid workers that Dr. Pearl insisted all his workshop attendees see are in cahoots and laughing all the way to the bank?*

I tried to relax. *Breathe, damnit, breathe! No, don't breathe, you're breathing all those germs floating around the airplane cabin.* I pulled a scarf over my mouth and tried to sleep. Early flights wrecked me. The night before, I had a lucid dream about sleeping through my alarm, then my brain told me it was just a dream and that I still had an hour to sleep.

By the time I arrived at the Sacramento airport, my head pounded like I had been at a rock concert the night before. I shifted my thoughts and tried to incorporate the airport noises into a positive experience conversing with my brain to the benefits of this trip: seeing my mother, learning new healing modalities to help Storey, and giving John a weekend with the kids without my sidling shadow.

"Hi Sista, how was your flight?" Cindy asked, looking in the driver's side mirror. "Okay, give me the address to this lady's house. I'm glad it's not far from the airport. I can't believe you're doing this. I'd never do something like this. What are you doing anyway?"

"Actually, I'm not really sure," I said at half the rate she spoke.

Twenty minutes later Cindy pulled to the curb of a house. We saw a lady walk toward us wearing long, flowing white clothing. I knew we were at Donna's.

"I'm so glad you're here, Sandee. Come in and we will get started," she said.

Tired and nervous, my legs felt like tree stumps. The energy in Donna's house was peaceful and warm, like I was visiting a favorite aunt who lived far away. All I wanted to do was climb on her massage table and take a nap while her magic fingers reconnected my meridian lines to the grid system of the planet, or whatever the hell she needed to do for me to take Dr. Pearl's weekend workshop. Donna led me into her treatment room. I saw a poster that looked like Leonardo da Vinci's drawing, of complicated sacred geometric lines stretching in a circle over a man's body hung on lavender painted walls. I had questions. Boy, did I have questions. But my brain was too tired for analytical thought, so I closed my eyes and melted.

In a hypnagogic state, I tried to track Donna's hands floating above my body. Lines and faces appeared in my choppy dreams, like I'd been drugged. For forty-five minutes it felt like her hands were lightly pressing on my body. I felt safe and cared for. But when the grid session was over, I still had a massive headache.

Cindy picked me up from Donna's and drove me to our mother's office in Sacramento. From there my mother navigated traffic efficiently through Sacramento and over the Bay Bridge while I talked my headache down and she yelled at drivers. We arrived at the foot of our skyscraper hotel where the seminar awaited our arrival. The hotel buzzed with San Francisco's energy. I looked around the hotel lobby for people with the desperate look like me who might be attending the workshop. To be less obvious, I left my crystals and silver bangles at home.

Dr. Pearl's Friday evening talk was free to all. Two hundred of us, including my mom, shuffled into a 1980s-style conference room. We watched a tall, confident man in jeans and a purple polo shirt walk on stage. The room filled with music and clapping like we were at the Phil Donahue show. For two hours Dr. Pearl entertained the crowd with a witty delivery of his incredible experiences. Several times my mother and I looked wide-eyed at each other and laughed.

The next day all eyes were on Dr. Pearl. The workshop attendees anticipated the reconnective healing techniques we had read in his book. An hour later I felt proud when he complimented me on one of my techniques.

I befriended a nice group of ladies, knowing that eventually we would be practicing on each other. When I was on the table and the students practiced on me, I involuntarily twitched and relaxed, like I read could happen. I understood that people with higher-than-average intuition gravitated to similar workshops, and I wondered if anyone working on me was able see Storey's beautiful face and my desperate plea.

That evening, after using Dr. Pearl's healing techniques all day, Mom and I walked around Chinatown. My unusually high burden of awareness was worse. I was unable to deflect the city's energy and noticed everything: puke on the sidewalk fifty feet away, a homeless man peeing on a building around the corner, men arguing over Chinese chess.

Dr. Pearl had mentioned that "things could happen." In the middle of the night, my mom's manual portable radio turned on all by itself. We both woke up and felt as though there was someone in our room.

The next day Dr. Pearl asked the group, "did anyone experience anything unusual last night?" Most heads nodded yes. A few stories were shared.

Dr. Pearl continued to entertain us with his rhetoric but reiterated that the two stages of grid alignments needed to be done two days apart. Mine were done two days in a row. I privately consulted him with concern to my grid timing—I didn't want to jinx myself. He said I needed to have my grids redrawn because they weren't drawn two or more days apart. I felt defeated, panicky. This seemed too technical, too linear in a world of fluid healing, but what did I know? I had to get it right, so I returned to Donna's after the seminar, and she redrew the second part of my grid before I flew home.

At the end of the long weekend I asked myself what just happened. I wanted to be home. I felt overwhelmed and empowered. Even my mother said she was proud of me for taking that chance. I reminded myself that miracles happened at random guided by love and courage—at least for the kind of miracle I was asking for.

Chapter 29

The second half of summer was dry and hot. We spent some afternoons at the pool down the road. To entertain myself while swimming with Storey in the water, I looked around and tried to guess which kids had peed in the pool or were about to pee. I glared at the young boys who grabbed their penises before jumping in, including Hayden. Contrary to popular belief, human pee is not sterile. But the water smelled like chlorine and was on the cooler side. Hot weather drained Storey's energy and made her symptoms worse, something the doctors never mentioned. The pool was good for us during the dog days of summer.

Hayden had various summer camps and Storey stayed at her winter school through the summer. It was 2002, and Hayden turned 6 years old and Storey, 4. Storey whined at home when she tried to walk for us, even with help. At school she did better. Most nights after I kissed her goodnight, I used the reconnective techniques I had learned. Not much happened, but I kept at it.

A few weeks before they started at Great Beginnings, Storey and I met Melissa during her interview to be Storey's new school aide. This was new territory for me. I had only interviewed babysitters and few at that. Melissa looked more like Storey's mom than I: bright blue eyes, dark hair, and a giant smile. At the interview Storey immediately crawled into her lap like they were best friends. Melissa's enthusiasm and love resonated with Storey. She was hired on the spot.

Under the love of Victoria and Melissa, and the support of Ron, the director of the Special Education Cooperative, I was relieved and grateful for their love. Storey was meant to be at that school across town. How serendipitous that Hayden's old school wouldn't accept her. No matter how hard we push or resist, I believe there are reasons some things do and don't work the way we think they should.

Hayden and Storey aways adjusted well to change. Hayden didn't protest repeating kindergarten; it was all fun and games to him. On their first day Melissa immediately picked up Storey and carried her to her new locker. Later that week Ron came to the school and talked to the circle of children about Storey, why she didn't walk and how they could help her. The innocent kids wiggled and listened. A few just picked their noses and fewer asked questions. After Ron's talk, children surrounded Storey and held her hands as though she were a princess.

Somewhere between being a kid and an adult we forget how to be around differences. We're weary, lose confidence, and we look away. I cried on my way to spin class that morning knowing Storey was stimulated and loved. Later, Ron told me how nervous he had been talking to the children because they were so real, so honest.

At the end of that first week of school John and I took Storey back to see Dr. Grabe in Billings for her awake EEG. It was a crisp, beautiful fall day. On the drive we left early enough to sit on the bank of Yellowstone River to toss rocks.

This time without anesthesia, Storey's EEG was easy. A nurse gently attached electrodes to Storey's head while she moved between John's lap and mine. We distracted Storey for more than an hour with markers and new stickers while the electroencephalogram drew red and black lines on a roll of paper like a lie detector. At one point I noticed Storey did one of her "drops" and was relieved to have it recorded.

"How's Storey doing? This EEG is very interesting, because her last two didn't show any seizure activity. This time her EEG is completely abnormal. Storey has a multifocal seizure disorder with predominant focus in the left parietal area. We classify this as myoclonus seizures. It's a severe form of seizures and most likely responsible for what you call 'drops'," Dr. Grabe said.

"I suspected those 'drops' were seizures," I said. "But I didn't want to believe it."

"We'll treat her with Depakote—valproic acid is the generic name. Given Storey's neurological condition, she is probably having other kinds of seizures you don't notice. Prescribing this basic seizure medicine is the right place to start."

"Geez, there's never good news. But I'm glad there's a treatment for the seizures, at least," John said looking away.

"I know you still want an overall diagnosis. I'm sorry. At least the seizures are telling us part of what is happening. Hopefully we can control her 'drops'," the doctor said.

"Do you think we'll ever know what is going on?"

"Unfortunately, there are many kiddos who never get a complete diagnosis. Looking at her file and extensive workup, Storey might be one of those mysteries. I'm so sorry."

Dr. Grabe scribbled Storey's prescription for Depakote on a blue piece of paper with instructions to safely increase the medicine to a therapeutic dose.

"Let me know how she does on this medicine. You probably won't see a change for a few weeks until the medicine is at a therapeutic dose. I want her back in eight weeks for another EEG."

Dr. Grabe's words felt like feathers and knives. I looked at John's sad eyes. I felt better under her care and confident I could call her with questions. Storey's future remained a mystery, but the blue prescription sheet in my hand was the first time I felt medically optimistic. I knew Storey's "drops" were seizures. I wasn't stupid, just in denial.

We had a child with a horrible disease; seizures were just part of the picture. I folded the blue piece of paper and put it in a secure zipped pocket in my purse. I hugged Storey and carried her outside, and John followed. The smell of wet pavement and moist leaves gave me a wave of déjà vu. In the distance, sandstone cliffs hid pictographs, and I wondered if our ancestors had had seizures or neurological problems. Were they considered honored deities or gods? We'll never know.

On the way home I pretended to carry the solution to *all* of Storey's problems on that blue prescription paper in my messy purse. The drive home felt like days. I craved a hug from Hayden. I needed his lightness.

Chapter 30

When our aspen leaves turned yellow and orange, I entered Dr. Marc's office carrying Storey and Dr. Perlmutter's book *BrainRecovery*. After reading his book, I was happy to report that Storey was already on a gluten-free and low-sugar diet something Dr. Perlmutter preaches for better brain health. Storey sat in my lap holding a highlighter and our yellow pad. Dr. Marc dialed Dr. Perlmutter's number.

"Thank you for seeking my knowledge," Dr. Perlmutter said. "After reading your daughter's health records, I understand your commitment to help her. Her medical file is very thorough. My heart goes out to your family."

I removed my foggy glasses and wiped them on Storey's shirt.

"I'm happy she is on a gluten-free diet because we know that rising and falling glucose levels, from all sources, stress the brain. Dr. Marc, I see you're already addressing free radicals in her body caused by environmental or dietary exposure. Continue with brain specific antioxidants, including Co-Q10, Vit E, Vit D, and Alpha Lipoic Acid."

"We've been doing that for a few months now," Dr. Marc replied.

"I feel Storey may benefit from using the unique formula Brain-Sustain. It contains Coenzyme Q-10, Alpha Lipoic Acid, N-Acetyl-L

Cysteine (NAC), Acetyl-L-Carnitine, Vitamin E, Gingko biloba, Vita-min D, Vitamin B12, and Phosphatidylserine, all of which add more of what you're already giving her. I developed this after years of exten-sive neurospecific research. This formula improves the energy pro-duction of the mitochondria and protects the brain from further radical damage. You understand this is a supportive care, not a cure."

"I have discussed that with Storey's mother. We also just sent in a long-chain fatty acid panel and expect the results any day now. I'm familiar with your BrainSustain formula. Thank you for your con-sult, Dr. Perlmutter," Dr. Marc said.

After further discussion between the doctors, I created a picture in my mind of a clear, soft, thick protective bubble that enveloped Storey and me and bounced negative words away from our essence. But, consistently, ten minutes into any kind of appointment I was unable to see across the room, and my notes hid between Storey's highlighter scribbles. That day was no different, but I was cautiously optimistic about Dr. Perlmutter's research.

It stressed me to introduce BrainSustain two weeks after Storey had begun taking her seizure medicine. The results could be confus-ing and inconclusive. The Depakote was the first thing that seemed to be helping her since the beginning. Seizures were only part of Storey's picture, and BrainSustain could be supportive of her overall brain health. But buying something Dr. Perlmutter had developed, even though he was a board-certified neurologist, felt like a conflict of interest. It left an unpleasant tickle in my throat, but I bought it anyway. I wanted to support Storey from all angles.

A few weeks later, on a Friday afternoon, Dr. Pranzatelli left a message on our landline: "I just read Storey's latest EEG report from Dr. Grabe and I'm very concerned, because if Storey *does* have a mitochondrion disease, she should not be taking Depakote. It can be very dangerous and toxic. I want to put her on Topamax. Please call me back. Thank you. Have a good weekend."

I dropped to my knees, then reached my right arm up and pushed the replay button again and again. Finally, I stopped crying and called Dr. Pranzatelli's office.

"Hello, I just got a voice message from Dr. Pranzatelli. He said my daughter's seizure medicine might be toxic, but it seems to be working, and now I'm panicking. What am I supposed to do? It's Friday night!"

The receptionist handed the phone to Dr. Pranzatelli's nurse. She assured me that he would call me back on Monday and not to worry about the Depakote for a few days. I let out a small sigh of relief, but the constant worry pulled me from being present with Hayden and Storey that weekend. Right then I decided it was time to cave in and buy a cell phone so I wouldn't miss another important call.

By Monday I was drained. I took the kids to school and then came straight home, trading my gym workout for cleaning the house while carrying our landline phone in my pocket like a desperate girl waiting for a boy to call. John worried the same. He picked the kids up from school and I never left the house. The call never came in. Right before five o'clock, I called Dr. Pranzatelli's office again.

"I'm sorry, he left for the day. I gave him your message, but it has been crazy around here. I will personally make sure he will call you tomorrow," the nurse said.

"Please understand, I'm going nuts. I know he has a lot of kids he's helping, but he left a message on my answering machine practically giving my daughter, Storey a near death sentence on Friday afternoon. What was I supposed to do with that information all weekend?"

I slammed the phone down on the receiver. I wanted to scream on the porch, but I was worried the college kids renting the farmhouse next door might think I was being murdered. I leashed Chisel and ran a fast five miles.

Tuesday afternoon I got the call.

"Hi, Mrs. Mills. So sorry I didn't get ahold of you yesterday. First, how is Storey doing on the gluten-free diet?" Dr. Pranzatelli asked.

"I'm not seeing any big changes since the beginning the diet. We switched to a different pediatric neurologist and that's who prescribed the Depakote. We increased the medicine to a therapeutic level over a week. But it hasn't completely stopped her seizure 'drops.' She still has one or two 'drops' every couple of days. Sometimes two a day, but that's better than two an hour."

"It can be a guessing game with seizure medicine," he said.

"She does seem a little more alert and happier. I don't know what is working or what isn't because we're trying medicine and diet changes at the same time. At least she's still happy on gluten-free because she will eat anything. Also, under the guidance of my naturopathic physician she began taking Dr. Perlmutter's formula, BrainSustain. Are you familiar with his research?" I asked.

"I understand you wanting to try everything. I don't know that much about that supplement. I remain skeptical and am concerned with her continued 'drops.' I think that adding the prescription Topamax while continuing with Depakote is worth a try. Topamax has been on the market for a few years and was just approved in children two years and older for epilepsy. One side effect we need to watch for is cognitive delay. I'm still concerned about using Depakote because we haven't ruled out a neurodegenerative mitochondria disease."

"We just started her on the Depakote. I don't know what to think. The medicine has helped her seizures. Now you're suggesting another pill that might help but has bad side effects, and the one drug that's working might be toxic. What are we supposed to do?"

"Let's add Topamax for a couple months and see how she does while still taking Depakote. We'll know more after that, taking both drugs for a short time will be alright."

My throat began to close. I couldn't wait to hang up the phone that connected me to a dimension of guessing games.

"Okay, Dr. Pranzatelli, thanks for calling," I said.

Topamax just approved. That didn't sound reassuring. Another unknown experiment to a complicated algorithm. Experiments stacked on experiments spun before my eyes while we watched Storey slowly decline. I was hoping to see greater results from something, anything.

Working with Eastern and Western healing practices made me feel pulled in opposing directions, like the two-headed pushmi-pullyu llama from the 1967 movie *Dr. Dolittle*. Or a mouse in a maze frantically searching for a chunk of cheese behind the correct door. Nothing we tried so far felt completely right in my heart. Storey felt my pain and frustration. She often said, "Mom, quit lookin at me."

Every night I wracked my brain. *Was it MSG in those stupid Cheez-Its crackers she had eaten at preschool? Was it bad water from leaking gas tanks from the gas station next to her preschool? Was it her immunizations? Was it a dark spirit following her around? Was it because the head of her crib faced north rather than, south, west or east? Was my collection of antique red Fiestaware emitting radioactive uranium oxide in*

the house during the winter? (I got rid of all red except one piece.) Was
I not loving her enough....?

Even though I followed through on my self-care—yoga, chi gong, meditation, and running—I couldn't turn off my monkey-mind. Every day I came up with a new obsession. When I noticed my mind going down that scary rabbit hole, I flipped my thoughts to visualize Storey healed and walking independently across the floor. This worked in bite-sized minutes. John was much better than I at putting those awful thoughts under lock and key. He also had to focus on supporting us.

A couple days later, with the overpriced Topamax in hand, I read the entire three-page list of drug information and side effects: dizziness, coordination problems, loss of memory and cognition, and of course, nausea and diarrhea. *Oh, great.* A pill that causes all the things we're trying to control. But I had faith in Dr. Pranzatelli. He was a reputable pediatric neurology movement specialist and seemed to be keeping Storey's mystery close to his heart.

I'll give this drug combination a couple months. But if the side effects
lower her quality of life, I'll stop, I told myself.

Months before it was confirmed that Storey was having seizures, a friend of mine gave me a 600-page book on seizures. I read parts. I tried to read other parts. I skimmed. I tossed the book off my deck and watched the pages flap in the wind. Between the lines, all the words said the same thing: *Treating seizures is a very complicated science. Here are 600 pages that will leave you more frustrated and confused than ever before.* Topamax wasn't even listed in the 600 pages; it was too new—too new to trust.

Chapter 31

Each morning when I handed Storey over to Melissa, I felt a grateful sweetness in my heart. Storey loved her and school equally. Hayden was always happy and up to the challenge of navigating his new school and new friends. However, he wasn't thrilled when I picked Storey up after lunch and left him at school for a few more hours. He wanted to come home and throw the ball for the neighbor's golden retriever.

A month after starting Depakote we went back to Billings for a second awake EEG. Thankfully the medicine had done its job—her scary "drops" had decreased significantly. But the side effects of Topamax made Storey's hands tremor like a person with middle-stage Parkinson's disease. She withdrew and cried often, and her eyes grew glassy. Physically overall, she went from getting better on Depakote to worse after introducing Topamax. Dr. Grabe concluded that the Topamax was toxic to Storey. She eased my fear of using Depakote with a "possible" mitochondria disease. Conflicting theories between medical health care providers were hard to decipher. It was part of the game.

Over the next month we slowly weaned Storey off Topamax. I couldn't wait to toss those expensive pills into the garbage. Once it was out of Storey's system, her shakiness decreased and her eyes lit up. Her smile returned. Dr. Grabe was empathetic to our frustration

and invited us to join their March neurology department's free bian-
nual metabolic clinic. It was a round table of experienced minds like
a mini-Montana Mayo Clinic: a retired pediatric neurologist, a brilliant neurologist from the Denver Children's Hospital, a social worker,
a nurse, and herself. Together the group evaluated Storey's records
and brainstormed new ideas, testing, and support.

Most kids were transported to afterschool activities, like soccer.
Hayden missed out because it was hard on Storey and we needed to
get home to do her exercises. While Storey and I did her exercises,
Hayden ran around with the dogs next door—a black lab named
Cub and a ball-obsessed golden retriever named Chauncy. Hayden
spent hours swinging a hammock tied between two aspens, talking
to himself, and tossing the slobbery ball for Chauncy.

Storey's favorite exercise was bouncing on the large exercise ball—
we kicked out of our way around the living room. I held her hips
while she sat on it and we bounced to Shania Twain's song "Up!" She
laughed the entire time exercising her core. We had fun. She thought
it was just a game and not physical therapy.

One day Storey squirmed and moaned at the first bounce. *Ugh,
what now?* She was in pain. At dinner she uncharacteristically ate
only a few bites. The next day in Dr. Feist's office, when the nurse
stuck Storey with a catheter to check for a bladder infection, I almost
fainted. Tests showed Storey had a double kidney infection. She and
I spent the next three days in the hospital. We snuggled, watched
our favorite cartoons, read, took naps, and waited. Storey's pain tolerance amazed me. She smiled when John brought ice cream from

Dairy Queen. *Fuck the "no dairy." We didn't have proof it was a problem anyway.* Ice cream was all she felt like eating for two days. On a beautiful hot fall day, we pulled out of the hospital parking lot four days later. Our pediatrician reiterated that we needed to keep an eye on bladder infections due to her neurological condition, and because the seizure medicine lowered her immune system. My mind wondered if this was all to test my stamina and strength.

Three generations of the Mills family gathered for Christmas 2002 in Grandma and Grandpa's log cabin in Big Sky. The cousins were Kathy-the nurturer; Noa-the sensitive brainiac; Alea-the independent; Hayden-the inquisitive; and Storey-the love. Although we had all been together six months prior, I saw sadness in the eyes of the adults and heard their whispers. But the cousins were blind to Storey's differences; they played well and loved each other.

The adults loved Storey, but they were at a loss. They were scientists; faith was the antithesis of their belief system. I felt like the odd right brained person who climbed an unknown mountain for answers. I believe just thinking about praying—whatever that means individually—couldn't hurt. Praying didn't cross their path.

The few days of Christmas were equally joyful and stressful. I tried to relax and appreciate moments like the kids giggling when Hayden tape-recorded the sound of Grandpa snoring as he napped on the couch.

On Christmas afternoon, I sat on the edge of the stone fireplace and drank hot cocoa to warm my cold back after skate-skiing at Lone Mountain Ranch. I closed my eyes and listened for the kids' laughter by blocking the political banter coming from the kitchen.

Without warning, it felt like my soul had split in two. I was watching a movie scene in slow motion of Storey playing dress-up and running around barefoot in the warm grass with Chisel. She held a magic wand in her hand, spun circles and tapped Chisel on her forehead and whispered, "There, Chisel, you are now the King of the Forest." Then Hayden appeared and kicked a ball next to Storey. They laid in the grass and pointed at cloud animals. A second later they hung their bellies over swings and spun in circles.

In the next scene Storey was laughing at a Barbie birthday party. Cake was stuck to the faces of the party girls. I saw Storey drawing brilliant colors and displaying her masterpieces to stuffed animals arranged at a tea party. The scene flashed to Storey at preschool, taking lessons off the shelf and pouring water from one tiny pitcher into another without trouble. Suddenly she was at home brushing her long, curly black hair and asking, "Mom, may I use your lip gloss?"

John's voice brought me back.

"Sandee, do we need to give Storey her medicine now? Sandee!"

My body jumped. "What? Yeah… before dinner," I said, almost dropping my cup. My head was dizzy. My back was hot. Voices echoed from the kitchen. I felt misplaced.

"Who wants ice water? John, get the coffee ready!" Grandma said.

Dazed, I made Storey's plate of food and John gave Storey her medicine. Dinner was a Rocky Mountain version of a Norman Rockwell painting, minus the pipe Grandpa gave up years ago. The kids laughed; John's dad told "funny" jokes; we stuffed ourselves. After dinner we watched the classic, *Jeremiah Johnson*. The kids played in the loft where they slept, except Storey, who slept on the floor next to my twin bed downstairs. I needed her close. Before bed she and I snuggled on the floor reading *The Lorax* and pretended we were camping. Soon we were both asleep beneath echoes of laughter.

That Christmas weekend I made sure Storey wasn't just a mystery patient, or my project to heal. She was a kid playing with her family by the fire in a log cabin in the woods.

At the end of 2002, Storey was 4½ years old. She was not running around the yard in dress-up clothes playing with Chisel. She walked a few steps with a lot of help and foot braces. When she sat on the floor during circle time at school, she wore knee braces. For standing therapy, Storey was strapped into a stander and lifted like a lever. She fell behind in school. Her hands tremored and tightened up. The seizures and seizure medicine slowed her down. But she loved school and loved Melissa. Her classmates were drawn to her light and her contagious smile.

Medically, we knew little. Two seizure medicines were introduced; one made her better, one made her worse. We were grateful for Depakote and trusted Dr. Marc's knowledge of nutrition. I used coconut oil on buckwheat waffles instead of butter. I put fish oil in her goat's milk and fed her a gluten-and-dairy-free diet. I gave her two drops of Cell-Food Drops—formulated with colloidal minerals, amino acids, and enzymes to detoxify her body of free radicals, every night under her tongue because it sounded like a good thing to do. I gave her Sleepytime tea at night to calm her nerves and magnesium to help her poop.

I consulted a medical intuitive who said she felt Storey's illness wasn't the result of immunizations but rather a genetic mutation. I consulted two different intuitives to bounce their different feelings against one another and to measure my sanity. We found a different neurologist in Montana that we liked and hoped she had fresh ideas and a tendency for epiphanies.

To find anything that might help, I continued to try crazy things and investigated any new idea. I flew to San Francisco to learn Reconnective Energy Healing with other lost souls. I had a geopathic survey done on our house and property by mailing a map of our house and land to a dousing and meditation group. For fifteen dollars they neutralized negative earth energies, ghosts, underground water, and ley lines. I began hot yoga and made new friends. We started and ended marriage counseling. We got a hot tub, and a couple of new guinea pigs. Hayden made new friends; three were dogs. Storey loved school. She gave everything her best, and she learned how to hide pain and confusion. She giggled the way a 4-year-old should.

Storey taught children inclusion.

Storey received craniosacral therapy, physical therapy, occupational therapy, laser therapy, supplemental and prescription therapy, eye patch therapy, water therapy, music therapy, gymnastics therapy, sledding therapy, horse therapy, Play-Doh therapy, family therapy, energy healing and Reiki therapy. The kids and I took deep breaths and *ooommmmmed* on the top of our hill and "did candle" before bed. We found Eagle Mount and met families with similar challenges, and I didn't feel so alone. We continued to walk up the road, Storey in the baby jogger with our black cat, Licorice, in her lap, and Dark Cloud trailing behind. Hayden walked next to me and talked about Transformers and truck wheels. We counted birds and spotted snakes, yelled at cars to slow down, and picked up garbage.

Storey and I stopped working with Tara when Storey suddenly pointed to a picture of a family in the book: *The Day You Were Born,* reached up for my hand and walked perfectly out of the room like she was healed, and I thought that was it! My hope went through the roof. *Tara was right, all those cards, effort did it. Storey was healed.* But like all the other sessions it didn't last—the walking didn't last and I lost most of my hope.

I ran more and cried less.

Dear *Storey*,

Remember that Christmas morning you put on a Santa hat and climbed on the rocking horse Grandpa had made fifty years before? Your delicate fingers squeezed the small handles. You giggled, then Hayden pointed and said, "Look, guys, Storey is rocking all by herself."

Your physical ability that morning was uncharacteristic, like a memory from a different life—a tease of what could be, what should be. Our hearts opened to the miracle of possibility the way many people feel while sitting vigil and watching a loved one exhibit terminal lucidity.

I think Grandpa made that horse just for you without knowing.

I love you always and forever,
Mom

Dear *Mom*,

Riding Grandpa's horse is one of my happiest memories. I named him Wonder. He knows why.

I love you too,
Storey

Storey on the horse Grandpa made a generation earlier.

CHISEL

Whoa, whoa, Nellie! I can't believe Mom forgot to tell you what happened to me that summer when the family gathered in Big Sky for Storey and Grandma's birthday weekend.

With a keen memory I knew what it meant when Grandma and Grandpa appeared at our house. Party at Big Sky! Naturally I was in heaven when I caught whiffs of hot dogs and sauerkraut. Hunger is my middle name. Being a mastiff, I need extra helpings to keep my muscles in tip-top shape while I lounge around guarding my family. Well, with five messy kids, I assigned myself the BOF (Boss Of the Floor). It was apparent the other black dog there wasn't going to overpower my intimidation. He left the floor to me.

When the family sat at the table, I sidled under the kids' dangling toes. "Don't feed Chisel any scraps. She might throw up," I heard Mom say. I knew what that meant, so I ate the crumbs out of the kids' laps and licked their scrumptious feet.

"Chiseeelllll!" they said and giggled. I don't know what Mom was talking about. Me throwing up hardly happens unless I indulge in too many horse apples.

After dinner we went to the firepit. Mom caught me a couple times licking fingers and snatching brown crackers. Jeez, what does she expect?

Then, suddenly, "BANG, POW, POW, POP!" What in the tarnation was that? It sounded like an explosion in my big head.

Mom told me I was fine. Then everyone screamed when fire sticks exploded in the air. It smelled like rotten eggs. I thought the sky was falling, and I ran down the hill and trees rubbed against my body like ghosts. I saw a familiar road and kept running. I found people. I wanted to tell them the world was ending, but they didn't care; they were laughing at the sky. A boy looked at me and accidently spilled stuff on my face.

"Who are you, big guy? Are you scared?" he said.

"Yea, dude, I'm scared as hell, the world is ending, and I didn't get to eat any burning balls of bliss. Why can't you hear me?" The boy patted my head. I relaxed. Then he grabbed my collar. BANG! It happened again. I pulled away. I tried to leave but that boy held me. I put my paws over my ears and curled up. Where *was* my mom?

When I woke, I was still there. I sniffed the boy and nudged my muzzle under his arm. He took me to his house-box. I jumped on his bed but he pulled me off. Then he gave me some of the best smelling food I could imagine. Of course, I swallowed without chewing and showed him the whites of my eyes for more.

"Okay Chisel, that's enough bacon, tomorrow I'll call your mom."

In the morning all I got was water and a couple pieces of dry bread. He led me to his small car. The world moved past the window, and I saw places I knew. The car stopped. "Bye Chisel, I'll check on you later."

I jumped from the front seats to the back and watched him walk away. Out the window was very short grass with very long sticks coming out. Mom had never taken me to do my business on that grass, it looked like heaven. I tried to sniff out the windows but all of them were closed. I panicked. I was hot; I couldn't breathe. That boy wasn't a good boy at all. I squeezed into a ball on the floor and thought about running up the hill with my mom and swimming in the creek.

Hours later, the door opened. I fell out onto the hot road. *"MOOOOOOM, DAAAAAD!"* I squealed. Mom cried. She hugged me and poured water over my head. It felt so good. Right then I decided that I will always do what my mom says.

"Chisel, I'm sorry I had you out during fireworks. I'm never going to let you out of my sight again."

That night I got lots of good scraps and Mom put pieces of hotdogs between Hayden's toes—just for me.

Chapter 32

Time continued without my permission. In January, when the kids returned to school, I was eager to get back to our routine, but not so eager for holiday viruses to find Storey.

After the holiday paraphernalia was put away, I had time to think and admitted that the alternative stuff and the twelve weeks of fish oil wasn't healing Storey. In fact, she was worse. I counted on balancing Storey's Omega-3's to make a noticeable difference.

At the end of January, I called the Children's Hospital of Colorado and managed to get a new patient appointment for a recommended pediatric neurologist in February. Hayden's enthusiasm for a plane ride was milk and cookies to my fear. Hayden was oblivious to what he did for my mental health.

We continued to swim on Friday nights and go to gymnastics Saturday mornings. Storey's favorite were the rings. Her little fingers grew white holding on so tightly. She gave it her best, kicking and smiling. Storey was still in the 10th percentile for growth, and it made assisting her easy.

One day out of the corner of my eye, I noticed Zuzana, whom I hadn't seen in months. Zuzana assisted Sara, holding her hands the same way I helped Storey. We gave each other sympathetic half smiles, silently comparing our precious girls and their wiggly bodies working tirelessly to stay erect. When open gym was over, kids ran past us. Zuzana and I met near the doors. We paused. Our ataxic girls reached out and hugged one another like they belonged to a special club. Zuzana told us that after two years Sara was finally diagnosed with Batten Disease—a no-cure neurodegenerative disease. A timed life.

I studied Sara, then looked at Storey, then back at Sara. Zuzana and I teared up watching other kids move past us, asking their mothers if they could have fish crackers in the car. My body was numb; my lips couldn't move.

"Aww, Sweetheart," John said, looking at Sara, who was trying to pull her mom to the door.

"I'm so sorry Zuzana. We still don't have a diagnosis," I said, gazing away.

John picked Storey up and kissed her cheek. Hayden asked me if we could go toss rocks after Storey's nap.

On Tuesdays, Storey stayed home from school and we went to see Sheri for private physical therapy. Afterwards I drove through my favorite coffee hut and rewarded myself with my weekly vanilla latte (skim, extra hot, half vanilla). The first few sips of coffee reset my presence and warmed my spirit. After that, the lukewarm coffee was just a waste of money.

In the afternoon we went to a craniosacral therapy appointment or to Eagle Mount for equine therapy. At Eagle Mount Storey sat on a horse led by a volunteer and two side-walkers. I sat in the sun next to other parents. We watched our kids smile and wave from the warm backs of horses.

The more people we saw—medically, alternatively, or spiritually— meant more information I had to decipher. At the time, there was little information on the internet, and I felt like Alice in Wonderland in *Through the Looking Glass*. New information had scary faces; few had medical treatments and researching alternative methods made me feel like the Mad Hatter. By then I trusted few, including some days, myself. However, it was all up to me to investigate. I was Storey's voice, her advocate. All I wanted was a medical doctor who was so enchanted by Storey's story that it haunted them day and night.

Nine weeks after balancing Storey's fatty acids with extra fish oil, Dr. Marc sent a fatty acid blood sample to BodyBio Corporation via the Kenney Krieger Institute. A few weeks later, four pages of results with explanations arrived outlining what fatty acids do and don't do for the body, and which to avoid for ultimate cell production and health. I learned more about fatty acids on those pages than I wanted, and a new obsession grew out of their confusing protocols. Storey's blood test showed that her Omega-3s were now too high, her phytanic acid was a bit high, and other fatty acids were out of balance. Understandably, too much of a good thing isn't always good—even fish oil.

High phytanic acid in the blood can indicate Refsum's Disease—a leukodystrophy— classification/storage disease which is an inherited or mutated condition lacking the enzyme peroxisomes. In Refsum's disease, the cells store and build up phytanic acid, which causes problems like ataxia and eye problems (to confuse everyone, these symptoms are also common in many rare life-threatening diseases). We all know that many diseases aren't a cookie cutter fit. I almost hoped Storey had Refsum's, since there was a possibility of supportive care including dietary restrictions by removing foods from a diet which contain higher amounts of phytanic acid.

Knowing the results, Dr. Marc advised we cut out all Omega-3s and foods high in phytanic acid, which were most meats and dairy and all greens. That left Storey on a diet of beans, rice, and fruit. I felt like I was chasing a ghost. Refsum's was a serious disease, and this fatty-acid panel was inconclusive at best. Storey was already on a restricted diet, and now no greens or meat. I had a hard time with so many speculative diet changes that I couldn't tell if any made a difference.

Maybe Storey's phytanic acid was high because she ate a lot of spinach the night before the test? Ambiguities drove me nuts. Obviously, if the medical field had given us a diagnosis, I wouldn't have sought any alternatives.

Many times, diseases show a false negative in the beginning because there aren't enough markers in the blood for a correct positive, which is what happened with Storey's friend, Sara, early on. And in theory it also happened to Storey, who was retested for a handful of diseases.

My Refsum's disease obsession was just one example of the many dark holes I Googled until I was on the verge of psychosis. Then I'd take a break, or not; then relax. It was all too much, and I felt like I was drowning.

I wondered why the doctors hadn't mentioned Refsum's disease. I called Dr. Grabe and asked for Storey to get a phytanic acid test done by a medical pathologist, but she was skeptical and obviously tired of my calls because at our next visit she handed me a list of diseases for which Storey had already been tested (see addendum).

The reason I hadn't heard about Refsum's was because Storey had been tested for so many diseases, I couldn't keep my notes straight. I was grateful for this list and decided to trust the doctors and my own intuition a little more, instead of Googling each disease only to find myself sliding down the rabbit hole of endless detours.

I wanted to try the next diet Dr. Marc suggested, because Storey would eat anything without complaint. We settled with a plan I could manage for a while: take away Omega-3s (no fish oil, hemp oil, flax oil, olive oil, or high-oleic safflower oil) and increase her Omega-6 fatty acids (nut and seed oil—but not peanut oil—sunflower oil, high-linoleic safflower oil, or polyunsaturated oils). I sat on my hands to keep my fingers from Googling all those fucking oils and laughed instead of cried while waiting to consult with the sixth neurologist at the Children's Hospital in Denver.

I let myself relax a little and enjoyed what Storey could do. Every morning I fell in love with her again. She giggled from her bed like she was entertaining a sleepover friend. When she asked for milk, I peeked into her room and cherished her free smile.

In letting my guard down and giving up control, life didn't seem that hard. My yoga practice strengthened, and I noticed small wonders—Hayden's effulgent eyes as he watched truck tires roll down the road; Chisel's cowlicks on the back of her hips which made smiles when she pranced ahead; the sound water made when Storey splashed her open palm in the pool; the smell of worms and the colors of the rocks on our road after a storm; the wordless love Storey shared with strangers. I wondered what I had done to receive such an honor, to be trusted with these teaching spirits I introduced as mine.

Chapter 33

We arrived at the Denver International Airport after my wipe down ritual and without delay. Hayden's passion for new adventures blanketed my nerves as we lugged two car seats and colorful bags through the underground transportation toward the car rental, then to Hotel Monaco's lobby.

"Mom! Is this a *faaancy* hotel?" Hayden's eyes sparkled.

"Yeah, and the best part is that they will bring us a pet goldfish swimming in a big glass bowl, to our room. Should we name the fish, 'Little Jerry Seinfeld?'" I said. "We're going to have fun."

"Mom... I like goldfish," Storey whispered.

I leaned over, lifted her onto my hip and kissed her forehead.

"Storey, tomorrow we are going to see another doctor. We hope he has new ideas and after that, we will ride the Light Rail Bus downtown and have so much fun," John said, rubbing her back.

Our unique room felt spacious with high ceilings, yellow-and-white striped wallpaper, cozy throws, and a large bright bathroom. Hayden laughed, jumped up and down on one of the beds, then stiffened his body like a plank and fell on the pillows. I laid Storey next to him and they giggled together until the bellhop arrived with Little Jerry Seinfeld. I balanced Storey against the night table so she could watch the fish zip around plastic seaweed. Hayden continued jumping while we unpacked.

The Denver Children's Hospital entrance had high ceilings and several giant ball machines with complicated moving parts—a brilliant design to distract kids and families.

Since we were there for another opinion and didn't have tests scheduled, I felt more relaxed than previous appointments. The receptionist spoke like she was a ventriloquist, asking for Storey's insurance card and handing me a stack of papers to fill out before sliding the plexiglass window above her computer.

I had fantasized that this doctor might receive a spark of brilliance and come up with a new theory the other doctors were unable to find. After almost an hour of agonizing pen tapping, the nurse took us back to a stark and windowless exam room with hard plastic seats—an artless contrast to the hospital's entrance.

Storey's goldfish friend at Hotel Monaco

"I see you've seen other neurologists. What are you doing here?" the nurse asked, looking down at Storey's thick file.

My jaw opened and my head went blank. I wanted to say, *What's wrong with you? Can't you see we are desperate parents? We want to know what's going on in our daughter's body. We've consulted numerous neurologists, naturopaths, psychics. I've prayed to the universe and to the god up there. Obviously, we are going out of our minds and this doctor was highly recommended.*

Instead, I mustered up, "Well... we were hoping for another great mind to be thinking of our daughter, Storey, and what might be happening to her."

John played with the kids on the floor. The nurse looked bored and stiff, unusual for a pediatric nurse. She continued with the same questions without looking at the forms I had just filled out. Hayden pointed to medical tubes hanging from hooks and a few dirty toys tucked in plastic bins. My face grew red. When the nurse left, I was furious, so furious I was silent for a few minutes.

Two and a half hours after walking into the neurology department, we saw the neurologist. He looked into our eyes and apologized for our wait. By then I was angry and exhausted from keeping Storey and Hayden safely busy. The doctor's caring nature didn't reel me in.

"It's all there in that stack of papers. At 2 years she began to walk wide legged, and then..." John said.

In the middle of John's narrative, the doctor's phone rang and he answered it. I looked down at Storey, then up at John. *Okay, keep it together. If I had a child with an emergency, I'd want to be able to get ahold of the doctor, too.* The doctor apologized and John continued, but the doctor was distracted and at that point I realized he had only skimmed the first couple pages of Storey's two-inch-thick medical file that I had mailed a month before. He tucked Storey's MRS films under the wall light table hooks and John continued.

I couldn't form my words. The doctor came ill-prepared, and because Storey was a new patient, he hadn't fostered an emotional investment. We were just another mysterious case in his endless workload.

"Well, looks like your daughter has had a thorough workup and has been tested for just about everything I can think of for now," he said.

His phone rang, and he answered it *again*. John raised an eyebrow my way, wondering when I was going to make some rude comment.

"I'm so sorry," the doctor said, closing his flip phone.

"We have a friend whose child had similar symptoms and an enlarged cerebellum. Their doctor prescribed steroids. But Storey doesn't have an enlarged cerebellum—hers is getting smaller," I added.

"I *could* put her on steroids, if you want," the doctor said.

I rolled my eyes and took a breath.

"Please tell us how experimental steroids could help if you don't know what you're working with. I'm *not* interested in trying something that's physically invasive unless you can give me some positive statistics behind it," I said grumpily, wishing I hadn't mentioned our friend.

"I can't tell you if it would help. I do think a skin biopsy and muscle biopsy is your only next option. I don't know what else to tell you," the doctor said.

"Okay, thanks. We just wanted another pediatric neurologist thinking about our medical mystery. We're trying to avoid the Mayo Clinic because of the stress of traveling and retesting with anesthesia, which we know from experience would make Storey worse. We are hesitant to do a muscle biopsy knowing that, as of today's knowledge, the remaining diagnoses have no treatment. I was just hoping you knew something the rest of the neurologists we visited don't."

I tossed the sticky trucks back into their toy box.

"John, let's go!"

I couldn't wait to get the hell out of there and back into the rental car and into what was left of our "normal" life. Hayden and Storey had been beyond patient and their stamina was amazing.

Outside the hospital I felt like the person in Edvard Munch's painting *The Scream*, which he painted after watching his family members die slowly of tuberculosis more than 130 years ago.

"Well, sweetheart, it's good you're doing all that other stuff for Storey," John said as we walked out of the hospital.

I knew John really felt that way. He still had a small reserve of hope that something I was doing might shift something within Storey's body.

We spent the rest of the day riding the transit. Hayden's enthusiasm never waned. We went to the Denver Zoo, rode the train, took pictures, and watched a baby hippo follow its mother. I stared at the mommy hippo and felt the love she had for her baby. My throat tightened. Instinctually I reminded myself what was happening in our lives must be part of a larger plan, and that I needed to listen to my heart the same way the mother hippo listened to hers. Their presence reminded me of what was important: to notice and enjoy life's simple pleasures. And to appreciate our story. My soul thanked the mother and baby hippo for living in the zoo for our entertainment and lessons.

Dear *Mom*,

That baby hippo looked into my eyes. I felt his heart and empathized with him. Like me, he too was afraid of life before he was born.

I felt like we knew each other before that day at the zoo. My heart warmed seeing the mother and the baby hippo's love. The kind of love we share.

Mom, I know you felt it too.

Thanks for taking us to the zoo.

I love you,

Storey

Dear *Storey*,

Grandma Pat used to collect little hippo figurines. Now I know why.

I love you too,

Mom

Never one to be extravagant, that night, I splurged and scheduled a massage at the hotel's spa. I didn't realize how physically and spiritually I needed to reconnect with myself. The masseuse found all my frustration points and guided them off the table. At the end she sealed the experience by misting orange lavender water over my face and chest. The droplets slid down my face like tears and carried away the last bit of my residual fear. I couldn't move for ten minutes after she left. My intention was to savor the peacefulness, knowing I'd need it soon.

Our goal of making an unpleasant trip into a fun adventure was successful. Hayden and Storey were giddy when we arrived home.

"That trip was way funner, it had so much action. When I grow up, I'm going to live in a big city like Denver," Hayden informed us.

Thoughts of the homeless teenagers we saw begging on the 16th Street Mall and flying to Denver during winter months to visit future grandchildren made me queasy.

Chapter 34

Alone, on a moonless night, I drive down an unfamiliar winding road. My car seems to accelerate on its own. My headlights flash on and off against the high canyon walls. Everything grows into a thick darkness. I can't see the road. I slam my brakes over and again, nothing. I flip my headlights in panic, nothing. I anticipate the next curve, gripping the steering wheel, hoping I make the right turn in the blackness. My voice is gone, no one hears my cries. I can't see anything. Where am I going? In my lucid mind I say: "This better be a nightmare or I'm dead."

Seconds, or maybe an hour later, I woke sweating. The clock read 3:33 a.m. My body lay stiff. For once John's snoring brought comfort. I was alive. Storey was alive. I took five deep breaths and glanced out the window and saw a light at the base of Mount Ellis. I begged my brain for the delivery of that dream to be the last time, but I knew better.

The doctor from Denver promptly sent a follow-up report to Dr. Grabe. In his report he reiterated a skin and muscle biopsy. He also mentioned repeating the Fatty-Acid Panel to compare the results to the tests from The Kennedy Krieger Institute. Additionally, he suggested a repeat MRS and nerve conduction test, restating that these tests were, at this point, strictly for informational purposes, not for treatments. At the appointment, I thought I had made it clear to the doctor that I had promised Storey I would never authorize another nerve conduction test. John and I agreed long ago that sedation was out of the question unless there was a possible treatment from different results.

And that was that. I was right when I doubted the Denver doctor would follow up on the Fatty Acid research like he said he would during our visit. I had had enough; there wasn't hard evidence that Storey had Refsum's disease. After a few weeks of depriving Storey of greens and some meat, she beamed when I handed her a bowl of frozen peas, her favorite snack.

A month later we drove east, past fields of crusty snow that followed the Yellowstone River to Billings for our first metabolic clinic. The metabolic team consisted of a retired pediatric neurologist, Dr. Guggenheim; a pediatric neurologist from the Children's Hospital in Denver, Dr. Turner (a different doctor than who we saw when we went there); —the 8th neurologist—a counselor; a nurse; and Dr. Grabe. The clinicians gathered to brainstorm about undiagnosed patients and to support families in their battles.

Out of habit, I took a deep breath before I lifted Storey out of her car seat. My stomach twisted. I was both nervous for new information and nervous that we wouldn't learn anything new. Storey interacted with the group. She sat in everyone's lap, flipped through board books and ate snacks. We began our story at the beginning. It was refreshing that the clinicians were prepared. They had studied her file and films. They listened.

Clearly Dr. Turner was the kind of doctor you want to be thinking about your child. She did most of the talking. It was a challenge for me to keep up without a hard copy that listed the diseases she talked about: leukodystrophies, recessive genes, epileptic encephalopathy, supranuclear ophthalmoplegia, lysosomal, carbohydrate deficient glycoprotein syndrome (CDGS), Nieman-Pick C, etc. The doctors talked about the possibility of one of the Nieman-Pick C diseases, because of Storey's ophthalmoplegia (upward gaze muscle weakness and ataxia). I never noticed Storey had a hard time looking up. More often she looked up and pointed to the heavens. They wanted to retest for Nieman-Pick C, which required a skin biopsy. I cringed, picturing them taking a tool like a carrot peeler to her skin. We brought up the issue around Refsum's disease and they all agreed that Refsum's patients consistently have retinitis pigmentosa—legal blindness. Had I known that significant bit of information, I wouldn't have dove down the Refsum's hole. This reminded us why it was important to get several professional medical opinions and to ask a lot of questions.

Dr. Guggenheim held Storey in her lap the second hour of the clinic visit. Then came to the dreaded subject of a muscle biopsy. The team reiterated its importance to further the investigation of a possible mitochondrial disorder. But they agreed that since Storey's levels of alanine, serum amino acids, lactate, carnitine esters, peripheral lactate, pyruvate, and central lactate were all normal, her symptoms were inconsistent with a mitochondrial disorder. The doctors also talked about a conjunctival biopsy to determine a neurodegenerative storage disease. I didn't like the sound of that. I knew what *conjunctival* meant: eye. We wanted to find a name for what was happening to Storey, but at what cost? There were almost no treatments for neurodegenerative storage diseases. Why would I risk one of Storey's good body parts to find a name with no cure? None of the diseases the team explored had a treatment. They were a death sentence. I carefully explained to the clinicians that a conjunctival biopsy was not going to happen. John and I agreed to another lumbar puncture (spinal tap) to test a category of pediatric neurotransmitter diseases. We were all too tired.

Pediatric neurotransmitter diseases were completely new to us until Dr. Turner mentioned it. I thought I had heard them all. Unfortunately, when Storey received a spinal tap in Springfield two years before, Dr. Pranzatelli didn't mention pediatric neurotransmitter diseases. Maybe it would have been easy in Springfield for the doctors to take a little more cerebrospinal fluid and test for those diseases? My mother compass of protecting her from invasive procedures ranged between: is it worth Storey regressing, perhaps permanently, for the possibility of learning something new? Or will she be fine after she eats an ice cream cone for being so brave?

At the end of the clinic, we authorized blood tests for phytanic acid to rule out Zellweger syndrome (similar to Refsum's), and to test for carbohydrate deficient glycoprotein syndrome (CDGS), a unique family of newly discovered diseases. I agreed to talk about a skin biopsy during our next visit if this bloodwork was inconclusive.

Storey sat in John's lap, and we squeezed in a little counseling time while they prepared to draw some of her blood.

"Do you have any lidocaine?" I asked. "You're going to have to put a warm compress on her arm. She doesn't have good veins and I'll need to distract her because she might pass out or throw up," I babbled.

My head pounded. I needed food. While I watched the nurse massage a vein in Storey's arm, the counselor slipped in the idea that a wheelchair might be our next supportive move. I began to cry. Storey turned white and looked like she was going to pass out, so they gently set her arm down and quickly stuck a needle in her foot before she knew what had happened. Storey's body stopped giving blood after 5ml; they wanted more. Somehow, we survived.

"The nurse is right. I think we need to get a wheelchair and a fucking van," I admitted to John in the parking lot.

Most medical diagnostic tools are through a process of elimination. The same disease in one person can be mysterious in another. It gets more complicated because often, a variety of rare diseases share symptoms, then toss in everyone's unique genetic code, personalities, and life experiences—it can be like untangling a spider web.

There are around thousands documented rare diseases, and 80% have a genetic component. Top that with all the mysterious diseases yet to be named, much less the autoimmune reasons or the genetics responsible. Once I realized the complexity of genetics and genetic diseases, and what could go wrong during gestation with just one wrong letter in a gene of many letters, it was astonishing to me that humans have evolved at all. And I wondered why people don't believe in miracles.

Time ticked on. John's business thrived and he still managed to ski on powder days. We lived to celebrate life's small wonders and wins in what we knew as normal and tried to ignore the darkness sidling in the corner. Hayden began to understand the complexities of living with ADHD and completing homework. I continued to drive Storey around to various therapeutic appointments. Storey and I consulted Elaine a few more times that winter; she lightly performed energy healing and cleared negative vibrations.

"You will never know how much you have helped Storey. I feel so much love around the two of you, and your love is keeping Storey here," Elaine said to me more than once.

I realized we visited Elaine equally for my benefit and Storey's. I craved Elaine's light, nurturing, and support. After our sessions Storey smiled more and tremored less, and I walked a little lighter.

Chapter 35

Hayden and John continued to ski most weekends through March 2003, making it home in time for me to go to yoga or cross-country skiing before it got dark. Storey and I spent our days playing and reading to the tune of Mozart, or we watched *Clifford the Big Red Dog* and *Sesame Street*. Storey played alone without fuss. I'd sneak peeks of her laughing while cutting up pieces of old magazine pages and carefully placing pieces into the waste basket—she never liked a mess. However, her favorite activity was "playing balls." Her hands shook dropping balls into a plastic toy chimney. The balls mazed around and appeared at the bottom. Storey did that for hours. She did everything slowly and deliberately. I didn't know if that was her personality, her disease, or if the seizure medicine had just slowed her neuropathways. Beyond her beautiful spirit, I didn't truly know who she was without symptoms.

That winter, one baby breath at a time, Storey slipped from us. Her head tilted more to the right, and her eyes glazed through space. We'd snap our fingers in front of her face, saying, "Storey, straighten your head." Immediately she'd smile, giggle, sit up straight and come back to us. Some days she was so shaky and out of it, my shoulders rolled forward and I felt like I was in the movie *Groundhog Day*. Some days Storey tremored less and was bright and alert. Then I'd overan-alyze cause and effect: What did she eat yesterday? What activity did she experience? Did I show her more love and encouragement, and her soul decided it wasn't too bad here? I developed a list of environ-mental conditions that might result in better days. And the opposite was true when things went south. I rewound bad days in my head and beat myself up if I convinced myself I could have done better.

I'll never forget a particular cold, overcast spring day when I needed good news. At preschool pickup Melissa greeted me with Storey in her arms. She told me that Storey seemed to have lost her pincher grab movement using her thumb and index finger on her right hand. At dinner the night before, Storey was able to pinch food with her thumb and index finger. The next morning, she couldn't. I lifted Sto-rey out of Melissa's arms and walked to the car as fast as I could. The car shook in unison with my sobs. I wanted to scream, but I didn't want to scare Storey.

My princess was slipping.

After a few minutes of sobbing with my forehead on the steering wheel, I looked around, hoping no other parent was watching me. I glanced in the rear-view mirror, and Storey smiled. I smiled back and thought, *at least she can still smile!*

"Hi beauty queen, we need to make one stop before going home for a nap," I said and drove to the coffee hut even though it was a Thursday.

A month later, Storey lost the ability to pinch with her left hand. She learned to adapt by grasping food and toys using her remaining three fingers against her palm, a harder movement, but easier for her. Her forefingers and thumbs stuck out when she picked up something.

Every day my heart broke again and again. So, I looked for a horse.

That March the east wind snaked its way down the Bozeman pass and over the saddle of our property and rattled our house, just because it could. Storey and I hid behind drawn blinds, squeezed home-made play dough between our fingers and baked cookies. By April I found my courage when the wind calmed, and I watched light peek between dancing rainclouds to cast golden light, florescent hues, and shadows around blades of new grass.

I carried on.

In spring of 2003, Storey continued to ride horses at Eagle Mount once a week. She smiled and sat straighter from the back of a horse. It made her strong and filled me with reverence. I longed for Storey to ride every day, but she couldn't unless we owned our own horse.

There's something very special about humans, mostly girls, and horses. Maybe it was their smell, their strength. I didn't know for sure, but for centuries horses have healed us. Ronald Reagan and others are known for saying, "There's nothing better for the inside of a man than the outside of a horse." And that was true for me.

Growing up in Salt Lake City we didn't have horses, or friends with horses, or any prospective friends with horses. However, I remember the intense yearning I felt watching trail riders from the Diamond P Ranch come over the hill toward our cabin outside of West Yellowstone. I'd negotiate with my dad, in exchange for crappy all-day chores, for a trail ride at the Diamond P. The feeling of sitting on a warm horse while it moved through colored aspens and open pastures was a gift I still cherish. I wanted Storey to carry that feeling longer than an hour a week. I listed the benefits of having a horse at our house to John, which included a fire break of trimmed pasture grass.

"I'm not interested in ranching or fixing fences," John said. "But, if you do all the work and it will help Storey, I'm for it."

I had a few horse friends, so I called Kristin and we got the horse acquisition rolling. She suggested that I lease a horse before committing to horse ownership.

A few weeks later John and I loaded up the kids and drove thirty minutes to meet a horse leasing company. When we arrived, a man wearing a salt-lined cowboy hat and riding a palomino greeted us at the gate.

"Hello, Sandee, follow me to the corral."

We parked next to a muddy enclosure packed with whinnying and kicking horses. A rough-looking sorrel stood perfectly calm tied outside the corral, clearly relieved to have space.

"This here might make a great horse for your daughter. He's mellow, been a dude horse for many years. Lazy, moves slowly, solid feet. He's 'bout sixteen hands, his name is Dagwood. He lives up to his name, I tell ya," the cowboy said, pointing to the tied horse.

I'm sure I had a deer-in-the-headlights expression. I kept looking over at the horses packed like sardines.

"Don't mind them horses. They just got home from winter range and are itching to hit all that green grass over yonder. Let's get Storey up on Dagwood. Sandee, you can lead, and me and John will sidewalk next to Storey to check whether Dagwood is okay with people walking right next to him."

I told Hayden to stand next to the fence and away from the palomino the man had been riding. I rubbed the sides of Dagwood's neck and pulled off some dried mud. Storey squealed with excitement when John lifted her on Dagwood. She rested her small hands on the saddle horn using three fingers and giggled. The horse took a few steps.

"Dagwood would be a good one, he doesn't mind side walkers," I said, looking back and trying not to trip in the mud.

"He's a good boy, worked real hard for us. I'd be glad to lend him to you verses leasing him to a 250-pound hunter come fall. A good brushin' and he'll clean up real nice."

"What about that one?" I said, pointing to the palomino.

"Sure thing, you know what they say—don't buy the first horse you see just because you feel sorry for it. She's a sweet girl, fun ride. Let's give her a try," he said.

Dagwood looked ratty compared to the palomino. John lifted Storey up, and I began to lead her away from the corral, but the palomino protested. She pulled away from me and tried to lift her head to walk backwards. The cowboy nudged her side. Clearly, this horse wasn't fond of having people that close to her while being led.

"This horse is beautiful, but she doesn't feel right to me," I said. "Dagwood is a much better choice."

"Yep, you're right, little missy. I think Dagwood would do just fine, like I said before and I'll say it again, he's a good boy. He'll be perfect for what you need him to do."

I shook the cowboy's hand and handed him a check to lease Dagwood through November.

In our back pasture, I lifted Storey onto Dagwood's saddle in front of Kristin and took a few steps backward and clicked my camera. Hayden jumped up and down outside our new electric fence. John smiled at Storey from a distance. Suddenly I heard what sounded like a bottle rocket. Because horses are unpredictable, especially a horse you don't know well, I felt a rush of fear and reached for Dagwood's halter, but he remained perfectly calm.

"Oh my god, Storey just shrieked!" Kristin laughed.

That shriek was the first time I had heard Storey squeal with excitement. In that moment I knew Dagwood would change our lives.

Storey on Dagwood in our front yard. John is standing close.

By the middle of May, it was light until nine o'clock. We ate dinner early. I'd brush Dagwood and sniff his muzzle while John buckled Storey's helmet before lifting her onto the horse. John wrapped his arms around Storey's front and back and I carefully led Dagwood around the front yard. At the end of her ride, she'd lie back to rest her head on his hind quarters. Her closed eyes told another story. Or she'd lean forward and hug his neck. Hayden got a turn after Storey.

Storey looked stronger after just a few weeks of consistent riding. Even though she continued with private physical therapy, and occupational therapy during school, Dagwood's presence inspired me and seemed to empower Storey.

Hey *Mom*,

I loved Dagwood so much. He was brown with a white streak down his nose. He was very patient with me and walked carefully when I rode on his back.

I love you,
Storey

Dear Cowgirl *Storey*,

My favorite part, besides seeing you smile on Dagwood's back, was rubbing my nose against his and sniffing. He smelled good. Only horse lovers know what that means!

I love you more every day,
Mom

Not long after Dagwood arrived, I was handed an article (people often gave me articles) from *People* magazine. The article was about a little girl who seemed paralyzed at birth from premature complications. Their doctor told the baby's parents that there was little hope of her walking. But the doctor didn't know what kind of parents the little girl had. They didn't buy in to the doctor's theory. They researched and found a doctor studying spinal cord regeneration using electrical muscle stimulation and repetitive exercises, or locomotor training. The parents enrolled their daughter to receive this new therapy. She hung above a treadmill and was able to walk with the help of a therapist manually moving her legs. The girl walked like this several times a day—the idea was to rewire her brain. She also rode a tricycle with her feet strapped to the pedals, and someone would push the tricycle. The little girl continued to progress. I stared at the pictures of this girl hanging above a treadmill and I knew that was what Storey needed.

This revolutionary therapy illustrated that the body wasn't always hardwired as previously thought. And through stimulation of repetitive movements, the brain and nervous system—depending on the injury or illness—might regenerate neuropathways. Of course, like any therapy, it wasn't a complete cure and took an exorbitant amount of perseverance. After I read the article ten times, I asked Sheri, Storey's physical therapist, what her thoughts were. The timing was serendipitous because Sheri had just purchased a treadmill with a contraption that held a harness above it, like the one in the article. She had planned on using it on Storey that day. I was so excited my head throbbed. Sheri strapped Storey into the harness and buckled her in above the treadmill, just like the little girl in the article. Then Sheri lifted Storey's legs to walk while the treadmill moved slowly under her feet. Storey walked. Not only did it stimulate Storey's nervous system, it energized her whole body. Storey smiled and laughed the entire time she was "walking."

I cried. And visualized our future.

Like a horse, we needed that kind of treadmill suspension at home for daily use. Sheri owned the only one in town. I researched and figured out how to buy one. I named the equipment our "walk-a-bout." We set it up in our bedroom. I also found a tricycle with an extension bar on the back, like the little girl had. Every morning and night I played fun music, and John buckled Storey above the treadmill. I held her ankles and we walked and walked. During errands and around town I pushed Storey in her special trike with her feet strapped to the pedals. On the tricycle Storey looked like a regular kid just having fun.

My self-care of yoga and running kept me mentally and physically strong for everything I needed to do for Storey and Hayden. It pained me that Hayden wasn't involved with after-school activities like soccer, but I couldn't drive him around and make Storey ride along when she was always tired. When I saw moms who drove SUVs with "Soccer Mom" bumper stickers, I felt jealous. How dare they have normal lives. A soccer mom was a time suck that I didn't have. I also envisioned late nights of frustration and exhaustion after soccer practice helping Hayden with homework that took most kids half the time. Hayden rarely complained; he preferred to play with Chauncy, the golden retriever, next door.

Nightly the kids rode Dagwood, then Hayden turned up the music and we all danced and sang while Storey "walked" above the treadmill. She loved it, but often grabbed the bar in front of her and swung back and forth, holding her legs above the treadmill. John shook his head in frustration and Storey giggled.

CHISEL

I tell you what, those dogs next door are so stupid. They run around like they own the neighborhood. Some evenings suspicious dogs join their pack, and they act like no one cares. But I care. I care very much that they cross into our property to leave their mark. I show them who's boss by pinning them to the ground and slobbering and growling in their scared noses.

I don't mind Chauncy and Cub because they visit Hayden. Hayden is just like Chauncy with endless energy, they play fetch until the sun goes down. But I'm not crazy about Cub. He pulled a fast one on me and killed a guinea pig, who was minding her own business in the grass behind her guinea pig-sized fence.

The best part about all those college kids next door is that they have parties. That means mystery meat and chips hidden between blades of grass. Their last party I turned my radar on high. Mom said no, but I snuck out at the beginning of the party.

"Chisel, you cannot go over there, you'll eat stuff and throw up. Sorry, it's kennel time," Mom said, pulling me home.

I didn't mind the kennel; I had a good view of their yard, and I knew I'd eventually find an opportunity to sneak back over. Once the party was at a roar, ten dogs tromped over and laughed at me through the steel bars. I barked and lunged at the door. Mom yelled and sent them running.

Later the party had high-pitched noises that echoed, and I saw people wiggle their butts at each other. Those humans looked as dumb as most dogs. Mom and Hayden went to the house without me. The audacity! Doesn't she know it's my responsibility keeping all those dogs in line and to clean the grass? Plus, there were college girls who wanted to run their fingers through my wrinkles.

Once the sky darkened, I heard Hayden say, "Mom, that was great music, and did you see all those dogs running around?"

That's it, I'll show Mom. I'll sneak away when she's not looking. Over the next few days, I had a hard time getting away. Mom kept me leashed or buzzed my necklace. Then one night I found an opportunity. I ran toward meat smells. Jackpot! There was a heap of pig grease on the boy's driveway. I went to town licking as fast as I could. Such delight!

"CHISEL!!!!!! Get over here, you're in big trouble," Mom said.

I licked faster and faster.

"OH MY GOD, CHISEL, you are so dead, what the fuck were you eating? Those idiot boys poured pig grease right on the driveway?"

Mom grabbed my collar and pointed home. She locked me in the kennel. It was worth every lick. Soon I saw her drive down the driveway. A half hour later my stomach ballooned in and out, and then I knew... Ugh! My kennel was a mess with piles of black greasy gravel.

"Chisel, are you okay? I'm calling the vet."

For a week all I got to eat was rice and stuff that tasted like cardboard. I laid around with little interest in guarding the house. Mom gave me a lot of wrinkle attention. Eventually everything went back to normal. Mom smiled and cried a lot. Storey smiled and giggled. I don't know what's wrong with Storey. She still smells and looks different. Mom and Dad fuss over her with sad faces.

About ten days after I redecorated my kennel, Dad let me out of the house (he doesn't pay much attention) and I bolted. I searched and searched for the grease pile, but it was gone. Then the wind blew just right, and I followed a smell. Bingo! There it was behind the shed—the PIG CAR-CASS—Mom will be so proud of me!

"CHHHIIIISSSSSEEELLLLLLL!!! YOU'RE SO DEAD!"

Chapter 36

The first week of June 2003, nine mothers chased their graduating kindergarten kids, who wore red gowns, to slick hair under awkward graduation caps and bouncing tassels. All the kids from Hayden and Storey's school sat on stage to sing. The graduation class stood in the back row. Hayden, the shortest boy in his class, stood behind Storey. I eagle-eyed her, praying she wouldn't suddenly "drop." She was almost fine, but I sensed her struggling and knew how hard it was for her to stay upright.

Diplomas were given and sticky fingers released celebratory balloons. The kids screamed and ran between bites of hamburgers. Storey sat and played with a 9-week-old puppy most of the time. She was happy. I was happy.

At kindergarten graduations, you realize that you had let time take your power long ago, when you thought your baby's nonstop cry defined the rest of your life. But when you watch a small rolled-up diploma handed to your kindergarten child, you wake up and realize that high school graduation is just a nap away.

Our traditional summer kick-off-hummingbird migration-birthday party was a few weeks later. When I asked Hayden who he wanted to invite to his 7th seventh birthday party, he rattled off six names;

four of them were neighborhood dogs. We invited his graduation class, and some of Storey's friends and their parents. I expected some to say no, but everyone came.

Parties were as stressful as they were fun for me. It motivated me to get my house picked up, my flowerbeds planted. However, it challenged my judging ghost. *I can't believe you didn't dust; they're going to judge you on your messy garage. You'd think you could have finished painting the kitchen.* A lovely pattern I inherited from my mother.

Before I knew it, my car was full of Costco pizza, Dollar Store plastic, and a Dairy Queen ice cream cake topped with a hummingbird icing creation. John's mother, Joan, followed me around the house, asking, "Where should I put these plates? Where is everyone going to eat? Etc."

In the chaos, love grew. Kids ran to Storey, who was wearing her princess headband, to hug her. Beautifully wrapped gifts randomly decorated the yard and kids' shoes were kicked into the air around the bouncy slide. Gummy fingers offered Dagwood old carrots. The swings never stopped. Wasps flew in and out from under the porch railing and ants climbed near the hummingbird feeder and entertained young eyes.

Two of Storey's friends joined her at her table outside and squished Play-Doh. Kristin kept a close eye on Storey, making sure she didn't fall out of her chair while John and I fed the kids before cake.

A couple times I carried Storey up the slide steps and placed her between my legs. We slid down laughing while the rest of the kids waited patiently. More than twenty migrating hummingbirds darted around kids playing on the porch; some landed on a few lucky fingers. The kids laughed and screamed and ran off the porch leaving half-eaten pizza for the wasps.

Dear *Storey*,

    I was glad the parents didn't listen to me when I said "no gifts" for your 5th birthday party, because when it was time for you to open your gifts, your friends crowded around you like you were Princess Diana. Your lightness of being made your body look as though nothing was wrong, like you had suddenly changed into a goddess of love. Your friends carefully wrapped their arms around you after they offered you their specially picked-out gift because they felt your extraordinary love. You giggled and laughed opening your Groovy Girls doll sets, toys, and new art supplies.

    I watched and cried. I knew the scene before me was a fleeting valentine to be tucked away. It was your gift to me. How foolish I was worrying about the appearance of half-painted walls during a party that meant so much to you and Hayden. That day I wondered how many birthdays you had left. I paused and took a deep breath between conversations and the frenetic energy of this short-lived wild party to notice the tenderness surrounding you and Hayden. My heart filled with so much gratitude. The kind of gratitude that has come to my rescue many times.

    A couple weeks later, on July 1st, you, Dad, Hayden and I celebrated your real birthday. We had your favorite dinner: steak, artichokes, and gluten-free cake. You tilted your head and the four of us sang, except I couldn't get through the song without crying, but you sang as loud as you could. You were so happy. I filmed you singing and blowing out your candles. I still haven't been able to watch the video.

> I love you my goddess,
>> *Mom*

Dear *Mom*,

> My 5th birthday wish came true.
>> I love you, thanks for making me feel special,
>>> *Storey*

Chapter 37

At the end of June, *Good Morning America* aired one of their previous episodes. *GMA* had traveled around the states looking for heartfelt stories. One Saturday morning John and I watched a video of two siblings in wheelchairs. Like us, for five years the parents of these children went from doctor to doctor searching for the cause of their kids' disabilities. Through a chain of good fortune, they found a doctor who was researching newly found, rare forms of pediatric neurotransmitter diseases (PND)—an umbrella term for many neurotransmitter diseases. In Texas, Dr. Hyland from the Baylor University Medical Center, Institute of Metabolic Diseases tested and confirmed that both siblings had an extremely uncommon form of Dopa-Responsive Dystonia (DRD). This crippling disease affects one in a million caused by a lack of dopamine (to put it in simple terms). With a fine-tuned combination of L-dopa and Carbidopa, the siblings' dystonia (uncontrolled movements) improved after a couple months. It was a miracle of the highest. After watching the show, families, including us, hoped their children had this disease because it was completely treatable.

On our slow computer, we Googled again and again and watched Harrison and his sister Gracie Colegrove (their real names for your research) blossom from being unable to pick up a piece of paper to jumping on their trampoline. John and I couldn't speak as we listened to Harrison, who looked into the camera with tears, pleading to never give up.

Confused and irritated, I briefly remembered the mention of neurotransmitter diseases at one of the metabolic clinics and wondered why Storey hadn't been tested for this set of diseases.

Neurotransmitters are chemical messengers that are released during nerve impulse to either excite or inhibit nerves. Pediatric neurotransmitter disease is a category of genetic disorders affecting the synthesis, metabolism and catabolism of neurotransmitters in children. Many children are unable to walk, use their arms, or talk. Some are born that way; some start to degenerate as the nerve and cells turn over. The symptoms of PND are similar to many neurologic diseases, therefore hard to diagnose.

Harrison and Gracie's story opened a whole new door of diligence and hope for many families like us. I was relentless. I also read about Caroline, a 5-year-old who was undiagnosed and unable to swallow or walk. Her spinal fluid was tested at the Baylor and she was diagnosed with 5-methyltehydrofolate, a cerebral folate deficiency. Caroline was the first person treated with folinic acid (similar but chemically different to folic acid). After three weeks she began to walk and swallow. I remember in the video Caroline's mother describing how every morning felt like Christmas as Caroline improved.

Harrison's words, "Never give up hope, never give up," swam around in my head while Googling PND over and over. Of course, I made myself nuts dissecting each category under the drop-down menus from related websites like NORD (National Organization for Rare Diseases). I learned how differently the diseases can present in each child, often resulting in a misdiagnosis, and mis-hope.

We are all enigmas in the astonishing world of DNA, each of us carrying unique variants and mutations. I'm still dumfounded that we can reproduce at all. I felt like I was straining to solve a giant decagon Rubik's Cube to learn a pinch of Rare Diseases 101. I wasn't a scientist. I wasn't Lorenzo's father. But I was driven.

Being a human with a rare disease is like walking into a giant shoe store with a sore foot. You carry hope because you see stacks of boxes with your shoe size. You try on many pairs—some are too tight, some make your heel slip, some don't support your funny arch. None of them fit perfectly and you're frustrated because they *are* all your size. You purchase the one that feels okay because you're out of choices. The next day you wear the shoes with faith, but then your foot hurts worse. You lose hope and take the shoe back to the store and try on a few more. Now you're urgently gambling because no one can tell you why your foot hurts all the time. You see people in the store jumping for joy because they found a shoe that fits. Yet, you also see people in the corner crying because, just like you, they are losing hope. You're all out of options. You have consulted shoe experts all over the country. The unique shoes you need haven't been designed yet because it isn't cost effective to design a shoe for one person in a million.

After five years, the Colegrove children found their miracle slipper behind the right door. Their miracle was as rare as their disease.

That kind of miracle was what I wanted for Storey. What I hoped for all along. Then I would write a book about it.

Since we were out of disease prospects, I convinced myself that Storey had one of the PND diseases. And… I feared she didn't. (See addendum for the list)

These are genetic diseases, meaning something happened because of a variation and/or mutation in a gene or genes. The discovery of the rare PND is relatively new, within the last twenty to thirty years. However, because of the super rarity, hundreds to thousands of sick and disabled people are suffering from misdiagnoses. A couple of these diseases have hope for some improvements. Some gain a lot of improvement with the right combination of medications, like the Colegrove kids. But because of the grand variables within our DNA, many people are back at the shoe store, crying in the corner.

Researching these diseases, I found other families like us: desperate, alone, going to extremes, and praying for miracles. Before Facebook, everyone supported each other through email. I finally had the support group I desperately needed. Locally I had support through Eagle Mount, and I felt less lonely knowing I wasn't the only mother with a special needs child, although it often felt that way.

On the PND website, I educated myself and learned how I could get Storey tested. My heart raced with excitement when I took Storey to see Dr. Feist, pleading with him to order the tests. He said he had heard a little about these diseases and was happy to research and order the tests. I pushed the long bar attached to the back of Storey's tricycle out of his office with the kind of excitement I thought I'd never feel again.

Every night after dinner, I emailed my new "roller-coaster-mother-friends." I belonged. I didn't feel the need to scream bloody murder on our porch. My friends and I talked about our beautiful children, about seizure treatments, sleeping issues, dopamine, neurotransmitter therapies, poop, and ideas to make our lives with a disabled child easier. I learned more from these mothers than I had from all the doctors.

I held on tight to the lifeline of PND while I waited for Dr. Feist's phone call to notify me that the test kit had arrived. Storey smiled entering Dr. Feist's office because she liked to show off her bike. Little did she know a spinal tap was on the other side of his door.

"Is Dr. Feist good at spinal taps? How much is it going to hurt? Will Storey get a spinal tap headache?" I asked his nurse, unapologetically.

"If I ever needed a spinal tap, I would insist Dr. Feist perform it," his nurse said.

Spinal taps are no cake walk. Because the test wouldn't require sedation, other than a lidocaine shot, we were willing to go ahead.

John lifted Storey out of her tricycle and she gave us a scared look.

"Storey, Mommy and Daddy are going to be right here with you. Dr. Feist will feel your back, and you will feel a little pinch. I'm right here. This won't take long," I told her.

The nurse gave Storey a wrapped sucker to hold. They joked with us as the nurse held Storey on the table like a monster-size potato bug. Then she bear-hugged Storey so she couldn't move. It wasn't Storey's nature to protest, but I knew she might faint.

I held Storey's feet and sang, "Hush little baby, don't say a word, Mommy's going to bring you a hummingbird."

The ten minutes felt like an hour.

"Alright, that's done. I'll send this to Baylor University by FedEx today. I sure hope this gives us some answers. It will be two to four weeks to get the results back. We are all anxious, hang tight," Dr. Feist said. He shook John's hand and gave me a hug before I pushed Storey down the hall.

On the way home it occurred to me I might be ruining our favorite song, by singing it during every stressful situation.

Chapter 38

At dusk, I'm alone riding my bike down a dirt road. I notice a flash of blue out of the corner of my left eye. Semi-familiar ghost images approach and circle me. I stop. It feels like I know them, but their faces are a blur. The blue flash morphs into a large bird like a parrot with big eyes. I freeze because it feels like spiders are crawling up my spine. The ghosts move closer; a figure stands near my left side. I know it and I don't know it. I lift my left arm 90 degrees and the blue bird gently perches on my arm. Before my eyes, the bird changes like I'm looking through a kaleidoscope pointing at the sun.

From somewhere distant, I hear, "This is a sign that Storey is going to be okay. She's the indigo bird. An indigo child."

The bird climbs in my lap the way Storey does. A ghost to my left hands me a box with a small opening and instructs me to put the bird in the box. The bird looks at me with big, sad, godly eyes. I tell the bird it will be safe, and it climbs in. I hold the box next to my heart.

Every day I walked around feeling like I was dreaming, hovering over myself, waiting to either fall to my death or be saved by large loving hands. As kids we all heard the phrase, *If you're falling in a dream and don't wake up, you'll die.* I always woke up.

I wondered if my present dreams came from where I imagined Storey felt. Like most mothers with special needs children, their bonds are intense, a blessing and a curse. I knew Storey's sensitivity was sharper than most children, and that added to my stress. I worried that she absorbed my worry.

Storey was exhausted and not herself for almost five days after the lumbar puncture. She whined, she shook, and she had more "drops." I wondered if she had a headache the whole time. I felt guilty for putting her through another spinal tap, but John and I did all we could to make her feel comfortable while playing the waiting game for results we had grown to loathe. John and I didn't talk about the tests, but neither of us could forget Harrison's plea. Even though I had great friends when this journey began, I felt like an alien in my familiar group, and kept the mothers of the PND group at my heart's reach. *If those mothers can cope, so can I.*

All my life I'd envied people who were comfortable with "the five-second rule." Mothers who could hand their child a piece of cheese while they sat in a dirty grocery cart or didn't give eating County Fair food after rides more than a second thought. I justified that my worry was a special ingredient for protection. However, like most things in my mind, it became a double-edged weapon. Too much worry sent out stress energy and exhausted Storey; it sucked her chi and her "drops" increased. When I was able to leave my worries at the door, she was happier and more present. In the long run, I decided that leaving worries on the doormat was a unique skill reserved for spe-cial people like Buddhist monks—and they didn't have kids.

I did my best to appreciate life's gifts and worked hard to raise my worry grade from a D to a B, consciously breathing moment by moment to pass by dark corners. I told myself that everything was as it should be. Likely I inherited a larger amygdala, the stress gland in our brain, from my mother's side. I admired people who had so much faith they could surrender to God's will. But as far as I was con-cerned, *their* kind of God had been fucking up for thousands of years.

We tried to make the most of the rest of the short summer. Hayden went to camps and Storey went to school for three half-days with Melissa at her side. We watched sky gifts of translucent primary col-ors arch over Dagwood grazing in the back pasture when the sun peeked between raindrops. Storey sat in my lap, my arms folded around her like she was a porcelain angel, and we watched our tiny, buzzing friends who dove through the golden light for one last drink before returning to their walnut-sized nests. Each night I questioned how we deserved the gifts before us when there was so much suffer-ing in the world. I always felt guilty leaving before the sun had set, like we'd be disqualified from seeing the next watercolor.

During those perfect summer evenings, I listened for a message from the heavens. What I heard over and again was that because of Storey's disease she was here to ripple love across the lands. If she didn't have special needs, didn't look different, no one would truly notice her, or notice her love. Early on I knew she wasn't of this world; she was from a much higher place where few souls were invited. During the lightshows the heavens reminded me that whatever happens in the end, it was truly out of my control because love has no boundaries.

That summer life accelerated. Mystical evenings were shorter, and we still had a lot to do to keep Storey with us. I kept up with her therapies. Occasionally we checked in with Dr. Marc, the naturopath. Storey rode Dagwood most evenings and Eagle Mount horses once a week. She walked on the treadmill each night, swam on Fridays and on occasion visited Elaine for energy healing and grounding.

We entertained John's and my folks when they visited. We traded in my blue GMC blazer for a Toyota Sienna van, all-wheel drive with automatic sliding side doors—a well-deserved luxury. I became a "Van Mom" whether I liked it or not. A blessing really. I was tired of holding Storey on my left thigh while I put my foot on the rear tire, freeing my right hand to open the door. The van was a small thing that made life easier. Hayden and Storey liked being able to see out the windows, and the ride was smooth. Chisel sat between the seats to catch crumbs. *Why had I waited?*

At the end of August, Hayden followed most of his kindergarten classmates across town to a Montessori School for first-through-eighth graders.

On a late Friday afternoon in the middle of September, I noticed a missed call from Dr. Feist. My knees folded under me. I wanted to toss the answering machine across the room. This was the third time since Storey's beginning that there was an important missed call from a doctor on a Friday evening. A long, blurry, hair-pulling weekend followed. John and I tried not to think about the test results when we took the kids to the Gallatin River to toss rocks.

After playing the game of landline phone tag with Dr. Feist on Monday, we finally talked on Tuesday. "Hello, Sandee, I know you're anxious to hear about Storey's results. I spoke to Dr. Hyland from Baylor."

"Knowing that you were able to talk to Dr. Hyland was worth the wait," I said.

"It appears she is low on one of the tests. Dr. Hyland said homovanillic acid was below our reference range. He said there is a possibility of a defect in dopamine metabolism in Storey. He thinks she *might* have Tyrosine Hydroxylase Deficiency (TH), but this is a newly discovered disease with many variables. Let me do some digging and call Dr. Grabe with help on the medication. This might be great news, but I don't want to make any promises. Time will tell. It will take some time to get the medication for dopamine adjusted," Dr. Feist said.

I released my breath. "Thank you, I read a little about TH. We are anxious to get this started." I said, feeling a ball of relief roll down my back.

"Mom, why are you shaking on the floor? Is something else wrong with Storey?" Hayden asked.

"I just talked to the doctor. He told me they might know what is wrong with Storey and there might be a treatment. I'm just so relieved and happy."

I looked over at Storey. She looked scared. I wiped my eyes.

"It's okay Storey, I'm happy."

She smiled and I picked Hayden up and swung him around the kitchen. "You guys, I'm so excited!"

I called John immediately. I could hardly talk.

"Wow, I just can't believe it, that is great. Hopefully this is it," he said, releasing a long-held breath. "And this all happened because we saw that program on TV and Dr. Feist ran the test?"

I felt the wheels of the rollercoaster slowly ascend. This time I wanted hope to take its sweet time. I wanted to savor the ride to the end, but I saw a caution sign deep in my gut that I couldn't shake.

Googling Tyrosine Hydroxylase deficiency didn't produce many hits. I reached out to my new PND friends and found a couple kids who tested low for homovanillic acid with a possible TH diagnosis. It was still a guessing game, as diseases can show low levels of many things in a blood test even though it's not the primary cause of the disease.

Dr. Feist and Dr. Grabe collaborated and found a workable combination of L-dopa and Carbidopa. Ten days after we talked to Dr. Feist, I carried Storey into a local compounding pharmacy that I hadn't known existed and set her in a chair.

"Hayden, hold Storey so she doesn't fall over," I said.

I felt like my body was in slow motion talking to the young pharmacist. Then it happened: I let out months of tears, almost hyperventilating, and I told the pharmacist all about Storey and why she was taking this medicine. Whether she wanted to hear it or not.

"Storey, you are so beautiful," the pharmacist said, looking at her.

"This bag might contain the answer to our dreams," I said, sandwiching the bag between Storey and my arms. The small white bag sat in my lap like it was a bottle of gold while I spoke to the gal in the Dairy Queen drive-thru.

That night after dinner, John videotaped me squirting the magic liquid into Storey's mouth. I narrated the event before helping Storey walk on the treadmill.

That night I couldn't sleep. *Who knows, maybe our local newspaper will write an article about Storey's miracle, and her beautiful face will decorate the front page.*

We knew it wasn't an instant cure. We knew this medicine could take weeks, maybe months before we saw anything... if it helped at all. John and I had just tossed all our last eggs of hope into this basket. We couldn't help it.

Mother Nature invited us to her October gallery of oranges, dark pinks, and warm winds; a sweet stillness we cherished. After school we played outside, and the kids hung on the swings and spun in circles. Storey exercised her core muscles going down the slide while I held her waist. We looked for the slightest sign that the medicine was working.

My mother arrived with a full head of her own hair after years of cancer treatments. She and the kids carved pumpkins next to the sandbox in the stillness of an Indian summer. A few days later we went trick-or-treating in town. The kids were happy. We were happy. We cautiously waited for a change in Storey.

Then news hit: flu season came early, and young kids were dying at unusually high rates. I couldn't help myself—I read a newspaper article about a little boy in Colorado who wasn't feeling well one night. His parents suspected he had the flu. They put him to bed and when they checked him later, he was dead.

I panicked. I obsessed. Mentally I had been doing so well. Ever since I had worked at Kinko's Copies sharing air with coughing college students, I got a flu shot every fall. But in 2003 and before, flu shots for kids were not promoted like they are today. Because of Storey's health complications, vaccines worried me. I also knew that if she got the flu, the outcome could be grave. So, I lived in fear. And I waited. We washed our hands and used hand sanitizer until our knuckles bled. Fortunately, the 2003 flu season came in with a bang and left early. We got lucky.

Over the next month, I interviewed many of the PND mothers and learned their kids were under the care of Dr. Kathryn Swoboda, a pediatric neurologist and neurogeneticist from Primary Children's Hospital at the University of Utah. I knew we needed Dr. Swoboda to see Storey. She would be the ninth neurologist looking at Storey's chart. The idea of visiting another hospital felt auspicious. Once I put aside my discomfort around more doctors and traveling, going to Salt Lake City felt easier, a comfort, the familiarity of my home turf. I called Dr. Swoboda's office and got the first new patient appointment in the new year.

Storey gladly opened her mouth and smiled three times a day to receive the white magic of L-dopa/Carbidopa (Sinemet) that I squirted on her tongue. We continued with her exercises every day. The kids and I "did candle," then I whispered our special meditation to Storey before I tucked her into bed: "The healing yellow light comes down from the heavens into your crown chakra and goes down through all your cells healing everything in its path…"

Most nights I laid awake staring through my window at the stars, visualizing the medicine working. *What would it feel like to know she's healing? What would it feel like to witness?*

But my gut painted something different.

Chapter 39

The low afternoon sun warms my face, and I close my eyes. Behind a door I see Storey in the distance. She is walking, smiling, skipping in her favorite polka-dot leggings under a spinning pink dress. I reach out, but she's far away. Giggles float to the clouds. It's visceral, three-dimensional. Storey is healed. This place seems easily accessible, divine. I want to stay forever.

Storey's giggles travel downstairs to my meditation mat.

I ask the universe if this place is real for us if I focus on it hard enough. I hold on like a beautiful near-death experience. Then I hear a whisper: "It's not time, go back, you can't stay."

My meditation came from love and reminded me that reality is temporary. For years I heard: *"It's all about intention."* The next day in meditation I scrambled to find the same door as yesterday. I waited. It wasn't anywhere.

A few weeks into Storey's L-Dopa/Carbidopa regime, John and I reminded ourselves to be patient. I imagined that her legs looked stronger, that she talked more, was less shaky, and that her eyes were less red. My impatience demanded additional guidance. *What the hell, I've taken Storey to so many doctors, I might as well consult another psychic intuitive.* After I finished reading the book *The Psychic's Pathway* by one of my favorite spiritual authors, Sonia Choquette, I Googled her name and signed up for a personal reading. Her price was comparable to that of a one-hour counseling session.

"Appreciate being a happy dyslexic, because without dyslexia you wouldn't have developed the foresight to properly care for Storey," Sonia said.

She echoed my mother's words: "*You've been preparing for this all your life.*" Sonia reminded me that I had come full circle. She was compassionate, sweet, and encouraged me to explore my creativity for mental health.

Her advice was alluring but thinking about adding one more thing to my list stressed me more than its benefits. I'd have to give up exercising and I wasn't going to do that; there weren't enough hours in the day. So, I settled on creative spelling.

Sonia also reminded me that Storey felt the tension between John and me. One doesn't have to imagine the stress in a marriage when there's a sick child. She mentioned to just let John be the one right all the time. John and I had both came from families where everyone was always right. It was up to me to be the one to back down.

I couldn't help but think if I just "let things go," in general, Storey might have gotten a lot worse. When I heard those words from Sonia, I saw the image of Dr. Doolittle's pushmi-pullyu. When I was younger my mother gave me a stuffed pushmi-pullyu. I loved it so much that I buried it in the backyard with our first bull mastiff.

Naturally Sonia didn't give me any information I didn't already know in my heart. Nevertheless, I wanted to hear what she saw in Storey's body; I wanted her to diagnose Storey with 100 percent accuracy. Still, I knew that when she circumvented my question, it said a lot.

In November we went back to Billings for our second metabolic clinic. It was nice to see familiar faces. We spent most of the time talking about pediatric neurotransmitter diseases. Dr. Turner educated us about this group of diseases, yet she delivered medical terms so fast that I strained to keep up. They were all skeptical that Storey had a PND, instead leaning toward a mitochondria or storage disease. The group of doctors talked about the benefits of adding Selegiline, a monoamine oxidase inhibitor—an enzyme to slow down the absorption of Sinemet (L-dopa/Carbidopa). Like Sinemet, Selegiline was consistently prescribed to people with Parkinson's disease. When people asked what Storey had, I often said that it was like infantile Parkinson's because that's actually what it looked like.

During the clinic, the subject of a muscle biopsy was mentioned. We declined again. They understood. At this point we weighed our desire to find a name for her disease (knowing it was probably a neurodegenerative disease without treatments) against Storey paying the physical price for invasive testing and anesthesia. Then the group encouraged us again to get Storey a wheelchair. Those words set spiders running up my spine and into my gut. We knew they were right, but the idea made me feel nauseous—like we had given up.

"I'm still fine lifting Storey in and out of her car seat. She weighs less than a large bag of sunflower seeds, and she looks less disabled in her stroller," I told them.

Some might call this denial. I called it a floss of hope.

The two-and-a-half-hour drive home felt incessant. By the time we drove up our driveway at five-thirty, darkness and depression made me feel like an elephant. I just wanted to get the kids to bed, hide under my covers and eat ice cream with chocolate sauce. Kristin dropped Hayden off at six o'clock. His enthusiasm temporarily took me out of my funk while he and Storey splashed around in the hot tub, diverting me from images of Storey in a wheelchair for the rest of her life.

It took some negotiating with Dagwood's owners, but they agreed to let him stay for the winter. I adopted a retired Eagle Mount horse, Tilly, to keep him company. The horses helped my mental health more than they helped Storey physically. I found myself outside talking to them like a therapist; I relaxed. The perfume of wet hay, alfalfa noses and mud soothed my soul.

Winter arrived that fall with twenty-five below zero temperatures for a few nights. The evergreens on the hill could have sheltered Dagwood and Tilly, but they chose to stand next to each other in the open wind. Their heads hung like the steer in Charles Russell's 1886 painting *Waiting for a Chinook*. The next day the sun melted icicles from their bodies. They grazed like the rough night had never happened.

The short evenings fueled my sadness, and the rollercoaster jerked me dizzy: *Storey looked better, no she didn't. She's so tired on this new medicine, maybe it's the shorter days. Maybe more time. Maybe tomor-row will be better. What have I done? What haven't I done?* Then one evening I learned that our local TV channel had stopped airing *Sein-feld*. I Googled anti-depressants and stopped journaling.

Weeks later Kristin called and said she found me the perfect horse with soft eyes and a good price tag. I crawled out of my slump. On Christmas Eve Kristin dropped off Angel. She, Dagwood and Tilly ran around like old pasture buddies. A few days later Molly adopted Tilly, and everyone was happy.

Angel's sweet nature lifted my spirits even more. She loved Storey and Storey loved her.

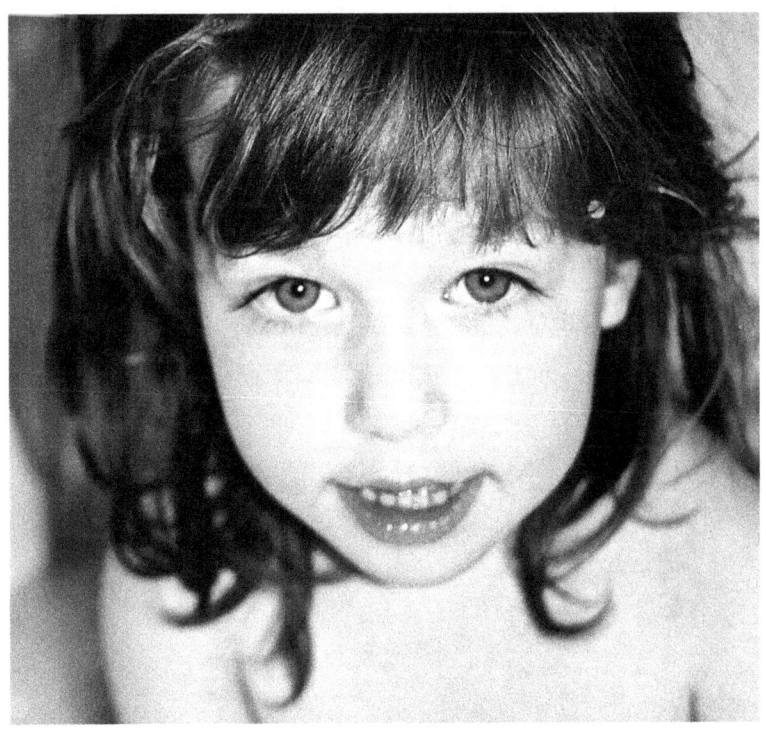

4½ years old.

Chapter 40

Dear *Storey,*

You're so fortunate to have inherited Grandma Joan's lustrous dark hair. Your father was the only other person in the family with her hair. At 90 years old her hair was still dark. She never knew what to do with the kind of hair many envied. You also have your father's dominant lower lip, and his translucent blue eyes. You have my smile, and unfortunately my cowlicks in the center of your hairline. Combing your hair was mesmerizing. To brush and trim your hair I secured you in your stander. Your curly hair would bounce up unevenly because I always forgot to calculate your cowlicks when trimming your bangs. I always wondered if you'd let me comb your hair when you're a teenager.

I love you forever,

Mom

Dear *Mom*,

Sometimes it hurt a little when you brushed my hair. But it was okay. Thanks for taking the time to make me beautiful.

Love,

Storey

B efore having kids, John and I annually trekked through my home turf, behind the Zion Curtain, on our way to Escalante. The first week of January 2004, we drove our new Toyota van south. Lagoon Amusement Park, where I had a couple birthdays growing up, passed on our left.

"Mom!!! How fast does that rollercoaster go? Do people fall off? Mom! Why isn't it moving? I want to ride it, Mom!" Hayden shouted from the back seat.

"Hayden, you can ride rollercoasters when you're over eighteen. I don't ride rollercoasters."

"Dad, do you like rollercoasters? Dad? Dad!!"

"What? I can't talk right now, it's rush hour. I need to focus," John said.

John found Hotel Monaco in downtown Salt Lake City, guided by the city's simple addressed grid system. If I had been driving, we would have ended up in Provo. The hotel lobby's interior motif was consistent with Denver's, but this hotel lacked the complimentary goldfish, much to our sadness. Regardless, I felt like a kid at an amusement park with exaggerated memories of my first experience of a Hotel Monaco. I was a little disappointed, until an oversized white-and-brown bulldog who sounded like it had a sinus infection bolted into the hotel lobby, pulling a stocky, middle-aged lady. Immediately

I asked if I could pet her dog. The lady took that as an invitation to share the dog's life story. Hayden jumped up and down and John gave me that rolling eye look—*Come on, it's just a gross, slobbery dog who can hardly walk.*

We arrived at Storey's appointment the next day with time to spare. I studied the busy waiting room and pointed at seats away from the path of least resistance for John and Hayden.

"May I have your insurance card, and please fill out this stack of papers," the receptionist said.

I took the clipboard and turned around. John and Hayden were in the seats closest to the receptionist—likely the most frequented seats. I rolled my eyes. It was flu season after all.

Dread moved through my nerves on the way to the exam room. Curiosity took over and I glanced through every open door. I saw children crying in their parents' laps, kids having EEGs in dark rooms, scared kids waiting on tables. The walk felt like a mile. I was glad John carried Storey because I worried that if Storey was too close to my body, she'd absorb my nervousness, the way a dog or horse does. When the nurse took Storey's vitals, she almost fainted. Dr. Swoboda arrived fifteen minutes later. Impressive in such a busy clinic.

"Hello, Storey. Look at those beautiful eyelashes," Dr. Swoboda said, shaking our hands. "I've looked at Storey's chart very carefully, and I'm still a little skeptical she has a PND since she's been on the medicine for over three months now without much change. There are other things to do, but let's go over everything."

Dr. Swoboda thoroughly reviewed Storey's chart without rushing. She spoke quickly and clearly and in medical terms I had come to almost understand. We were in brilliant hands. She was a mother who felt the pain of the families and a doctor who obviously read her patients' charts before each appointment. She cared. I decided right then and there she was going to be our last neurologist. When I asked about the Colegrove kids, she explained their miracle cure was an extremely rare variant within that category of diseases. Then she continued to go over all the other PNDs. John distracted the kids and I hyper-focused, scribbling readable notes.

After the initial review, Dr. Swoboda mentioned a skin biopsy and muscle biopsy and the possibility of another nerve conduction test. My heart sank. I voiced my feelings around anesthesia and biopsies and the promises I had made Storey. She explained how easy it was to get a skin biopsy—lidocaine under the armpit, a small skin punch smaller than a pencil eraser in a sweat gland. I felt foolish. For years I visualized a carrot peeler-type instrument was used to shave a layer of skin for a skin biopsy. I realized the doctors probably didn't explain the simple technique because of my cantankerous attitude toward invasive procedures. True, a muscle biopsy was more invasive, yet probably not as horrible as I had illustrated in my head. Finally, we consented to a skin biopsy knowing there was a slight chance for a storage disease diagnosis. And just like that, Dr. Swoboda whispered behind the exam room door and two nurses appeared. They worked their magic in getting a skin sample and some blood before Storey had time to throw up.

We said goodbye and knew that, in time, we might or might not know something.

Not wanting to go straight back to the hotel, I talked John into driving by my childhood home in Holiday. On our way, freeways that were two lanes had expanded to four. In my old neighborhood I stepped into a world of déjà vu. Memories of my neighborhood friends playing together most evenings appeared when we drove up our street. Once a brick castle, our old house looked small. The front yard had been the length of ten cartwheels, now just two. Across from our house was a massive boulder, Indian Rock, which we hiked to searching for petroglyphs. I-215 blocked by a concrete wall hid the entrance to our Indian Rock playground.

I recalled crazy things I'd done with a questionable crowd before moving away in junior high. I saw myself smoking cigarettes with Katie in her chicken coop, and riding in a large beat-up Cadillac on the freeway at midnight driven by my 14-year-old friend who laughed as I white-knuckled the armrest, scared shitless and wanting the nightmare of my last sleepover to end. I remembered going to keggers up Little Cottonwood Canyon and watching rebellious Mormon kids high on drugs, wondering if I was going to survive the ride home.

Running down memory lane distracted me from the tough truth. We weren't—I wasn't—going to find the kind of miracle the Colegrove kids had found.

Storey wasn't getting better.

Storey was getting worse.

This time around I didn't mind playing the test results waiting game. We knew at that point that if the skin biopsy gave us a name for Storey's disease, it came with a tragic future.

I'd always been honest with the doctors about the supplements and vitamins I was giving Storey, handing them a detailed list and hoping they would understand my logic or find any contraindications. For instance, Dr. Swoboda mentioned that carnitine might lower the effectiveness of her seizure medicine. I cut it out. Under the doctor's prescription, again we slowly increased the Sinemet to a more therapeutic level and waited for the skin biopsy results.

In the evenings I found false hope when Storey perked up after a meal with protein. Frequently she seemed a little hypoglycemic right after a nap. Every afternoon I slid my arms under her sleepy body and carefully placed her in her car seat to drive across town to pick Hayden up from school. It always took her a long time to wake up. If she was going to have any kind of "drop" seizure, it was during that waking up period.

One afternoon I turned to Costco after picking up Hayden. I looked into my review mirror and found Storey's body acting weird. She kind of torqued her body and squealed, frowning. Clearly, she was having a seizure, but it was a different type of seizure—she seemed almost completely conscious, like she was fighting for her soul. I had only seen this once before, in the car in Sacramento after the psychic reading, when it seemed like she couldn't breathe. I turned the car right, almost getting into an accident before parking. I reached my hand back to touch her leg.

"Storey, you're going to be alright. Hang in there. Mommy is here."

"I don't want Storey to die today," Hayden said, looking at me and then at Storey, crying.

I felt like I was going to throw up. My heart broke for Hayden. For Storey. For myself. Hayden was always such a beamy kid, taking everything in stride, doing his own thing when Storey needed so much attention. I crawled into the back of the van and hugged Storey, then Hayden. The episode was over. She seemed a little out of it, then smiled.

I took a deep breath.

"Hayden, Storey is okay. She just had a weird seizure. She is not going to die today. Let's skip Costco and head straight to Dairy Queen. That will make us all feel better."

In two weeks instead of the six I expected to wait, Dr. Swoboda called with the results of Storey's skin biopsy. The test didn't show any storage diseases. Per usual, the skin and blood tests showed nothing. John and I felt relief and dread—again.

The doctor scheduled us to come back for a follow-up appointment in the spring after Storey had been on the increased medicine. We liked and trusted Dr. Swoboda and we knew she was our last brilliant pediatric neurologist thinking about Storey outside Montana.

Chapter 41

Storey was 5½, old enough to ski with Eagle Mount. It was winter season 2003-2004. She skied in a sit-ski: a molded bucket seat with shock absorbers attached to a metal frame above two wide skis that were entirely controlled by a person tethering from behind. John, an advanced and strong skier, volunteered with Eagle Mount and learned to tether Storey in the sit-ski. They skied every Saturday morning for five weeks. Hayden and I happily tagged behind. We were skiing as a family, something I didn't think we would ever experience. Storey watched us ski around her and giggled.

"Storey, isn't this fun? Do you like skiing? You're doing a good job," Hayden said.

Occasionally John's folks picked Storey up and took her home for a nap while John, Hayden and I skied together the rest of the afternoon. It felt a little normal those hours on skis.

The Sinemet helped Storey tremor less, and "drop" less. But it made her more tired and sometimes she threw up after a dose. Many of my friends at the PND support group shared similar stories about their children who took this medicine, which was a miracle drug to some and complicated for others. Although Storey looked better, like on Topamax, her cognition declined. Her voice decreased to a whisper.

An Eagle Mount volunteer, Storey in a sit-ski and John (Dad).
It was crazy-hat-day.

Storey still loved preschool and seeing Melissa three mornings a week. Storey tried so hard on lessons; she wanted to please. The sicker she got, the more love she shared with family, her classmates, and strangers.

"Mom, I love you, I love you, I love you," she often said to me over and over.

In grocery stores Storey looked into strangers' eyes, like she knew their story, their struggles, and whispered "I love you, I love you," repeating it until they heard her or I wheeled her away. The strangers didn't know whether to smile or cry. Neither did I. One day at her physical therapy appointment she looked at an assistant and repeated, "I love you." The therapist was struggling. Her son had begun having seizures. Of course, Storey didn't know this. Or did she, somehow? The more physical strength Storey lost, the bigger her heart grew.

When I witnessed and felt the aura of Storey's love expand, I recalled what some of the spiritual teachers told me. "She knows things before they're going to happen. She experiences the suffering of others. She is put on this earth to share love. She is a master-in-training; she is a Bodhisattva," they had said.

The opposite was also true. She felt scared around certain people, and a few times began crying without a visual cause. And although it would be a lot easier to have a healthy, boring child without special needs, I felt honored to have Storey under my wing.

At the end of February, I flew to Seattle for a Salon conference with the (then) famous psychic, Sylvia Browne. I felt like I already knew her. I'd read many of her books and had watched some of her videos. I liked her mantra: "Take what you need and leave the rest behind." I decided the Salon in Seattle was a great opportunity to ask someone famous what they saw wrong in Storey's body, even though she wasn't what was called a "medical intuitive." It was a small group of thirty people, mostly women, who had the opportunity to ask Sylvia questions in an intimate setting. When I saw her in person at a Hay House Publishers event the summer before, she'd seemed down to earth (except for her very long fingernails). A large woman with a round grandmother lap.

As I walked in the Seattle rain, I remembered flying there with Storey to visit the psychic surgeon a few years earlier. My desire to go to extremes to help Storey was still unwavering. There I was again, seeking any way, shape, or craziness. Even the pink cherry blossoms in Seattle reminded me to keep going, learning, searching. I loved my daughter so much that everything reminded me of her and of our fight.

I waited for the hotel shuttle and looked around for other women who had the same desperate look in their eyes as I did. It didn't take long before I spotted a beautiful gal with long blonde hair. I asked if she was attending the conference. A few minutes later she and I were like long-lost friends. We stuck together all weekend. We felt safe sharing our stories. During the conference we all sat and listened to Sylvia talk about the "other side" and the history of spirituality. It was all fascinating, but each person had showed up to ask her one desperate question.

My new friend sat next to me; we glanced at each other and rolled our eyes a few times during Sylvia's talk. Some questions were answered, others evaded. All I knew was that I didn't really care about the history of spirituality or anyone else's question. I came for one reason only.

Then came my turn to ask my million-dollar question: "What is wrong with my daughter and how am I going to save her?" My body shook and my voice cracked. I tried to hold my flood of tears. I'd come so far, so desperate, like a drug addict searching for one last high. Between semi-hyperventilating sobs I managed to tell Sylvia a little about Storey.

"Honey, your daughter should not be eating any dairy," she said.

"I don't give her dairy, except maybe one spoon of Dairy Queen ice cream."

"You're more intuitive than you give yourself credit for. You're right—another nerve conduction test would send her out of her body and leave lasting negative effects. I see her walking again, but I can't tell you when or how," Sylvia said.

"Really? No one can tell me what's wrong. What do you see?" I asked.

"She's here to teach us compassion," she said. And then she finished. "Best of luck. She's a beautiful spirit."

Basically, that was that. I had no words. Immediately Sylvia called on someone else, like she didn't want to tell me the whole truth, or like she was just making stuff up. *No dairy? I came all this way for that.* It took me the rest of the afternoon to recover. Not only from my disappointment in Sylvia, or my stupidity, but from my gut-wrenching, never-ending fear that the worse thing in the world was happening before my eyes.

I didn't really know what I expected to hear from her. Maybe Sylvia was only as psychic as her followers wanted to her to be. Maybe she sensed in me that I just wanted someone to tell me that Storey would walk again. Regardless of Sylvia's questionable reputation, during those few hours I still felt a little comfort. She was kind, empathetic, and didn't judge. The weekend was unforgettable. I made a new friend and I "took what I needed and left the rest."

The Seattle pink cherry blossoms told me that spring winds might end, with new beginnings just over the hill. A week later, I looked in the guinea pig cage and found four little balls of fur bouncing like popcorn.

Chapter 42

Spring 2004 meant that Dagwood had to go back to his owners after leasing him all winter. When his owners arrived in their old horse trailer, I was having friends over and didn't think twice about handing over his red lead rope because Angel and Tilly were in our pasture. I made the mistake of turning around to see Dagwood's red tail waving goodbye in the low golden light.

Dagwood had been my first horse-love. The day after he arrived, I rode him down our road with ignorance and confidence tucked under his saddle. He quickly learned his job with Storey, respecting her needs and overlooking our inexperience. His name was the first of many written on the weathered boards in the shed. He was one good horse. Why did I look back?

Few things are more miraculous than watching a new foal trying to stand next to its mom in a wet pasture. In the spring, every morning I looked out our bathroom window for Angel and Spirit (Tilly went to Molly's house). How lucky I was to see that heartwarming sight whenever I wanted and needed to be reminded that dreamy wonders were possible. Spirit's lightning bolt whipped back and forth on the hillside like she was playing with ghost friends. Angel grazed from a distance like a mother who lets her children out to play until dinner is called.

Five days after Spirit was born, I noticed Angel walking oddly across the pasture. I just figured she was still sore from giving birth. The next day I noticed her entire right hind leg was swollen. Many phone calls later, Kristin's vet arrived. He said Angel had an infection in her leg caused from the shots she received right after Spirit was born. At that time, I remembered thinking how odd it was that the vet techs injected Angel's vaccinations in her rear end rather than her neck. The shots caused an abscess that ran down to her fetlock. Twice a day for ten days I chased Angel around the pasture with a giant syringe full of antibiotics. Angel was unusually calm and very little startled her, yet after a few days she ran away when I opened the door. I managed to inject her neck with the entire antibiotic prescription. Her leg looked better for about two days. On the third day, her leg swelled to twice its size and the abscess oozed puss. Spirit got her first trailer ride to the vet at three weeks old. Two times a day for ten days the vet washed Angel's abscess from the inside out with Betadine. Angel could have died if it weren't for the skilled vet (a different vet than who gave the shots). Home again, Spirit entertained us by running back and forth across the pasture with speed and jubilation, just like in the movie *Spirit: Stallion of the Cimarron*.

Then the spring rains came.

Still, no horse shelter. I listened to the rain all night, worrying about little Spirit shivering and hoping Angel would lead her into the trees for protection. On the second night I couldn't stand it. After dinner I cleaned the garage, put in a bucket of water and a bale of hay and brought them in for the night. My horses were warm and happy, and I got some sleep. But hay against smooth concrete is like marbles under their feet. Spirit quickly learned why she had legs. Hayden and Storey laughed every time we opened the door to the garage when Angel and Spirit stuck their heads into the house. I can't believe I never got a photo of that, but we always thought there would be another time.

Chapter 43

"M mmmmooommm! The hummingbirds are back. Mom! Did you hear it?!" Hayden announced.

At the beginning of May we headed to Billings for our third metabolic clinic. Dr. Turner reviewed old and new tests. She clarified diseases recently discovered and answered questions about PN Diseases. The clinicians recommended retesting Storey for many of the diseases. We felt like the clinicians were grasping, and they were. So were we, that's why we returned. Storey had been tested up to three times for many of the same diseases. The results were consistent throughout. One of the clinicians mentioned getting a *nerve* biopsy. I was frustrated. I thought they knew us well enough by then. *Did they really think I'd change my mind?*

In the spring of 2004, at almost 6 years old, Storey weighed 38 pounds—average for growth in the tenth percentile. She had poor circulation, her fingers were shiny from inflammation, and her legs were swollen most of the day even though she continued with physical therapy and home exercises.

Since the beginning, when the doctors tapped her leg with a rubber hammer, none of them were able to find reflexes. The doctors weren't worried. None could tell us if that was a symptom or not. "No reflexes" were always in her chart and that was that. Her "drops" improved to once a week on average, instead of one or two an hour. Her face and stomach were a little puffy. Her tremors had improved since taking L-dopa/Carbidopa. She sat well on the floor with her back supported and her legs straddled to balance. Sadly, her cognition had plateaued. Once talkative, using complete five-to-seven-word sentences at eighteen months old, now she whispered short, incomplete sentences. She had forgotten all her colors except for pink. But she was happier, less scared, and more outgoing since the beginning. She shared her smile. She lived in the moment, in peace. She didn't seem to be in pain. Adults, strangers, kids, and animals were attracted to her.

She and Hayden played well together; he helped her with toys and her ball machine. He brought me pull-ups and wipes. He played Fleetwood Mac's "Rumors" for us.

A few days after the metabolic clinic, we headed back to Salt Lake City for our spring follow-up with Dr. Swoboda. It was exhausting having the two appointments so close together. It felt like my old coat pockets had holes and at the medical and alternative appointments the possibilities and ideas just slid through those holes.

Dr. Swoboda noticed improvement in Storey's tremor and suggested we increase her Sinemet, bartering for additional improvement. She still suspected a storage disease versus the possible TH diagnoses because Storey had improved a little, but not a lot. Dr. Swoboda reminded us that neurotransmitter testing may show low neurotransmitter numbers like that for Tyrosine Hydroxylase (TH) in other complicated neurological diseases. She said that frequently there's more than one neurological problem with most neurological diseases.

Dr. Swoboda suggested the next level of extensive testing, which included sedation. She recommended a dilated ophthalmologic test, a funduscopic exam, electroretinogram, and again, the dreaded nerve conduction. I reminded Dr. Swoboda the promise I had made Storey when she hinted at another nerve conduction test to rule out neuropathy and neuroaxonal dystrophy (INAD—a neurodegenerative disease involving degeneration of the nerves and cognition resulting in death before age ten).

I had learned to listen *and* to trust my "mother's intuition" with confidence, degenerative disease or not. My gut told me the test procedures would shorten her life.

At the doctor's visit we *expected* to have our hearts broken, but it was never something we got used to. John and I had learned to be realistic and to accept that Storey didn't have a curable disease like the Colegrove kids did.

We still admired Dr. Swoboda, but we left there with no more information than when we had arrived. To lift our spirits, we went to Trolley Square and Utah's Hogle Zoo, where I had had birthday parties as a child and silky deer tongues licked popcorn out of my fingers. I wondered if my mom had wiped my fingers before cake.

Drained and tired of searching the fog of guesswork, blood work, and mystical work, by the time we pulled into our driveway I decided we had had enough doctor appointments and alternative promises.

I needed a break.

I needed to live.

We needed to live.

Chapter 44

During summer solstice, light beamed around four-thirty in the morning and set at ten-thirty at night. Our kids laughed under the gracious light. For just a few moments each night, light cast shadows in the fields of aspen clusters, then reflected in the irises of Angel and Spirit. The show's ending presented a portal of gold and pink that I dreamed of passing through many times. It felt like I was under a spell where possibilities and sadness battled on the horizon.

Those nights Hayden, Storey and I sat on the porch and wept with gratitude. I dreamed they were learning how to save this lightness to use on a dark day. I couldn't put them to bed until the heavens loosened their grip.

That summer the heat rose to triple digits for weeks and zapped Storey's energy. Many afternoons we stayed in her room with the only air conditioner and longed for her physical energy to return when the temperature dropped. For me the heat was bittersweet. I wanted summer to last. I wanted Hayden and Storey to see their grandparents longer, to toss more rocks in Yellowstone Lake at Pumice Point. I wanted to see more popsicle-juice smiles. Eventually time brought cooler days and the smoke from forest fires cleared. Storey looked better, and we shopped for snow boots. It was the last summer Storey and Melissa worked together.

When we built our house in 1993, we had mixed feelings about LaMotte School down the street. We liked the rural school idea, but its coffers were low. Teacher wages bought little more than beans and rice. A rusted barbed wire fence framed a playground of three swings and a steel slide that faced the afternoon sun. We hoped that by the time we had kids LaMotte School would be a better version of itself. The image of walking to school, led by Chisel, was a rural dream. When it was time for Hayden to start first grade, we decided to let him continue with the Montessori method at a school across town, where 6-year-olds write reports about cnidarians.

LaMotte's principal invited Storey and me to the interviews for Storey's new personal aide, or paraprofessional. Immediately we fell in love with Serena's giant heart and gentle nature. I was disappointed to find out that half-day kindergarten was in the afternoon instead of morning—the least productive time for a 5-year-old to learn. I had to rework Storey's naps and medicine schedule to make the best of it.

After Labor Day, Hayden and Storey started at their new schools. John dropped Hayden off on his way to work (his basement office had moved thirty minutes across the valley). In the morning Storey and I did her exercises. At the school's first assembly, the principal compassionately introduced Storey, I leaned against the door frame as tears dripped down my cheek watching sixty-two classmates, from kindergarten to eighth grade, turn their heads in Storey and Scotty's direction. After the meeting, the kids huddled around Storey like she was a princess.

As though no previous student with special needs had ever attended LaMotte, a converted storage closet became the special education room. Between stacks of colored paper and dusty boxes, Storey, Scotty, a boy with Down syndrome, and a few of the other kids received tutoring and therapy in that closet. It wasn't ideal. But luckier, I figured, than being stuck all day in a large, noisy special education classroom with underpaid aides just trying to get through the day.

Storey's day was split between the closet and her kindergarten classroom. Unknowingly, Storey and Scotty taught their schoolmates how to love and accept differences. Every morning Storey smiled and squealed in delight when I pushed her baby jogger through the door of LaMotte School.

Hey *Mom*,

I loved school. My hands hurt, but I still liked to cut construction paper and make pictures for you. And I loved story time. Probably because when the teacher said they were going to have story time I thought they were talking about me.

All the kids were nice. I knew that many of my friends had emotional struggles and I sent them love.

I love you to the moon and back, and back, and back,

Storey

Storey,

I'm sure all your classmates felt your loving energy.

I love you to where the hummingbirds go and then back to us,

Mom

Chapter 45

A week after school started, a friend of mine invited me to a lecture by Judith Bluestone, the founder of the Handle Institute in Seattle (Holistic Approach to Neuro Development and Learning Efficiency-HANDLE®). The institute provided an effective, non-drug alternative for identifying and treating an array of neurodevelopmental disorders, specializing in Autistic Spectrum Disorders (ASD). HANDLE has helped thousands to overcome many disorders and to live peaceful, productive lives.

Judith had big eyes, a bright smile and spoke softly to a standing room of optimistic viewers. She unwound the fabric of her own story growing up with autism, seizures, chronic pain, paralysis, hypersensitivities, illnesses, digestive issues, and an inability to talk or hear early in life. She grew up in a time when kids like her were sadly sent to institutions.

"I mapped my neurological irregularities from fetal insults and early neurotoxic exposure of environmental pesticides my father brought home on his shoes and clothes from working as chemist," she said.

Clearly, she was gifted on both ends of the (now wider) autistic spectrum like the well-known Temple Grandin, with extreme neurological challenges and a higher-than-average I.Q. The audience dropped their jaws listening to her stories and how she overcame challenges in a time of little tolerance of kids on the spectrum. For example, she "walked" using a pogo stick as her mode of transportation for two years because the rapid movement and sudden stops shut down the overstimulation in her sensitive inner ear and vestibular nerve. Using her intuition and intelligence, Judith taught herself ways to organize and rewire her brain. Later she dove into neuroscience, neurorehabilitation, neurodevelopment, neuropsychology and counseling. She helped thousands with neurological challenges through HANDLE.

Judith spoke deliberately to an audience drinking every drop of information like we were listening to Gandhi. She wasn't there to brag about herself, she was there to offer hope—holding a bible to the spectrum as far as I was concerned. Her 2004 book *The Fabric of Autism: Weaving the Threads into a Cogent Theory* outlined and demonstrated gentle methods and effective therapies to help children like her. The stories she stitched together rolled around in our heads as we thought about our children and family members. Frozen by her words, I sat and wiped my cheeks. An opportunity, which I thought was nonexistent, stood before me. I couldn't look away. Although Storey wasn't diagnosed with autism, I knew Judith could climb into our world and understand.

The whole evening was serendipitous. I learned about Judith's talk hours before she spoke and almost didn't make it because John came home from work late. At the end of her talk a long line weaved through the room to purchase her autographed book. Sheepishly I stepped to the end of the line. I had time to rehearse my plea. I worried Judith would be exhausted and overstimulated from grasping hands. When it was my turn, Judith looked into my eyes and saw

Storey. Without words she reached out and gave me a grandma hug. I crumbled in her arms and my voice went mute. She paused and caressed my back and gave me time to gather myself.

"I have a daughter who's 6 years old and… her cerebellum is shrinking. No one can tell me why. Do you think you can help?"

"What is her name, Sweetheart?" Judith asked.

"Storey."

"I helped a boy with a dry cerebellum and uneven cerebrospinal fluid, and with a unique treatment plan we were able to help him function again," Judith continued. "Sandee, I'd be honored to see your daughter." Knowing Judith had a full client schedule during her visit, my friend Gwen offered Storey her son's appointment.

Judith's words made me feel like Storey had just been found after being kidnapped.

Two days later John and I walked Storey toward wizard-like doors at the house Judith was staying. Behind the doors danced two smiling blonde girls. One turned around and yelled, "Judith!" Danielle, the owner of the house who spearheaded Judith's involvement with the Bozeman community, had arranged the book signing because she was so impressed with the progress her daughter had made while working with Judith. Danielle gave us a hug when we entered her warm home.

We followed Judith through a maze of thoughtfully decorated halls to a room where she saw clients. My path to heal Storey, taking her to so many different people for help, caused Storey to grow wary. Storey immediately reached out and hugged Judith like she was her grandmother. Storey stared at Judith and repeated "Hi," giggling away.

John and I shared Storey's story with Judith, who listened attentively while evaluating Storey through play. At this point Storey looked like she had cerebral palsy; her entire body was in a constant state of physical stress and sitting upright was challenging. She had low muscle tone and muscle weakness, she tremored, she looked at people with a crooked head, and she spoke in soft, short sentences. Her feet were always cold and stiff, as if she were paralyzed from the knees down. But Storey could smile. She could look into your eyes and hold toys using her last three fingers against her palm. She could walk a little with help, stand in her stander, and push a ball across the floor. She could laugh. Most importantly, she felt love and could tell people she loved them.

Judith spoke tenderly to Storey, who was trying to stay upright. She picked up Storey's cold feet and affectionately rubbed them. She took off Storey's socks and applied light pressure on acupressure points to warm her feet and stimulate circulation. She did the same to her fingers and they relaxed under her touch. Storey's extremities looked alive again.

Judith worked patiently for more than two hours evaluating and organizing a dozen simple exercises for us to do at home. In a complicated neuropathic way, these exercises encouraged Storey's brain map to turn back on and to reorganize her nervous system. A few examples of her new exercises included face and skull tapping. Judith taught us how to lightly tap her face at the temples, sides, forehead and above her mouth to wake up Storey's tactility, muscle tone, auditory and interhemispheric functions, and to calm her amygdala. Joint tapping her shoulders, arms, and legs supported proprioception, muscle tone, differentiation, and visual functions. During "Jiggle Bridge" we rested Storey on her side with her knees bent and my hands on her knees and elbows, then jiggled her hips and shoulders as she laughed. This supported differentiation and calming. "Buzz Snap" was when I ran my hands down each finger and toe with a little giggle saying, "buzz snap," and I'd pull my hand away at the tips. This encouraged muscle tone and circulation.

There were more exercises. Storey's favorite was the two-finger spinal massage—I'd run my fingers down the sides of her spine to support her autonomic nervous system. Who knew these simple exercises and a few more through play aided so much in neurodevelopment?

Since Storey began school at eleven-thirty, it enabled us time to include these exercises and a few more before school. "Gentle enhancement" was HANDLE'S philosophy, a concept I had to consistently remind myself. *If a little is good, that doesn't mean more is better.* I tended to push. Patience at every second felt like a lifetime. Nevertheless, these new therapies felt right. Judith knew ways to reorganize Storey's damaged and complicated nervous system.

John and I were grateful for this new discovery. It was harder for John to climb his way out of his melancholic heart when it came to watching Storey lose function. My determination augmented his diminishing hope. In the end he chose to remain skeptical.

Three days later we returned to meet Judith for a quick follow-up before she went back to Seattle. Sheri, Storey's physical therapist, came with us. We reviewed Storey's exercises to make sure I was doing them correctly. Storey was already less shaky. She worked for an hour then said, "I'm tired."

Was Storey calmer? Sitting up straighter? If she slumped, all I had to do was tap lightly between her shoulder blades and it sent a message from her muscles to her brain, notifying her to sit up. Her tremors lessened. She sat unassisted longer and seemed to be more present in her body.

Unlike the guessing game of Storey's medical prescriptions without easy access to the doctors, Judith gave me continued support. She returned my emails quickly even though she had hundreds of client emails to return each night.

No doctor diagnosed Storey with autism, but we watched her withdraw and come back and withdraw again over the years. Storey spoke in short, slow sentences versus babbling full sentences like she had at 2 years before she got sick. I asked Judith about this.

"It's like Storey is walking on a high tightrope with a chair on her shoulders, and her entire body and brain is working very hard to balance on the tightrope. There is no time for her brain to answer what is two-plus-two. Her cognitive brain has been compromised because her nervous system is in survival mode," Judith explained.

What Judith said made complete sense, yet I still wanted my pre-disease Storey back.

Judith felt Storey's condition might have been triggered, not caused, by immunizations and other environmental neurotoxins. She suggested I place castor oil packs on Storey's stomach while she napped. As Judith described the process, my shoulders sank and I had a little déjà vu from some of Tara's weird suggestions. The idea was that castor oil packs would help to detox and reduce inflammation: the body would absorb the beneficial elements of the castor oil and draw toxins out of the body that interfere with normal bodily functions. Upon further investigation, it seemed to be a messy process. I tried it anyway. I warmed Storey's stomach for a few minutes with a heating pad, then placed a cotton washcloth soaked with castor oil across her stomach and layered it with plastic wrap, then placed the heating pad back on. The instructions said to do it three to four times a week. It was a mess. Naturally, Storey didn't seem to mind. I followed the directions on and off for a few months. I don't know if it ever helped. Storey's HANDLE exercises became part of our routine.

She tremored less and was more alert and happier. Most importantly, she had a lot less "drops."

Before we knew it our favorite season arrived. Storey wore a Costco tiger costume and Hayden wore a lightning bolt costume I had made using cardboard. We laughed because Hayden's seatbelt barely fit around the lightning bolt. Like most years, we met at a friend's house in town then walked up and down the "Halloween Street."

A week later it was time for John and me to dress up for the Eagle Mount Gala/Fundraiser.

CHISEL

Mamma Mia... suddenly I smelled the best smell from the kids' toy box. I gave Mom my starving eyes and suddenly I caught a pig ear flying in the air. Mom sent me outside to enjoy my tasty treat. I laid in the warm grass and rolled over the ear so I wouldn't forget that luscious smell. Then I chowed down. Oh man, that was the best chip ever. I must have been a good dog to get that. I rolled on my back and boxed the air when I was done. Then suddenly a pain punched my stomach. I tried to walk it off, but it got worse. I tried to barf; nothing came up. I tried to poop. Nothing. The pain was different and worse than when I ate pig fat and gravel.

I heard Mom's voice in the distance, but I couldn't think or make my legs work. My stomach felt like a basketball. Hayden kept calling me.

"Moooommm! I'm over here," I tried to bark. I found Mom pushing Storey's stroller to me. "Mom, what is happening?"

My stomach felt like I got kicked by a horse. She found me... she was going to rescue me. I knew she could.

Dressed in ball clothes and heels, my shoes echoed against the concrete floor as John and I passed barking dogs in kennels at the vet. When I saw Chisel's sad, drawn wrinkles I smeared my makeup. She looked like a drugged inmate in a concrete cell without water.

"Chisel, you're going to be fine. You survived. I am never giving you another pig ear, ever. Those hard, greasy things should be taken off the market for making your stomach bloat and twist. I'll put my coat under you, so you know I'm near. You're going to be fine. The vet fixed your stomach in time. I will be back tomorrow."

John nudged me to go. I know he was thinking that the sooner we got to the gala the sooner we could leave. I had flashbacks of saying goodbye to my first bull mastiff, who died of a heart-based tumor the night of my high school senior ball, and how I was able to compartmentalize my sadness and grief long enough to have fun instead of getting drunk and crying in the women's bathroom like a dumped date.

The next day I waited for the call to see if Chisel made it through the night. At ten in the morning I sobbed.

CHISEL

My family never smelled so good. My mom loves me so much. From now on I'm going to be extra careful. I almost walked across the rainbow bridge to see my furry mom, who smelled like sweet milk, and to play with a couple of my siblings. But when my other mom visited me and tucked her favorite coat under my head, her love pulled me back. My job isn't done here; Mom and Storey still need me. Mom tells me I make her and Storey feel better. I love them so much, as much as food. No... more than food. I'm never going to take spooning with Storey for granted.

"Spooning with Chisel"

Chapter 46

By Christmas 2004, Chisel ran around like nothing had happened a month earlier and joined the extended Mills family in Big Sky. I still felt a little uneasy around John's family, but by then everyone was used to Storey's uniqueness. They knew we were, *medically,* doing everything we could. They loved her just the same. She was happy to sit next to Grandpa on the couch playing board puzzles for hours while John, Hayden and I skied.

That holiday I reflected on the past years replaying the encouraging words I'd heard from intuitives, psychics, Sisters of Light, Tara, Judith, energy healers, Elaine, Dr. Marc, therapists, teachers, and friends. My favorite encouragement was from Hayden: "Storey looks really good today." Their words kept me going, but I still waited to hear the words *Storey will grow out of this, you'll look back on this, even write a book about it and your family will live happily ever after.* So, I scheduled my last psychic reading with Kenny.

I knew I was pressing my luck, going too far, testing our destiny. The first thing Kenny said was that we'd be moving. *Why do they all say that?* We had no plans to move. In fact, we had architecture plans drawn up to include an elevator in our existing small house. Kenny

First row: Chisel, Sandee (me), Storey in baby jogger, Alea, Kathy, Hayden, Noa. Second row: John, Grandma Joan, Cindy–John's sister, Kyria–David's wife, David–John's brother, Grandpa John. Hiking Ousel Falls trail, Big Sky. Photo by John's uncle Pete.

had credentials but he was the only one of my crazy psychic consultants to lay out the good, the bad and the ugly.

"I see Storey is happy, she seems to be on the spectrum. She's intelligent. Her immune system is very weak. Her brain can't send proper signals to her nervous system. As you know, she's here to teach. This is her last life. The disease she has is one in a million, that's why it's so hard to diagnose. I'm sorry, but she won't ever walk on her own again."

"What? Will she die?" I said, immediately regretting the question.

"She has about four years to live," Kenny said.

Die… DIE? Why did I ask that question? Even if he is wrong, which I'm sure he is, I'll hear his words forever. Why do I set myself up to be taken down? I'm so stupid!

That was the first time I had heard that word, which would never be repeated. No one else, including the doctors, mentioned *die* even though they stumbled around a possible terminal disease. At the end of the day, they never really explained the consequences of a progressive neurodegenerative disease.

Those words were all I remembered Kenny saying. *How dare he?* Psychics were supposed to tell you what you wanted to hear front and center. I was the only one who could think those thoughts. I had that right, he did not. But I had called Kenny to ask what he saw.

I called John and told him what Kenny said, even though I'd been too nervous before to tell him I had scheduled a final psychic appointment.

"Sandee, why do you keep torturing yourself? Psychics aren't real. They just want your money," he said.

"I know, I don't know why I do that. I just want some truth. I'll try to forget what he said. What time will you be home?" I asked quietly, pretending to make light of the situation even though my heart raced.

"Yeah, right... give Storey a hug. I'll be home around five."

What did I really expect anyway? Since Storey's second birthday we'd been dodging a real-time nightmare.

Believing or "knowing" that Storey and I committed to this symbiotic fight a lifetime ago, I still doubted my guiding qualifications. But when Storey smiled and looked in my eyes, I remembered our sacred oath. Like most mama bears, I was here, now, to support Storey in all that she did and didn't do. She was a shining star under my protection.

Our passage became clear when I came across a book Wayne Dyer and his wife wrote in 1996 called *A Promise is a Promise*. The book was a love story between a mother, Kaye, and her daughter Edwarda when she went into a diabetic coma as a teenager. My heart ached for Kaye. I admired her dedication. She promised never to leave her daughter's side. She slept in a chair next to her daughter's bed and awakened every two hours to adjust Edwarda's body. Her unfathomable love and hope that someday Edwarda would fully wake to tell her mother where she'd been kept Kay going for years and years.

When Storey became sick, Edwarda had been in a coma for almost thirty years. Their story enthralled me. I knew few mothers who would dedicate every minute of their lives keeping their daughter alive in bed that long while falling into insurmountable debt. Edwarda was able to breathe on her own and her eyes opened and closed, but she did not talk or move. She was fed through a tube and everything else was done for her by her parents until her father died of a heart attack seven years into Edwarda's coma. Kaye became the only caregiver. She only left the house two times: once for her husband's funeral and again for her other daughter's wedding. This dedicated mother knew Edwarda's life was a blessing, not a burden. Strangers visited Edwarda's bedside and were healed from illnesses just by being in the presence of unconditional love. Sometimes Edwarda's mother saw the apparition of the Divine Mother.

This story had stayed with me. I wanted to support this mother's dedication knowing her love was in a different class of mama bears. I signed up to receive their newsletters and sent money when they had fundraisers. In the end, Edwarda never regained full consciousness to tell her mother where her spirit had been. Kaye died at eighty-one, after taking care of her daughter for thirty-eight years. Edwarda's sister took over her care until Edwarda died in 2012 at fifty-nine years old, after being in diabetic coma for forty-two years. Every day Kaye prayed to receive a miracle for Edwarda. About thirty years into Edwarda's coma Kaye realized that Edwarda *was* a miracle, all along.

After finishing the book, I felt guilty for not doing more for Storey. Guilty that I couldn't be more like Kaye. And guilty that my relationship with John was strained. I didn't want Storey to worry about us.

So, I emailed one of the Sisters of Light whom I had met at the hotel more than two years before, hoping for some reassurance that Storey's decline wasn't because of me. Days and weeks went by, I had forgotten I emailed them. Then one day I received this letter:

Dear Sandee,

What's happening with Storey is not because you and John are stressed. Her body is her vehicle. She had to be in her body to spread love and healing. She's an avatar who's doing important work on the planet to fulfill a very large contract. She is clearing planetary karma. Some days she is better or worse depending on what she is working on. Her work goes on when she is awake and asleep. You're doing a great job keeping her healthy and strong through diet and grounding activities for her physical body. We know this is a tremendous strain on you and your family. We also know you understand this. Please take care of yourself and find time to relax, to find grace, and know you're doing everything you can out of love for your daughter. Storey's work is similar to the work of Mother Theresa, but behind the scenes. She has many guides and angels. We know this is very hard to understand, but in time you will realize the importance of your role as Storey's mother and guide. We love you greatly and thank you for the

*great contribution that you are making in completing this
great work, and for such a loving mother.*
         Blessings,
              Sisters of Light

The letter surprised me, and it didn't. I felt connected to these Sisters through an invisible web. Simultaneously their message and images flowed through the intuitives and spiritual counselors I had seen, completely unaware of one another. Storey's responsibility became clearer to me, not because of the letter but because it triggered how I felt during Storey's first year of life; a knowing tucked deep in my cells. When Storey arrived in this world I had a feeling it wasn't going to be easy. I sensed that I had signed up to solo climb, void of any instructions.

Storey changed people. She changed my friend Bob—another advanced soul—when he "accidentally" saw her in the hospital moments after her birth.

Strangers and friends said, "She's an old soul. I will pray for her."

She healed people just by being present. Life seeds germinated and grew in her path. Sometimes I could see her wings like an effervescent hologram out of the corner of my eye.

In the beginning I ran my errands without her because I didn't want people to feel sorry for us. I didn't want to start a lengthy explanation of why she was growing differently until I realized she tapped strangers lightly with her invisible wings, giving them the love they needed. Later I realized that the people who stared or felt sorry for us were new souls beginning their marathon, unable to see Storey's light. I saw similar light and love, or spiritual contracts in the eyes of other disabled children and adults. They healed others just by being. Their whole life was to heal and to love. We all know people like this. In truth they are more important to this physical world than we are.

I really don't know what happens before we are born or after we die from our planet, but obviously all of us feel a calling for something bigger than us, to make our mark. We wander through our spiritual path trying to mend the holes in our hearts. We attach to the wrong truths, looking to hide our pain in an addiction, excessive exercise, poor choices, or choosing to keep our burdens, etc.

We want to understand our reason, our pain.

We want to understand our hell.

We all want to make a difference.

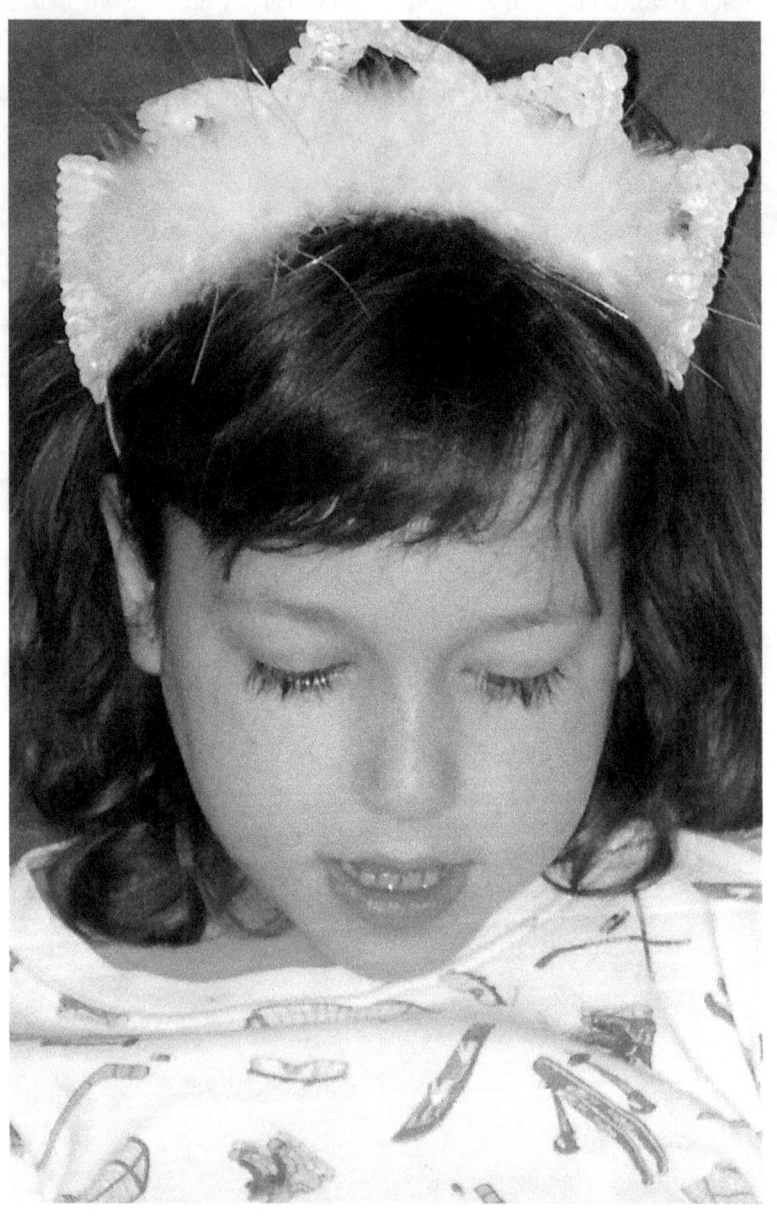

Storey 5, Easter Sunday

PART 3

2005-2006

CHISEL

My feet hurt. My toes have spread apart like an old lady who never wore shoes, and my face has turned white. Considering I almost met my maker getting pancreatitis from eating rotten meat, seizing in front of Mom when I was a puppy after eating Sudafed, and a twisted stomach, I've calculated my time in sunny spots to be mighty high.

I watch Mom most of the day. Her body moves in predictable ways. She races around, talks to herself, talks to Storey and yells at Hayden.

She depends on me to clean the dirty dishes but after I got my necklace stuck in the silverware tray and pulled it across the floor screaming bloody murder, I fired myself from that job.

Dark Cloud is the favorite cat around here and a great mouser, I'll give him that and he knows I'm the boss. I gave Mom the whites of my eyes and looked in Dark Cloud's direction when he pulled the Christmas tree down.

Mom and I have our own love language. I know being around me breaks her life into moments and she returns her love with wrinkle rubs.

I worry about Storey the most, she's growing wings.

Chapter 47

A round the holidays, information about Lyme disease came to me from many directions. I stumbled upon news and random articles. Many people inflicted with Lyme disease shared a variety of symptoms as Storey. Borrelia Burgdorferi Bacterium (Lyme) was caused by the bites of black-legged deer ticks, and for example symptoms can be chronic fatigue, cognitive problems, neuropathy, joint pain, depression, and migraines. Of course, symptoms varied in each person.

If Lyme disease was diagnosed in Montana, that meant it came from a tick bite outside of the state. This information didn't matter to me. I remember removing a tick from Storey's hair one spring when she was 2. I created scenarios in my mind: maybe a tick hitchhiked in John's folks' bags from Wisconsin, or maybe Montana ticks really do carry Lyme disease and it hadn't been discovered yet—there's always a first. Regardless of the slim chance that Storey had Lyme, I took the information and raced.

I had a new obsession. A new high. A new hope.

I read about a lab in Florida that claimed to be the most accurate in diagnosing Lyme disease. Dr. Feist, once again, listened to my plea and voiced his doubt. A week later Storey and I were back in his office. I hid Storey's face from the needle. Fifteen milliliters of blood were sent overnight.

A week later the test results were faxed to Dr. Feist. The results were positive for Lyme. Initially I was elated, a possible treatment! But something didn't sit right. My high had worn off and my intuition put on the breaks. Dr. Feist felt the same. He called the lab; they were adamant that we treat Storey with the intensive Lyme antibiotics immediately. We both knew Lyme disease treatment was not to be taken lightly. If we got it wrong, the treatment would make Storey sicker. Dr. Feist consulted the neurologist in Helena, who said he'd never found a child with Lyme disease from Montana. We put the brakes on right there. This lab didn't seem as convincing as their glossy pamphlet.

Dr. Feist suggested we run another test, a regular enzyme-linked immunosorbent essay (ELISA) and Western Blot test. To our relief, the traditional Lyme Disease test came back negative. I was satisfied with that, and my obsession stopped there.

Desperation and hope had, in the beginning, guided me to the muscle testing people, to Tara, to medical intuitives, to doctors and neurologists; to test after test, only to be disappointed and heartbroken. I felt like I was being guided by Gollum who laughed when he saw the words *precious sucker* on my forehead.

I knew life was fleeting, floating, melting in the sunset. When I stopped racing and lived moment by moment, like watching Storey pick up a noodle or watching Spirit's lightning bolt zip across the pasture, it felt like everything was going to be all right. Then seconds later I'd be in my frenzy, looking for something that might give Storey a future.

A future together.

That January Hayden came down with influenza. I jumped back into the dark hole of worry, fighting to function like a regular family, staring at Storey for the slightest sign of the illness. We were all prescribed Tamiflu to stop it before Storey developed life threatening symptoms. Quarantining at home, I got sucked into signing Direct TV's two-year contract. I felt like I had graduated with the average household with hundreds of useless channels at our fingertips when all we really wanted was *PBS Kids* and *Seinfeld*.

"Mom, I can't believe we get to watch the funny guys again," Hayden said from the living room while I made dinner.

Seinfeld had, once again, worked its magic. Thankfully the Tamiflu worked, and Hayden was the only one who got sick.

Caring for a special needs child is a never-ending worry. Soon it was Storey's swollen hands and feet. Worried about Storey's edema, my mother introduced me to a man who sewed compression bands. I took measurements of Storey's shiny, swollen hands and feet and ordered his socks to help with circulation. Storey wore the compressions at night looking like she was ready to fend off a police dog. We laughed every night. Then in the middle of the night when I got up to roll her, I'd remove the compressions. They seemed to help a little but not as much as I had hoped.

We continued to see Sheri for physical therapy once a week and craniosacral therapy every couple of weeks. Storey skied with Eagle Mount at Bridger Bowl Saturday mornings, January through March. Friday nights she swam with our friend Leslie, and every night we had twenty minutes of HANDLE exercises.

The day Sheri brought out the wheelchair catalog, I slumped over. Sadness became my guide. Storey had grown out of her glorified stroller, and I couldn't carry her all the time. I knew once Storey graduated to a wheelchair she was never going to want to walk. She'd surrender to her decline.

The adaptive catalogue with smiling children in wheelchairs surfaced thoughts I'd had four years earlier during our girls' weekend about pushing Storey around in a wheelchair. My worst-case fear stared at me from the glossy pages. *Be careful what you wish for.* I felt guilty for thinking the worst in the beginning. To my relief, my brain led me to remember that I spent way more energy visualizing Storey healed.

It was time. I knew it. John knew it. Nevertheless, I cried when I signed the insurance papers for Storey's wheelchair. Storey picked purple for part of the frame since they didn't have pink.

Riding in a wheelchair, Storey would look disabled. I'd have to smile through the pain and appear as though I was Superwoman. People and kids would look at us differently. Storey would draw more attention. There would be questions. Parents would whisper to their kids, "Don't stare." But the kids would stare. I stared as a kid because I wanted to know what was wrong.

Storey tried as hard as she could in the walk-a-bout and worked fervently at physical therapy. It was obvious all this work was to help her maintain what she had, not make her better. So, I decided to focus on her gifts—the love she spread to ones in need.

She didn't have to be healed to teach us how to live, or love.

Not only was The Gallatin Madison County Special Education Cooperative funding Storey's school aide, but they also connected me with other resources like Family Outreach. This local non-profit

Leslie, a volunteer and a good friend with
Storey during Eagle Mount swimming.

provides services to children and adults with special needs. It educates
and teaches skills to families, individuals and their caregivers. They
help with evaluation and processing grants and general federal funding. As required by Family Outreach, Storey went through hours of
testing and evaluations to determine where she stood on an average
scale. Memories returned of the rigorous tests I had gone through as
a child before I was properly diagnosed with dyslexia. When I took
tests, to me the examiners seemed so stupid, nerdy and smelly. The
results were always the same: "Sandee is very creative and appears to
be smart but incapable of understanding phonics. We don't know why."

Unlike me, Storey didn't mind the tests. She liked the attention.
Storey tested below average on everything, except she was 100 percent aware of her surroundings and her environment. Of course, the

results focused on what Storey could *not* do, rather than what she could do, or who she was.

Family Outreach requires in-home checks when a child applies for in-school services. Without a choice, a support staff member came to our house to make sure Storey was loved and cared for and that I wasn't a mentally ill mother. I understood the reason. Once a week a nice gal knocked on my door and asked questions for an hour. I grew to resent the meetings; they made me feel inadequate and took time away from playing with Storey. I felt like I was being evaluated to see if I had cracked under the pressure. But truthfully, I *did* need these meetings. They helped me process our reality and offered choices. Rarely did I burden my friends with my frustrations. I kept quiet when they told me of their kid's accomplishments while I was home helping my 6-year-old daughter with a mysterious disease.

In one of the meetings, the gal decided one of our goals should be to call the doctor and ask for a swallow study. Storey had begun to choke when she ate and many times it sounded like she couldn't clear her throat.

A swallow study consists of drinking what looks like white Pepto-Bismol while photos are taken. On the X-rays, barium sulfate appears white where the metallic solution moves down the pharynx and esophagus. I read that the substance is non-toxic in small amounts. It is toxic overall, because it is insoluble in water and can cause vomiting, diarrhea, constipation, and the possibility of additional problems stemming from underling health issues. I needed to understand the risks of the test against the good it would do. None of this sat right with me: the stress of handing Storey another questionable liquid to sip, then asking her body to expel the toxin just to show us what we already knew—that she had trouble swallowing. Dr. Feist agreed.

So, we made mealtime a game. We giggled, cleared our throat and said, "Storey, do this." Storey gave it her best. But I feared her future was like Lorenzo's, whose parents constantly sat next to his bed and sucked mucus out of his mouth because he couldn't swallow.

Chapter 48

Storey's decline was hard to ignore. We chose to focus on and cel-ebrate her smile, her love, and her willingness to work hard at physical therapy. On good days when she seemed brighter and stron-ger than the day before, I still envisioned her healing.

Denial and hope were like battling twins. Denial fed hope and hope enabled denial—they fought over the same truth. At this point, denial was beating me down and its twin was disappearing with the setting sun. Giving up and letting the truth come forth felt like I was giving up on Storey. She deserved better.

A slow progression, or regression, or degeneration—no matter how it's expressed, it is heart-wrenching. When you live with some-one's regression, it's easy to overlook and deny the small changes. You anticipate the expressions and whispers of friends you haven't seen in a while. But you know that over time small changes add up like a slow water drip in the bathroom faucet.

After more than a month of wearing the leg compressions, the back of Storey's heels developed red spots like bed sores. I didn't think too much about the four-millimeter spots until Lori, Storey's craniosacral therapist, voiced her concern. Lori used a low-level Q-1000 laser on the sores at each session. Just like so many things I had tried with Storey, the compressions seemed to make things better, until they backfired. I stopped using the compression socks and had a new challenge of healing potential bed sores from the back of Storey's heels.

The Q-1000 was originally developed to use on horses and animals; it reduced pain and sped recovery. Lasers have been used in the medical field since the 1950s. Dr. Marc used various lasers on Storey and Hayden to desensitize their allergens.

Taking Storey to see Lori six days a week for two minutes of laser was unrealistic. So, I ordered my own Q-1000 low-level laser. It was an expensive purchase, but I was happy to do it and grateful that we could still afford to buy groceries. Those bed sores had the potential to turn deadly. I lasered her heels several times a day and used the laser on my animals when they had an injury. Of course, John was skeptical until he saw a football trainer use a laser on a Green Bay Packer's injured hamstring. The laser healed Storey's sores. The compression socks stayed in the closet.

Early spring 2005, we headed back to Billings for another metabolic clinic with the same group. During each new visit the clinicians tried to hide their broken hearts studying Storey's physical and cognitive loss. The meetings always began the same, reviewing everything we had done including naturopathic support and the latest new tests, like Lyme. The group still felt Storey's condition was a rare degenerative disease and obviously, at this point, irreversible. The group showed relief when they learned a wheelchair was on order. We didn't stay long. Everyone had run out of suggestions. There wasn't a brilliant Dr. House coming up with a lifesaving wild idea at the end of the hour. Before leaving an eerie pause-filled room, everyone stood and pushed the noisy chairs under the table. I lifted Storey and hugged her tight. We hugged the clinicians through swollen eyes. The room knew the truth. We wouldn't meet again.

John carried Storey and we walked out the front door.

Hope went out the back.

Chapter 49

Spirit's lightning bolt streaked across the pasture for a year. I never got tired of watching her performance. We had named her perfectly; her energy matched the horse, Spirit, in the 2002 animated Disney movie of the same name. At one year, horses act like toddlers in horse maturity and Spirit weighed approximately 600 pounds. Right after her birthday, I received a call from the gal who had sold me Angel, Spirit's mother. She informed me she had found Angel's and Spirit's father's registration papers. Spirit's father, Moon Flash, was a half quarter horse, half thoroughbred registered with the American Paint Horse Association. Spirit's mother was a full blood registered blue roan quarter horse. After reading the papers I renamed Spirit "Spirit Moon," but we mostly just shouted "Baabbyy" over the fence and she'd trot to us.

That first year I devoured horse training books. My favorite was *Groundwork* by Buck Brannaman. The movie *The Horse Whisperer* was based on Buck's training style and gentle approach of waiting for the horse's give and take, in contrast to the old cowboy way of whipping a horse into submission.

Intuitively, I touched Spirit as much as possible. I rubbed tarps over her head. I hung loose ropes around her neck and tied one of

Storey's giant dolls to her back. I hugged her often and she learned how to move away from my energy. A local horse trainer gave me more gentle tips. Spending time with Spirit was therapeutic. In the pasture with her and Angel, I felt like I could handle what might come next.

Horses are known to mirror your emotions moment by moment. They don't live in the past or future (unless, like us, there was trauma). Their reflection and awareness grounded me to this life and to the earth. Storey lived as they did—in the present. Storey glowed while hugging Angel's back as we led her around the yard, even though Storey had lost the ability to sit up on her own. Dancing with these powerful beings felt like I had unlocked a door of my ancestral memory working and evolving with horses. My connection ran deep, and I knew it was the same for Storey. Her soul came alive when she was on Angel or watching Spirit from the other side of the fence in her stroller.

Out of the horse pasture, accepting Storey's decline and staying present were my greatest challenges and priorities. Not only were Storey's issues demanding, but so were Hayden's. At 7 years old and in second grade, his Montessori classmates were studying the genus and species of animals while he frolicked for an hour looking for a pencil sharpener.

Several times John and I rolled Storey's stroller to meet with Hayden's teachers to discuss his ADHD. One teacher voiced her opinion on the magical properties of Ritalin. "It worked wonders for my son," she said more than once. His teacher thought he would learn better sitting quietly in a chair like a zombie instead of nurturing his kinesthetic learning style. Again, these conversations took me back forty years, when I sat in meetings looking down at my dirty Keds while my parents glared at me, listening to my teachers talk about my inability to sit still or how I just stared out the window. My teachers labeled me disruptive and suggested to my mother I take Ritalin, which hit the market in 1955. I just wanted recess time to burn my energy doing back flips and cartwheels in the grass. Back then, educators didn't understand that some kids needed to move their body to learn, and it surprised me that Hayden's Montessori teachers encouraged their archaic treatment. My mother used her intuition and sent me to tutors and gymnastics instead.

Hayden didn't have dyslexia. He spelled beautifully and memorized verbatim when he finally sat down to read. He just had an inquisitive brain that got bored with subjects of little interest to him. John and I came up with a plan for Hayden. We took him to a local HANDLE therapist and an occupational therapist to calm his nervous system. Hayden burned up his energy skiing, swimming, hiking, jumping on the trampoline, and tossing a ball for our neighbor's hyper golden retriever. The difference between Hayden and me was that he was always happy.

Dear *Mom*,

    I loved Spirit. She was cuddly. I loved it when you parked the baby jogger next to the fence so I could talk to her while you watered the flowers. She liked to remove my socks, one by one. Then she'd sniff my lap for a carrot. She came into our lives at the perfect time.

    She came for you.

      I love you,

        Your *Storey*

Spirit a month old, with her mother Angel.

Chapter 50

Our county recycled some road mix and paved our road in summer 2005. We were all happy, especially Chisel—it was easier on her aging paws. Storey's wheelchair arrived five months after Sheri ordered it. It took the insurance company that long to decide if Storey truly needed one. By then Storey looked miserable in her glorified stroller. At 6 years her large front teeth, inherited from my family, began to punch through her gums. Her smile grew crooked and her face lacked muscle tone. Without complaint, she picked things up with her three last fingers against her palm. She was beautiful. She laughed when she felt well and gazed to the heavens when she didn't. Dark Cloud, our grey and white cat's favorite resting place was in Storey's lap when she was in her wheelchair, or on top of her feet dressed in beaded Crow moccasins a friend had made just for her.

Under the direction of Dr. Swoboda and the metabolic team, Storey was prescribed Artane, a prescription some Parkinson's patients took to relax stiff muscles and nerve impulses. Many of the PND patients had tried Artane. Some were helped, some were not.

Like so much we tried, Artane backfired with Storey and her symptoms grew worse. She threw up, shook, and felt terrible. We tapered her off the medicine, which took weeks, and after the medicine was out of her system, the side effects continued like her reactions to anesthesia. It took everything I had to keep my shit together.

My sister's daughter Meredith arrived to help me at the beginning of summer when her college semester ended. Hayden's 9th and Storey's 7th annual birthday party was fun, but Storey was miserable. Her eyes were heavy and quiescent. We sat on the porch fanning her and offered her small bites of Dairy Queen cake (I had given up on no gluten or dairy). Hayden ran around in circles with his friends. That birthday contrasted with Storey's magical 5th, where she glowed all day and sang with her friends.

Two weeks later we headed to Big Sky to see the extended family and celebrate the Fourth of July and Storey and Grandma Joan's birthdays. I knew in my gut this was going to be Storey's last birthday. I kept that feeling tucked away. I wanted it to be perfect. Storey always shared parties with Hayden and Joan. For Storey's 7th, I wished the celebration could have been just for her. When the gifts were piled on the dining table, I audaciously asked Grandma Joan which gift was for Storey from her and Grandpa.

"We didn't get Storey a present, we don't know what to buy her," Joan whispered to me.

Heat rose from my feet to my head. I held back tears. My voice quivered. I knew they loved Storey.

"How about a book? This could be her last birthday!" I managed to say.

I walked outside where no one could see me and cried. Joan always gave her grandkids at least one gift. Joan and John were generous— one year Grandpa made Storey a dollhouse, another year, bunkbeds. They put three of their grandkids through college. As a mother it felt like my child was being excluded for being different.

A few weeks later my best friend growing up, Katie and her daughter, arrived from California. Their stay helped to pull me out of my slump. Twelve years had passed since I saw her last at our wedding. Katie's hug reminded me of life before kids. Their visit diverted my attention for a few days with their happy-go-lucky positive ways. We gagged on cigarettes and Coors beer for old times' sake. A week later a good friend from high school, Sheryl, visited with her two girls. Storey loved having them around and they were fun distractions.

At the end of July, the heat wave arrived. We huddled around Storey's air conditioner in the afternoon. Hummingbirds drank extra at night. John and I tried to celebrate our anniversary and my 44th birthday, but I didn't have the energy. I ate a lot of Baskin Robins Grasshopper Pie and wondered how people could just walk around town, smiling and doing regular life when our child was slipping from this world.

Through the smoky heat of August, we drove south to Salt Lake City to see Dr. Swoboda for Storey's six-month follow-up. The Embassy Suites felt routine. We ate at Rodizio's Grill in Trolley Square. The restaurant was fun and lively, which helped to erase some of my anxiety until I watched lines of people at the buffet touch every serving utensil with their dirty hands—not to mention the waiters fanning meat skewers from table to table asking for your choice. John told me to quit obsessing and ordered me a glass of wine, then I passed around the antibacterial gel.

When Dr. Swoboda came into the exam room and saw Storey, her face dropped. She had seen enough kids like Storey; she didn't need a crystal ball to know her future. This brilliant doctor was out of ideas.

She couldn't tell us why this was happening to Storey or what to do about it. Like the metabolic clinic, at this appointment she reviewed everything in Storey's chart and noted the progression of her disease.

We talked about the Artane and its continued side effects, one being that Storey spoke less. It had been what felt like years since her vocabulary was that of a 7-year-old. We described a new symptom where Storey's eyes got stuck looking up, like she was having a seizure, but completely conscious. Dr. Swoboda explained that it was called Oculogyric Crisis (OT) triggered by an imbalance of medications, including L-dopa L-dopa/Carbidopa and most likely the side effects of Artane. The episodes lasted minutes to hours. Many of the PND parents shared stories of their children doing the same thing.

We didn't have an instruction book. There was no glossy pamphlet telling us what to expect. When we first gave Storey Artane, ten pages of side effects were stapled to the medication bag. I read them all. Storey already showed most of the symptoms. Artane was a trial run, a last ditch of hope, but as most things we had tried, whether medical or alternative, most backfired and Artane was no different.

Dr. Swoboda pulled suggestions out of her hat of knowledge. A muscle biopsy was mentioned again: "It might give us a name, but not a treatment." Storey had been through too much, so we declined. Dr. Swoboda understood. She suggested another drug to complement L-dopa's absorption but pointed out that L-dopa deficiency wasn't Storey's overall picture. Her disease was much more complicated. She worried about Storey's swallowing and mentioned genetic studies of unknown etiology, explaining to us that it was like fishing in uncharted waters.

Our shoulders rolled forward. We thanked Dr. Swoboda and walked out. Over the next weeks we changed her medication to the new L-dopa/Carbidopa ratio and that, too, backfired. Storey threw up often; her Oculogyric Crisis increased. After trial and error, we went back to her baseline dose of L-dopa/Carbidopa.

Before school started in the fall we saw Judith from HANDLE one more time. She had that same look in her eyes as Dr. Swoboda had, but Judith aired optimism. She spent a couple hours with Storey reviewing her exercises, adjusting some, adding more, holding hope.

I stuck detox pads on the bottom of Storey's feet while she slept. They were black in the morning, which maybe indicated that her body released toxins. Twice a week Storey and I sat next to each other reading books in Dr. Marc's office while she had her feet in an ionic detox foot bath. Storey splashed her toes in the water and watched it turn dark. Everyone we had seen was grasping onto one last handhold that might pull Storey to safety.

That fall we received little moisture to put out forest fires. Mount Ellis hid behind smoke. John drove Hayden across town back to his Montessori school for third grade. Storey returned to LaMotte School for first grade, and Serena returned as her aide. She and Storey were still in love. I was indebted to Serena. It felt good to get back to a routine and to something resembling normalcy.

Because of the smoke, Kristin and I decided to commit to a 60-day hot yoga challenge. For sixty dollars you took six classes a week for ten weeks, performing twenty-six postures of sweat and exhaustion for ninety minutes. The challenge offered discipline, commitment, grounding, and life changes. We had seen the changes of other 60-day yogis and both she and I needed to feel something positive. John wasn't too excited. Some of the classes were in the evening. It was a great distraction: no phone, time for just me. My biggest challenge was to forget about Storey before I stepped on my mat.

Storey grew worse. She stared into space more. She still loved to play ball by pushing it with the back of her hand across the floor. At school asking: "Pla ball wit Ron?" Her vocabulary shrunk. On the days she was bright, looking into our eyes and talking more, and swallowed without choking, I still felt hopeful. Other days, I stood dripping in sweat seconds after yoga class listening to phone messages from Serena: "The principal wants Storey to be picked up because her eyes were locked up and they can't have her in school when she looks like that."

I knew it scared the principal. It scared the shit out of me. But she had a right to be in school. No one knew what to do. When it was time to take class photos Storey's eyes locked up. I tried to snap her back to us long enough to get a class picture of her smiling. The photographer got frustrated and said he was out of time. An hour later, she was smiling. Sometimes I drove past Storey's school on my way to yoga and I'd see her giggling and being pushed around in her wheelchair on the playground by her friend, James. On those days my heart swelled, and I pictured Storey's joy and love rippling into the hearts of the seventy-two kids who went to her school.

Storey slept more. After her naps it was hard to wake her to drive across town to get Hayden from school. I questioned our decision to keep Hayden in Montessori elementary school, but then remembered he needed additional opportunities to learn than the traditional way of sitting in a seat. He, too, was different.

In the afternoon Storey and I blasted music and continued with her home therapy while Hayden tossed the ball for the golden retriever next door.

Looking for a creative distraction, I pulled out my 40-year-old bead collection and beaded like a mad woman. I became fixated. Beading was something I *could* control. A few times after picking up Hayden from school I drove to the bead store, locked the kids in the car (don't judge, we've all done that), and made a frantic ten-minute bead run. The sicker Storey got, the faster I beaded. By Thanksgiving, Storey's swallowing was worse. Not only did I resist getting a saliva suction, like Zuzana had for Sara, no one had suggested it. No one told me what to expect next.

Storey my pumpkin eater,

This is excruciating to write, and I'm sure it's hard for my readers. I can't take anymore reflecting.

I love you forever,

Mom

Mom!

Hush Little Baby... you can do it. I'm sending you love and strength. You need to tell our story. Also share that semi-funny story about the road, that might help.

Love your artichoke eater,

Me

On a beautiful fall day Storey was still sleepy after I lifted her from her nap. As usual I was running late. I put her in her car seat and Chisel jumped in the van, and we headed to pick up Hayden.

I loved our van in every way. It climbed our steep, curvy driveway on snow days and it had large windows and a video player. What we didn't know was that the tires were run flat tires, meaning you're fucked because there was no spare. When we went to the car dealership to purchase the van, the salesman, wearing tight pants and cologne, saw a family in need and failed to warn us about the run flat tires. The under and inner side of the wheels had pockets large enough to hold chunks of mud. Before our road was paved, the clay mud would attach itself to the inside of the wheels, causing the van to wildly shake and shim all the way to town. Because of this, I carried a two-foot-long flat blade screwdriver so I could crawl under the van and pry away the dried mud—something all mothers want to do after a rain.

That fall day I turned on the air conditioner and headed onto the freeway. SHIM!!!!! I pulled to the side of the freeway, put on my hazard lights, and kept the car and air conditioner running for Storey and Chisel. I grabbed my trusty screwdriver and told Storey what I was doing. I crawled around under the van, stuck my butt in the air, and hoped some moron looking at their cell phone wasn't going to sideswipe me. I banged, cussed, and pried away the mud long enough to keep the van from shaking its way to town. When I was done, I discovered the car had locked me out. My phone sat on the dashboard.

Frantically I danced for Storey, talked to her as much as I could through the closed window, and waved my arms and screwdriver in the air like I was dancing, at any car whizzing by at eighty-ninety miles an hour. After fifteen long minutes a man in a truck stopped. He didn't have a cell phone but was kind enough to drive five miles into town and call AAA.

I continued to talk and sing to Storey through the window so she wouldn't get scared. She just laughed. I never got the name of the man, but I'll never forget his generosity.

Of course, we went to Dairy Queen after picking up Hayden.

Chapter 51

In hot yoga, the instructors encourage us to stay in the room and lie down if we needed a break unless it was a physical emergency. One day in the middle of my class, a horrible fear came over me. My hands trembled. Storey's helpless face appeared. I imagined a 911 call from Storey's school. So, I did what few yoga students had done: halfway through class I rolled up my yoga mat and headed for the door.

"Sandee, is everything ok?" the instructor asked.

"I just need to leave, sorry."

I drove as fast as I could to Storey's school. *I'm so selfish for going to yoga.* When I arrived, Serena was sitting next to Storey. They both seemed fine, except Storey's lips looked a little blue. Serena said Storey seemed okay, maybe more congested, but happy. But I wasn't okay. I couldn't see and I couldn't stand. Storey's "drops" had grown frequent. Sometimes her lips and fingertips looked gray. And I knew without a doubt she wasn't going to be okay. Ever. I had tried everything; the doctors had tried everything. Storey had a constant frog in her throat and had been coughing for two months. We had visited the doctor twice to check for pneumonia. He said it was congestion, not pneumonia. Did they take an X-ray? I don't remember.

Serena closed the door behind us in the makeshift paper storage/ Special-Ed room where they spent most of the day. I sat in a red, plastic kiddie chair, dropped my hands into my face and sobbed. I confessed to Serena that I was scared to death. It was the first time I had admitted my true fears to anyone, including myself. I wondered how many years, months, days Storey had left. Serena said a prayer for us. I was able to relax enough to help Storey with her drawing, hoping she didn't notice my condition, but I knew better. Running my fingers through her silky hair, we shared crayons that she struggled to hold. I found my breath and knew being with Storey was where I most wanted and needed to be, not yoga.

We went home from school early. Storey ate a good lunch, and I lifted her over my left shoulder and carried her upstairs to our bedroom. I gently laid her on our bed; she looked so small in our bed among our eight pillows. I opened the worn pages to *Hush Little Baby*. My voiced cracked reading our favorite words. I kissed her right cheek, her left cheek, and her forehead and said, "Here is your triangle kiss, I love you so much, Beauty Queen."

"Mom, lie dow wit me," she said.

This was our routine. Most days, feeling overwhelmed, I usually told her I needed to put the groceries away and straighten the house. But that day, I laid on my right side to face her, and we weaved our fingers together before resting them next to our hearts. Occasionally I'd open my eyes and find her staring at me, smiling.

"Storey, close your eyes like Mom." Usually, I fell asleep before she did. That day the dirty dishes and messy house were trivial.

After what felt like just minutes, we woke late to leave for Hayden's school. Both of us were always groggy after napping, like our souls had taken a detour back home.

The lower sun of fall warmed my face through the car window as I headed onto the freeway. *Breathe,* I reminded myself. If I had learned anything from yoga, it was to breathe when I felt stressed. Halfway to Hayden's school, Storey looked as though she was on the verge of an OT crisis, but it passed. She attempted to smile at one of the kids who came to the window to see her. I was relieved when Storey smiled back. She was going to be okay for the rest of that day.

"Mom, I think Chisel needs a mini cone from Dairy Queen," Hayden said, climbing into the van.

"She does? Okay, but I need to run to the bead store because I'm making twenty-five necklaces. One for each of your teachers and Storey's therapists. I'll only be a few minutes and then we'll get ice cream," I said, feeling life speed by.

"Okay, but hurry." Hayden said.

When I returned to the car from the bead store ten minutes later, Storey smiled and Hayden said, "Mom, I saw a truck do this." He pointed up both of his index fingers, which meant the semi had spare tires attached to the sides of the truck. His expressive face always lit up when he told stories.

Two errands were our limit after school because it tired Storey. We used her stroller instead of her wheelchair for quick errands because it was easier and faster.

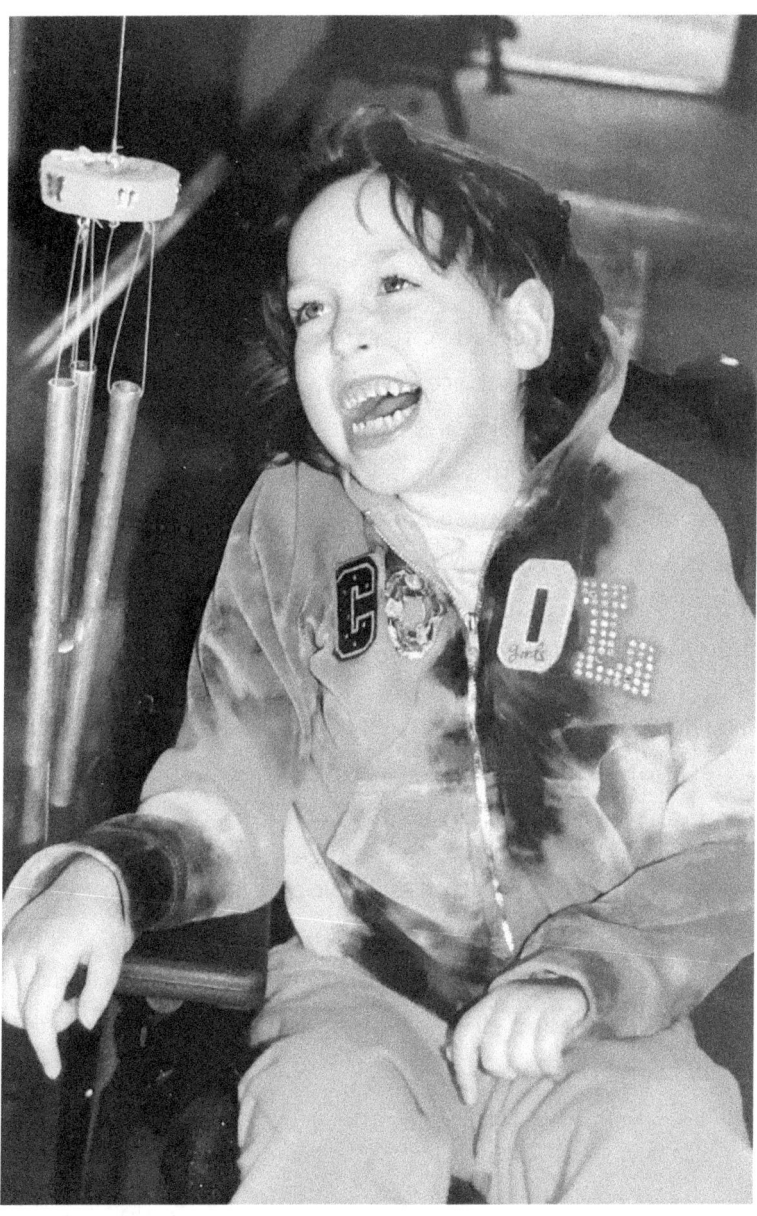

I don't have many pictures of Storey in her wheelchair
because she was so much worse by the time we got
it. But here she's at school having a good time.

CHISEL

I felt a particular bump in the road and knew where the car was headed. My mouth produced excess drool which made its way to car seats.

"Chisel, do you want a baby cone?" Hayden asked me.

Through the windows I noticed my favorite white-haired friend that worked there. She always gave me extra ice cream. Mom put Storey in her stroller and Hayden grabbed my leash; this meant we were going to sit outside and I'd have opportunities to lick melted chocolate off the payment. We used to sit under a big tree next to the parking lot, but one day the tree was gone. I remember that day well because Mom was in tears.

"They cut down our shade tree for no good reason," she said. After that it was a while before I felt that bump in the road when the van turned right.

We walked to the red tables. Hayden carried my cone and that little brat licked my cone even though he had a giant one for himself. "Sit, Chisel!" and I did as he asked. I fake-bit Hayden's hand and left slobber on his thumb for taking a lick of my cone.

"CHISEL!"

Mom was so busy wiping Storey's face she didn't see me sneak off to the side of the parking lot where other people held dripping cones.

I watched Storey, Hayden, and Mom pile into the van. Mom lifted Storey's stroller into the back and normally that's when she'd lift my legs up into the van (I pretend that I can't jump). Hoping for one last pavement lick, I waited for Mom to call me. I looked away for one second and the van was driving over that bump. THE VAN WAS GONE! They left without me. THEY TOTALLY LEFT WITHOUT ME.

Mom wouldn't leave me; she loved me too much. Plus no one in the parking area was giving me food, I'd starve. People kept telling me to go away. There was a very large man who tossed me one fry. ONE FRY! Then he told me to scamper. So, I walked around and showed strangers the whites of my sad eyes. It felt like a lifetime later when Mom came back. Mom was wiping her eyes and her face was red.

"CHISEL!!! I'm soooo sorry. At home I lifted the hatch to the van and realized I hadn't helped you up. I called Dairy Queen and asked for the old lady to keep an eye on you, but she had already left. I'm so relieved. I can't lose you. I need you," Mom told me.

Mom dropped her face into my neck and I felt her love.

"Chisel, Mom was so worried she cried all the way back here," Hayden said. "Mom, can I have another ice cream cone?"

Chapter 52

A few weeks later I put chicken thighs in the oven and we bundled up and walked. Storey giggled when Licorice jumped into her lap. I felt lighter walking. Minutes later Licorice jumped off and ran in the bushes when we stopped at the bottom of Libby's driveway.

"Hi Libby, can I play your piano?" Hayden asked, kicking off his wet snow boots before busting into her log home.

Libby could tell I didn't have the energy to lift Storey. "Just roll Storey right into the house, don't worry about the snow. I'll get a towel," she said.

Chisel laid against her couch, and Libby handed me a glass of pinot noir. She pulled Storey's jogger close to the piano and sat next to Hayden on the piano bench. She held Storey's hand and helped Hayden play. Libby knew our story; she knew I needed a few minutes.

Forty minutes was over in a flash.

"Shit! Hayden, we must go, look what time it is."

My body felt like a brick. I wanted to stay next to her warm fireplace.

Huge, stick-your-tongue-out snowflakes lit up in the light of the headlamp Libby lent me. We sang our way home to alert sidling animals in the chokecherry bushes. Licorice had waited for us on the porch. The chicken thighs were leather.

"Hey Dad, it was scaaary running down the road in the dark, we could barely see through the flakes, we didn't even run into any bears or mountain lions," Hayden said.

"Sandee, you shouldn't be on the road with the kids when it's dark," John said from the living room.

When fall folded into winter's darkness, Storey's cough intensified. Swallowing thin liquids, like water, was challenging. I fed her anything she could swallow; smoothies were easiest. Surprisingly she could still swallow a small piece of meat and noodles. Eating and swallowing turned into gagging and coughing, and coughing turned into choking. I had a flashback of Lorenzo in the movie who received nutrition via a feeding tube through his nose. I didn't want that. I didn't know what to do and neither did John. Then one morning we sat at the kitchen table. I lifted Storey into my lap and held her head low, tapping her back while she coughed.

"She can't live like this," I said, looking up at John.

"I know." His face went white.

He took Hayden to school. Storey and I stayed home. I thought she just needed rest, and she would get over this illness. I placed her on her side on the couch so she could watch *Toy Story 2* while I frantically beaded. I had a distraction. I was creating something positive; I had control over the beads.

On the night of December 14, 2005, I let Storey sleep with us, something John and I rarely did unless the kids were ill. I propped

Storey's head into the crease of my shoulder and tried to sleep. I woke when I felt Storey trying to take big breaths. She remained calm. I whispered how much I loved her. I didn't want to take her to the emergency room in the middle of the night because that's when bad things happen, and our ER didn't have the best reputation. I hardly slept. Storey was able to sleep most of the night and when she woke, she smiled. She knew it was special that she got to sleep with us. She felt safe, even though she wasn't.

In the morning, I spoon-fed her a raspberry smoothie with my right hand and dialed the doctor's office with my left.

"My daughter is having a hard time breathing. Can I come in right away?"

"We don't have any appointments this morning," the reception-ist told me.

"What? I need to bring her in right away. She can't catch her breath. She's in a wheelchair. Should I just take her to the emergency room?"

"No! They will just send her back to us," she said.

"Then why can't I just bring her to you right now?"

"Please hold," she said.

What the fuck? The receptionist put me on hold and Laurence Welk music played. Hot needles ran up and down my body. I couldn't believe what was happening. It was the kind of treatment I imagined having in the ER in the middle of the night. I wasn't in the mood for an inept receptionist.

"Bring her right in. Dr. Hansen will look at her," the reception-ist finally told me.

I said goodbye to John and Hayden, brushed my teeth and looked out the bathroom window for a second. At that moment, a bull moose jumped the fence and ran into the trees. It was only the third moose I had seen on our land in thirteen years. Chills ran through me again. I had imagined moose to be one of my power animals. I didn't know if it was a bad sign or a good one. Perhaps the moose came to remind us that whatever happens is still perfect. I knew in my heart that I was meant to keep the memory. Storey smiled when I told her about the moose.

"Oh, what a beautiful house," I said, wondering if that was going to be the last time Storey would see it, or the last time Storey would feel the van's tires roll over the bumps in our gravel driveway. We made it to the doctor's office in ten minutes. When I opened the door to the waiting area, I felt both relief and a wave of fear. Relieved because Storey was going to get some help, and fear because I knew Storey's condition was dire. I wished I was wearing virtual reality goggles that I could rip off when I wanted the scene to end. Just a week before, Storey and I drove into a handicapped parking space at the Nutcracker Ballet. We laughed because I had to lift her over a chest-high snowbank to get her out of the van.

The nurse hustled us to an exam room. The oximeter on Storey's finger read 60 percent. I didn't know how bad that was until I saw the nurse's face and watched how quickly she inserted a nasal cannula. Storey noticed the nurse's expression and cried. Considering what little oxygen Storey was getting, she still didn't miss anything. Dr. Hansen arrived and we were escorted through a maze to the ER. A different nurse with long, wavy hair taped wires to Storey's chest and kept looking at her oxygen levels. I studied everyone's expressions. White coats floated in and out of the room. Dr. Hansen checked on us between patients. She was familiar with Storey but didn't know us well. I knew her son shared a birthday with Hayden because they had attended the same school.

John came to the ER after he dropped off Hayden. We sat. We waited. We held Storey's hand. Suddenly, her oxygen level dropped further. Alarms went off, white coats rushed in, and Dr. Hansen ordered an intubation. Six people surrounded Storey's bed. Someone zipped the curtain across the bar to hide Storey from the rest of the world.

John and I froze.

"Everyone out!" someone yelled. "Mom, when was the last time she ate?" a white coat asked.

"She had a smoothie this morning," I said.

"She just threw up red stuff," he said, wondering if it had been blood.

"I gave her a raspberry smoothie. She doesn't do well with any kind of anesthesia." A lump formed in my throat. John couldn't find his words either.

"We gave her Fentanyl and Versed," a white coat said from across the room.

I worried that she aspirated while they stuck a tube down her throat, making her situation worse. I was out of my mind. I had no control. The nurse with wavy hair put her hand on my back.

"We can't keep Storey here. She needs to go to a children's hospital," Dr. Hansen told us.

The nightmare morphed both in slow motion and in record speed, then it came to a screeching halt. My stomach dropped. I looked past the beeping machines and out the window. *Maybe I can rip off my goggles now and take Storey to the car.* My head felt like it might explode. Dr. Hansen's words sounded like the teacher in a *Peanuts* film I had loved as a kid. I had to think. John and I paced like broken robots.

"I'm sorry, what?" I said in Dr. Hansen's direction.

"Do you want to go to Great Falls, Seattle Children's, or Primary Children's Hospital in Salt Lake City?" she repeated.

"Aww… what… why can't she stay here?"

"This hospital can't support a child who's intubated. She needs respiratory support at a children's hospital."

"Okay…" I stuttered. "John, what do you think?"

"I guess Salt Lake City, her neurologist is there," he said.

"But, but there's a storm—how do we get there?" I asked.

"We are going to order a flight-for-life to Salt Lake," Dr. Hansen said.

"A small plane in this storm?" I said, twisting my hair.

"Sandee, it will be fine, the flight will come from Salt Lake City. They do this all the time," she said.

"Can I fly with Storey in the life-flight to Salt Lake City?" I asked the nice nurse because Dr. Hansen was distracted.

"There is a weight limit on these flights, so I don't know for sure. You're lucky because you don't weigh much, and neither does Storey," she said.

"What do I bring? I need to gather her medications! Do I bring diapers?" I said while watching large snowflakes blow into the building when someone opened the ER door.

"It's a children's hospital. They have diapers," Dr. Hansen said, writing on Storey's chart.

The thought of flying through a snowstorm in a small aircraft with nothing but my purse was inconceivable, a galaxy beyond my comfort zone.

"John, what do I need to bring? Storey needs tons of stuff. She likes books, her stuffed animals, and her special quilt. She doesn't have those things right now."

I dropped my face on his chest. He and I paced between Storey's room and the waiting room where Kristin and Leslie—Storey's favorite

Eagle Mount swimming volunteer—waited. We mumbled, hugged our friends and tried to wrap our heads around what needed to happen next. Kristin handed us lattes and muffins. I felt like throwing up, but I knew a migraine would make everything worse if I didn't eat something.

It was Friday. Storey was supposed to be swimming with Leslie. I was supposed to be getting a massage. We were not supposed to be in the emergency room fearing our future. Storey was supposed to be like every other beautiful 7-year-old girl who loved pink and ponies.

Meredith called and said she'd fly to Salt Lake City right after her last final. She was always eager to help during her collage breaks. Intuitively she knew what needed to happen next, when to do it, and how efficiently it could be done. I depended on her more than I knew. And Meredith loved to travel. Once, without hesitation, she flew to Johannesburg to rescue her great aunt who was in the hospital with a broken pelvis.

Storey remained unconscious from the anesthesia, and I was grateful that she wasn't watching the madness of the ER or looking at our red, swollen faces. Of course, I couldn't help but worry about the long-term effects of the Fentanyl and Versed, which she hadn't had before. I didn't know that that was the least of our problems.

Mothers do this all the time, I told myself. The EMTs lifted Storey into the ambulance. "Her feet are always cold. Can you put an extra blanket around them?" I asked them.

The storm was worse. Everything had gotten worse. I tried to take a deep breath, but the sideways wind took it from me. I hadn't yet been given the thumbs-up for joining the life-flight. The thought of Storey waking up with strangers, in a smelly hospital, seven hours away from us was beyond any kind of a mother's comprehension. I cried in John's arms, said goodbye to my friends and walked into the storm.

The EMT opened the passenger's door for me. The ambulance driver looked like one of Elaine's boyfriends from *Seinfeld*. I rode to the airport where the pilot would make the final decision of me joining Storey and the flight crew.

We'll make it, they'll let me on the flight. Everything will be okay, I thought, distracting myself from having a nervous breakdown in front of this good-looking driver.

"Are these ambulances fun to drive?" I asked him.

He looked at me like I was crazy, but we both smiled. At least I could still try to get people to smile when I needed one myself.

Yet, everything wasn't going to be okay. The snow had turned to sideways sleet, and we would travel in a loud box right through it, heading into the twilight zone.

The ambulance drove to the tarmac and parked next to a small idling jet. I looked straight at the pilot, who was of generous proportions. He saw the look on my face and said, "Yes, you can go with us. There's a weight limit and you don't weigh much."

Relieved, I tucked my purse under my arm and climbed into the traveling skybox.

Two flight nurses were friendly and casual. They hid any concern about the storm. I reminded them how cold Storey's feet were. They turned the heat up a bit but failed to wrap her toes in an extra blanket. I envisioned a protection of white light around the airplane when the pilot coasted on the tarmac. Under my breath I summoned Archangel Michael for courage and a safe passage through the storm. Even if Michael didn't exist, it helped me relax in that moment. I sat at Storey's head and kept my hands over her ears to block the tremendous noise. Telepathically I told her everything was going to be fine. The plane grew louder and colder. I was buckled in so tight I couldn't get to her numb feet.

Storey was still asleep from the anesthesia when we landed on the hospital roof at ten at night. Once outside, my body shook uncontrollably. I wrapped my hands around Storey's feet hidden under a thin blanket. They were ice.

Why don't people listen to mothers!?

Chapter 53

Fat snowflakes followed the small jet from Bozeman. Storey was rushed into the Primary Children's Hospital Pediatric Intensive Care Unit (PICU). My world spun like I had ridden the 100-year-old rollercoaster at Lagoon Amusement Park. Storey's hospital room was lit with beeping machines. The people in white coats seemed to be speaking a different language, and their moves looked automated. A curtain was pulled, dividing us from a baby in a crib. Bits of broken colored images flashed behind my tired eyes the way I envisioned a high on bad drugs. Machines spoke. Down the hall I heard a child cry.

A smiling volunteer welcomed us and handed me a stuffed moose with a red ribbon that read 2005. *A moose, it must be another good sign.* I thanked her and asked for a heated blanket to cover Storey's frozen, white feet.

"Hi, I'm Linda. I'm going to be Storey's nurse tonight. This chair unfolds to make a small bed. You can sleep there," she said while inserting a feeding tube up Storey's nose. A pediatric respiratory therapist arrived with an apologetic look to suction Storey's lungs. The noise sounded like a helium balloon being blown up and deflated. It woke me from my stupor. Storey moaned. I sang "*Hush little baby…*" and

I thought that was it. I didn't know that the suction torture would happen every three to four hours.

At the 7 a.m., shift change, Linda introduced me to June, the day nurse. Storey was awake for the first time and tried to smile. June mentioned that Storey was doing well, considering. I asked questions about the machines and how to interpret the numbers. The oxygen machine became my new meditative focal point.

The next day Meredith arrived about the same time a new respiratory therapist walked in. He had kind eyes and a teddy bear nature.

"Hi, little one, you should ask your parents for a pony," he said apologetically.

"She has a big pony," Meredith and I said in unison, half smiling.

Then the suction began. The tube in Storey's mouth moved and woke her. I could feel her pain. Eventually she found a happy place and at times could sleep through the treatments.

John and Hayden walked in later that afternoon carrying Storey's favorite pink and purple quilt.

"Hi, Sweetheart," John said. His eyes grew big and teary. Hayden trailed behind him, flapping his stuffed black cat and holding Storey's white stuffed dog. Rarely at a loss for words, Hayden was speechless.

"Here, Storey," he said, waving her dog and ladybug pillow.

"Hayden, this tube is to help Storey breathe. This one is to feed her good things like smoothies," I explained.

After a few days on antibiotics Storey felt better. Her vitals were promising. We imagined being at the PICU no more than a long weekend.

Once John settled into the rhythm of the machines, I walked in slow motion to the parents' showers. It was the first time I saw the reality of the PICU—my head turned side to side observing small, still bodies in beds attached to breathing machines. Many were sedated, few cried. They didn't sedate Storey because of her history with anesthesia and her unknown disease.

How do all these children endure? How is Storey going to endure? These children should be outside running around on this sunny day.

I cupped my hands and closed my eyes under the trickling showerhead. For a second, I was just a mom taking a morning shower. When I opened my eyes, the shower was a stranger. All I knew was that I didn't want to get too familiar with it.

John made reservations for two hotel rooms—one for us and one for Meredith and Hayden to share—at a University Guest House next to Fort Douglas (ironically, my father worked at Fort Douglas while I was growing up). It was a ten-minute walk to the hospital. The Ronald McDonald house was a fifteen-minute bus ride. We wanted to be closer.

Meredith preoccupied Hayden. They rode the bus to the Utah Hogle Zoo. It was important for Hayden to be with us. Storey would want that. His positive outlook and sense of humor was needed to fill in the silence. He provided Storey lightness and gave us strength.

By the end of the weekend a doctor noted that Storey's vitals were better.

"She doesn't need as much assistance getting oxygen," he said. "We'll probably be transitioning Storey to a BiPAP machine."

Being new to the ventilator world, we didn't understand how important that was.

"Storey, you need to cough like this when they take the tube out," I said.

I made coughing noises and she laughed as much as she could; it distracted her and they quickly took out the tube. The look on her face went from trying to smile to very uncomfortable. They placed the BiPAP machine over her nose and mouth. Then her eyes rolled back, and she went to her place where I wasn't invited. She looked more uncomfortable with the BiPAP machine over her mouth and nose than with the tube down her throat. She gasped like she was trying to climb out of water. I couldn't do anything but hold her hand and sing our favorite hummingbird song.

John and I stared at the machine readings. The nurses continued with her feeding and medication schedule. I didn't know what kind of antibiotics she received; perhaps I should have asked and written it down. I didn't want them to know I was neurotic under my veil of calm. I needed to maintain a good relationship with the nurses. They were the lifeline between information and the doctors.

I asked to see Dr. Swoboda. A nurse said she was out of town for two weeks. I looked at John; our hearts sank. We felt lost. Dr. Swoboda was the only doctor who knew anything about Storey. She was our last connection to our reality. This was before efficient computer systems.

"John, I'm going to insist they call Dr. Swoboda wherever she is, to inform her that we are here." Suddenly I didn't care if I was "that" mom.

Less than two days later it was clear the BiPAP machine wasn't giving Storey enough oxygen. Her levels fluctuated instead of maintaining near 95 percent. When her oxygen readings suddenly dropped below an acceptable level, white coats rushed in. The curtain was drawn. John led me away and said, "I can't watch this."

My feet turned back in Storey's direction. I wanted to watch everything that was happening to her. It gave me a sense of control, knowledge. John and I were different that way. I jumped around the curtain to watch them work on Storey like I was at a rock concert.

I whispered, "It's going to be alright, Beauty Queen." I felt her spirit next to me. It was familiar. She was comforting me.

Minutes later, a breathing tube was back in place.

"She was prescribed stronger antibiotics," the PA said.

"Fuck! It looks like we're going to be here for at least another week, maybe through Christmas. It usually takes that long for antibiotics to kick in," I said, looking at John.

"I know," he said.

The respiratory therapist visited every two to three hours. But Storey wasn't waking up. Sometimes she slept for an entire day.

"What does it feel like to get one of these treatments?" I asked the respiratory therapist out of curiosity.

"Years ago, my father was on a ventilator. I asked him what it felt like to be on one and he said that it felt like your life is getting sucked out of you." His teddy-bear eyes looked at the ceiling.

I regretted my question.

The next day Storey remained asleep. Hayden was thrilled when the nurse rolled in a large gaming machine for him to play. I knew he would stay busy while Meredith and I went to Target to buy Christmas toys.

At 9½, Hayden still believed in Santa Clause because he didn't have older siblings to spoil the fun. I didn't want that to be the year he learned the truth. We vowed to make the most of Christmas 2005. I still thought Storey would be discharged before Christmas.

Meredith and I filled a Target shopping cart, and for a moment I forgot why we were there. For a moment, I enjoyed myself. We arrived back at the hospital with bags, smiles and plans. When we walked in Hayden hardly looked up from the giant Game Boy-on-wheels. To my relief, Storey's eyes were open and alert.

"Hi Beauty Queen, look what I have. We are going to decorate your room. You look good. The antibiotics must be working," I said, kissing her forehead.

"Dr. Swoboda was just here," John said.

"What? I thought she was out of town?"

"Kathy said the nurses know little about what is going on with the research doctors."

"When is she coming back? I have a lot of questions for her, and why are you calling Dr. Swoboda Kathy?"

"She will stop by tomorrow," John said.

Meredith and I hung sparkly things above Storey. We placed an artificial lit Christmas tree across from her bed and I draped her neck in a lavender neck warmer. Her room smelled like a spa. Storey tried to smile to show off her room when people entered.

I told Storey that Santa might make a visit. Our nurse Linda corrected me.

"Santa can't come because of the germs his costume might bring, and we can't display flowers or balloons or anything because of potential allergens," she said.

My eyes filled. Storey loved Christmas. I understood the hospital rules. But still, I wished for a Patch Adams-type person to show up. I thought about hospitals that had become second homes to children fighting cancer or other horrible diseases for days, months, years, and where Christmases had become just another day of surviving.

I glanced at Storey and at the machines keeping her alive and wondered how families make it. How many truly made it?

Chapter 54

When I rested next to Storey, the lights on Storey's Christmas tree became a meditative focal point. I pretended the lights were a calling and the machine noises were healing vibrations of the universe.

After Meredith and I turned Storey's room into a Christmas motif, we decorated her and Hayden's hotel room. Hayden asked me if Santa knew he wasn't at our house. John was disappointed that Hayden still believed. Once their room was decorated for Santa's visit, Meredith got out olive oil, gloves, and a hotel shower cap. She asked Hayden to sit in front of the TV. Hayden had forgotten we were still dealing with his head lice.

"Hey, Mom, look, the funny guys are on!" he said, wiggling out of the chair to jump in place. "It's the soup show."

Meredith and I looked at each other and laughed at the irony of the moment.

On my way out to return to Storey's room I glanced back at Meredith and Hayden and smiled. *What would I do without Meredith's help?* The timing of Storey's hospital admission was frighteningly convenient—Meredith was on winter break from college; Hayden and Storey were on Christmas break; I had delivered all my beaded necklaces I made for teachers and therapists; we weren't planning on being in Big Sky that Christmas; and the grandparents were flexible. In a weird way, I felt grateful.

The next day, John's folks arrived. Storey tried to smile when they walked in.

"Hi, Sweetheart," Grandpa John said softly.

John's parents looked troubled. They walked around the small room, fidgeting. Storey's eyes followed their moves. We needed their support, and I wanted Storey to see them. It was hard for any visitor, especially family, to visit a sick child with a breathing tube. We updated them on Storey's stats and possible outcomes. John's dad, now retired, was all too familiar with hospitals. He had always loved to play "spill the puzzle pieces" and laugh with Storey. But when they arrived, the silly Grandpa was replaced by a worried one. Neither of them said much. No one knew what to do. John asked them about their flights. I kept beading.

I always wished my kids—and me, for that matter—grew up with a grandma who had a warm lap, an objective ear, who was goofy, and who smelled like fresh chocolate chip cookies. A grandma who let you be who you were with little instruction even though you often spilled your milk at dinner. But like 99 percent of adults, Storey and Hayden's grandparents, on both sides, lacked experience when it came to a special needs grandchild. They felt helpless. They were distracted. But when we needed their support, they always showed up.

One morning in the hotel breakfast area, as I sipped my watered-down coffee and bit into a white powdered-sugar doughnut, one of Storey's grandparents sat down next to me. After expressing deep sadness, they said, "You and John need to get on with your life."

White powdered sugar flew out of my mouth. There was a pause of silence, wiped my face, took a sip of coffee and said, "This *is* our life."

That grandparent and I were a lot alike. I'm no angel, that's for sure. I, too, have been known to say the wrong thing at the wrong time. In that moment, I disliked them *and* myself. I exited quickly and made it to Storey's bedside in record time. I hugged her and hid my tears.

John's folks stayed a couple days. One day after they left, Storey's school aide Serena arrived with her son, sister, mother, and father. I couldn't wait for Storey to see Serena. They didn't get a chance to hug goodbye before Storey got sick. When Storey saw her, she blinked hello and tried to smile big. Serena held Storey's hand and visited with her like they were still in school. Before Serena and her family left, John, Hayden, Meredith, and I held hands with them and closed our eyes while Serena's mother said a beautiful prayer for Storey. I wished our families knew the power of prayer. To me that prayer felt like one last slice of hope.

When our eyes opened, I could feel how uncomfortable it made John. He couldn't set aside his opinions of religious dogma long enough to appreciate the power of love in a prayer, miracle moments, or the beauty of the unknown. He needed everything to be proven and real. He and I walked through this world differently.

My spirituality comes from mountains, sunsets, animals, and the mysticism of a universe with gods, angels, and guides. My faith works when life sucks. It offers me an understanding that does not include a god who sits above choosing favorites.

Serena kissed Storey's hand. "I love you Storey, get better," she said.

I walked with Serena and her family through the PICU doors that separated sick children from the sunshine. We stopped outside and leaned against the steel railing at the hospital's prayer fountain and looked down at the glowing coins in the water. Serena's dad handed his grandson a penny and he dropped it into the water. I could feel the energy of each coin holding a wish to heal a sick child. All the wishes were the same.

On this unusually warm December day in Salt Lake City, it seemed surreal in contrast to what was happening inside the hospital doors. I didn't want Serena and her family to leave; they embodied a life of normalcy. On my way back to Storey's room, I walked past children crying and laughing, children with bald heads and in wheelchairs, and people in facemasks wiping tears.

Everyone walked with their own shadows.

Chapter 55

My fantasy of driving home on Christmas Eve was just that. Holidays in the PICU were another day of sadness and optimism. On Christmas Eve day, my dad and Valerie planned to drive to Salt Lake City to see us, but the night before Valerie was called to her father's bedside. On Christmas morning my dad left without her and drove east on I-80. A few hundred miles later he got the kind of call no one wants to answer. Valerie's father had left this world on Christmas day.

Grandjack arrived to see Storey in time for Christmas dinner. A Mormon family of a previous patient volunteered and smiled behind steel trays to serve Christmas dinner at the PICU for parents and staff. Everyone sat in chairs arranged in a circle of Merry Christmas whispers and nods. Hayden, being his usual exuberant self, unconsciously performed his hop-skip-fly-through- the-air, across the middle of the circle. His sequence of movements was a welcome familiarity to us. Meredith, John and I looked at each other and cracked up. The rest of the sad faces either wanted in on our secret laughter or wondered what was wrong with this boy leaping across the room in front of everyone. His performance lightened our heavy burden—everyone's heavy burden—for a minute. I wondered if the other parents had a Hayden in their life.

We settled into a routine at the hospital. We gave each other necessary breaks. One of us was always with Storey, except for the middle of the night. John or I arrived around 7:45 a.m., after the nurse's shift change. Later, John exercised at the hotel and I ran the trails above Fort Douglas.

One evening when the sunset was casting the last gold shadows across the dirt trails, I stopped running and looked at the Salt Lake City valley. I wondered how many tragedies and miracles were happening under the same sunset. Then I looked to my right and saw a golden retriever puppy running toward me. I knelt and it ran into my arms. I cried and drank in his puppy breath.

"So sorry I didn't ask if I could pick up your golden. My daughter is sick in the hospital, and I needed some puppy-breath therapy," I said to the puppy's owner, who looked annoyed because I interrupted his dog training.

I wiped my eyes, and the mud from my clothes. The owner hooked a pink leash to his puppy and pulled it away. Storey never left my thoughts, but I'll never forget that second of puppy grace.

The historic brick buildings at Fort Douglas blurred past me when I picked up running speed on my way to the hospital. I admired people who could handle life's stresses without animals or exercise. I thought of my animals at home and wondered if Spirit, Chisel and our cats missed me.

Many evenings we went out for dinner during the nurse's shift change. Our favorite was a local microbrew pub where laughter echoed across the restaurant, contrasting the silent melancholic atmosphere of the hospital cafeteria. John and I found it hard to contain our stress. It usually showed up beyond the hospital doors, like when John was parking.

"There's a good spot," I said, pointing.

"Oh really? Why don't you ever for once in your life stop fucking telling me where to park?" John's face was turning red.

"Why are you so mad? I'm just showing you a good spot."

"Why do you always try to pick a fight?" he asked.

Suddenly I felt ill. Images of Frank and Estelle Costanza from *Seinfeld* bickering like us flashed across my frontal lobe. John usually parked as far away as possible just for spite. Aside from our underlying stress we needed dinners out. Hayden loved entertaining Meredith and the grandparents at dinner. I was always anxious to get back to meet the new night nurse and to kiss Storey goodnight. Seeing a familiar night nurse was always a relief—it meant I didn't have to educate them on Storey's supplement and medication schedule. Most nights John had to peel me out of Storey's bed to go back the hotel.

Having a child in the hospital and staying connected to friends and family was a challenge before good cell phones, CaringBridge, Facebook, or high-speed internet. The hospital computers sucked; my email rarely worked. I called my friends on my morning walk to the hospital and tried to sound encouraging. I didn't want them to worry, but the truth showed in my body. I held back tears around Storey; she was so sensitive. A psychosomatic ball of stress tears formed in my throat (in medical terms it's called a Globus Sensation). My eyes were like sandpaper, and I often felt like there was a clump of eyelashes stuck behind my right eyeball throbbing worse after each cry.

The PICU was always full. When I needed to walk around, I still glanced through open patient doors because... I was nuts and nosy. Across from the nurse's station I noticed a teenager who was always flat on her back. Her beautiful thick, blonde braid draped like Rapunzel's to the floor. Tubes and wires hung out of her body like a spider plant. Since I walked by her several times a day, I made up stories in my mind about her. Eventually curiosity got the best of me.

"Hi, I've seen you here for a while. What is your daughter's condition?" I asked the girl's mother at the morning snack stand.

"She needs a new heart. She has Down syndrome," she replied.

"I'm so sorry!" Both of us left dabbing our eyes with a tissue. I said no more.

Rarely did I see a child who looked like they were going to skip out of the PICU holding their mother's hand and an ice cream cone in the other. None of this made any sense to me. Why did God make snow if these children couldn't be outside building snowmen?

Dr. Swoboda returned and judiciously reviewed Storey's chart and recent history. She reiterated diseases and tests. We had heard it all before and my right eye hurt so badly my mind was mush. Dr. Swoboda never made us feel like Storey was just another mystery. We agreed to another skin biopsy. It was an easy procedure. But John and I remained skeptical.

The three of us discussed possible options and outcomes: an easy eye exam by an ophthalmologist to look for a storage disease; maybe surgically inserting a permanent feeding tube into her stomach; or a tracheotomy letting a portable machine breathe for her—most likely forever. Dr. Swoboda was forthright. She restated her belief that Storey had a progressive neurodegenerative disease, but we still didn't want to hear it. Storey was on her third round of strong antibiotics, and they weren't working. There were few miracles left for someone like Storey who had been intubated for more than ten days. Swallowing and breathing rarely returned as neurodegenerative diseases progressed. We were already doing everything medically possible.

Then Dr. Swoboda mentioned giving Storey a flu shot, something I was skeptical about because of her fragile nervous system. John and I got flu shots each year, but I worried that with Storey's condition a flu shot might wreak havoc on her already weak immune system. Even so, I knew what would happen if Storey got sick with the virus.

"If Storey doesn't get the flu shot, I guarantee you she will get the flu in this hospital. I understand your concern, but I still advise she get the shot," Dr. Swoboda reiterated.

There was no good solution. I looked over at John and then to Storey and realized Storey had thrown up. She understood more than we knew, how scared and trapped she was under machines and tubes that kept her alive. She couldn't even cry. *What are we thinking, talking about all this awful stuff at her bedside?*

Dr. Swoboda advised a procedure of injecting Botox into Storey's saliva glands to slow down the production of saliva and lessen the chances of future aspirations. The procedure sounded dreadful, but Dr. Swoboda's confidence in the staff made us feel better. We wanted her to suffer less in the long term. I thought of Lorenzo—the difference between him and Storey was that he didn't have a breathing tube. John and I agreed to the Botox procedure.

That afternoon, while Hayden was telling me about Fort Douglas and how Grandjack had worked in all the red brick buildings, the nurse arrived holding a flu shot for Storey.

"That looks like an adult vaccine dose. She only weighs 45 pounds. Is that a child's flu shot?" I asked.

"This is what the doctor ordered," Linda said, lifting the bed sheet up and looking for Storey's right thigh.

"Can't you just squirt half of the shot into the garbage and give her the rest?"

"It doesn't work that way."

I had a bad feeling about the shot. I distracted Storey and kissed her forehead. Luckily the shot was quick. Storey's eyes went big when the needle entered her leg muscle and then she closed them. She slept the rest of the day and through her respiratory treatments.

The next day the ophthalmologist arrived to dilate and examine Storey's eyes for any indication of ocular manifestations or systemic features changes (indications of storage diseases). He looked right at me and noticed the patch I had put over my right eye, which still felt like a rock was rolling around in it. I could only see out of my left eye. The ophthalmologist immediately made an eye appointment for me at the Moran Eye Center.

I studied his moves, but before I could blurt out, 'Please put gloves on," he had his hands all over Storey's eyes. I had visions of his hands touching the dirty phone all the visitors used to call for the PICU doors to open; her chart; his face; and tons more stuff on the way over. I felt sick. I shouldn't have had to police the medical staff about the importance of sterilization around a sick child. I was a pain in the ass to some of the staff. I had a right to make sure they were doing as they were trained. Storey's life was on the line. Dr. Swoboda was right; with this carelessness there *was* a high probability that Storey would get the flu. Every time someone entered the room I mentally and energetically pictured a thick bubble of protective healing light around Storey. That kept me a little sane.

The eye doctor prodded and poked in Storey's eyes, still gloveless. Later, his assessment to find markers of a storage disease was inconclusive. Dr. Swoboda continued to brainstorm.

A few days later, one of the good nurses realized Storey's feeding tube had come too far out of her nose, meaning that it wasn't far enough into her stomach. The nurse ordered to have it reinserted under an MRI camera without anesthesia. It took longer than expected and was excruciating for Storey and us. I sang *Hush Little Baby*. John and I were helpless. I wrapped white light around her, around the room and the entire hospital.

For the first time I was glad to be back in her room. I turned on the relaxing music on the TV set, placed Storey's ladybug pillow under her cheek and snuggled her purple and pink quilt around her breathing body.

"Storey, I love you. Now your feeding tube will be much better. I'm right here beading. Just rest."

She slept the rest of the day. I beaded like a mad woman and decided that, between the painful eye exam, Botox insertion, and feeding tube procedure I wasn't going to authorize any more procedures. All of us had had enough.

Hayden and John headed to the roof of the parking lot to drive his remote-control car Leslie had sent. Hayden deserved extra time with us. He never cried or complained about the long hours sitting with Storey. For a kid with ADHD, he sat patiently and lit up when we suggested doing something new. He could ride a city bus around Salt Lake City all day with Meredith and be completely content.

"Mom, do homeless people make enough money? Mom, you'll never let me be homeless, will you?" he asked.

"No, honey, I'll make sure you're never homeless."

Hayden's presence reminded us that our situation was what it was, and how we lived with it made all the difference. Walking through the dark halls to visit Storey after dinner always felt eerie. I couldn't help but wonder how many new kids had been brought in; how many families got bad news or received miracles. I wondered how many children got to go home.

I wondered how many kids were called home.

Storey was as happy as she could be with a breathing tube. When she was awake she always tried to smile, but it was clear to us by the look in her eyes that she wasn't getting better.

Dear *Mom*,

I want you to know I was having a lot more fun in the hospital than you and Dad. Some of the children and I left our bodies and floated around the PICU. We'd hug our parents and send love into their hearts. Sometimes we'd play Uno or Jacks and talk about our options of staying or leaving this world. Other times we played in the rooms of the sickest kids to keep them company. We were able to be more present than if we weren't sick. We could feel and see the love of our mommies and daddies and quickly returned to our bodies when they needed us. Many of us felt so much love it was hard to leave our bodies to go play.

Thank you for loving me so much,

Storey

My Dearest Pink Lover *Storey*,

My heart heals knowing you had fun with friends in the PICU. Sometimes I felt you leave.

I love you to the hummingbirds, to the stars, and to the universe and back,

Mom

Chapter 56

"Did you have a good New Year's Eve?" the nurse asked when we walked in.

New Year's Eve is my least favorite celebration dating back to the high school parties I thought I needed to attend. Back then, New Year's Eve meant dodging single teenage guys who thought the stroke of midnight was an open invitation to French kiss single girls. New Year's also meant a raging morning headache. Years ago, I made a New Year's resolution to always feel good on the first day of the year.

I thought the nurse's question was odd. It was no time for us to be celebrating and she knew it. We had plenty of time to watch the New Year's ball drop at Times Square before saying goodnight to Storey. When we heard a click from the overhead speakers, we assumed we would hear "Happy New Year." Instead, we heard *"Code Blue!"* Frenetic footsteps and flashes of white passed our door. I looked at the nurse, she bowed her head. I peeked behind the curtain to the 18-month-old baby with Down syndrome sleeping with a CPAP. His mother and I exchanged half smiles. We knew too much.

A few mornings later Grandjack, Meredith, and Hayden packed to head to Bozeman. Hayden's Christmas break was ending. Meredith offered to stay with Hayden until we came home with Storey.

They came to the hospital one more time to say goodbye. Luckily, Storey was lucid and smiling.

Hayden kissed her forehead. "Goodbye Storey, I'll see you back home later." He smiled and looked to John for approval. John and I felt our anchor pulling away. We walked to Grandjack's car with them.

"Hayden, Storey loves you so much. She is so proud to have you for a big brother. Do what Meredith says. Give the cats a lot of attention. We will see you soon, I love you." I loosened my hug and reached out my hand.

"Mom, can I play my Game Boy at home?" he asked, smiling.

"Yes, after your homework."

There's never enough time, and often too much time, for goodbyes. The space between Hayden's front teeth seemed smaller. I shut the car door, kissed my fingers, and touched the outside of the passenger's window.

I didn't want to go back to the hospital room. John and I walked past the pennies sparkling in the fountain next to the hospital entrance. I felt lost, confused, frightened. I pictured my dad driving too fast between Pocatello and West Yellowstone while explaining the different years of clear-cut forests to Hayden and Meredith.

Storey was asleep when we walked into her room. John opened *The Wall Street Journal.* I turned up the classical music channel on the TV, rested back in the chair/bed and stared at the pattern on the ceiling. Layers of dots jumped and danced like I was looking through a toy viewfinder. *What am I going to do without Hayden?* The teddy bear-like PA walked in.

"How's it going?" he whispered.

"Well, the last few days she seems to be breathing without a lot of aid. They have been running trials to see how long she can go without oxygen assist. Sometimes she can go four hours, so we are hopeful," John said. He let out a breath and looked up at the machines.

"This is good, considering she has a neurodegenerative disease," the PA said. "She will be leaving the hospital with a lot more equipment than when she arrived."

"She hasn't been diagnosed with a neurodegenerative disease," I snapped. "I wish everyone would quit saying that's what she has. She needs to get better so we can take her home." My body shook.

I knew he was right.

Fuming, I walked out to get a dry powdered sugar doughnut from the 10:00 a.m. snack cart. Storey was awake when I got back. I smiled and kissed her forehead, then read her the Sunday comics. When I chased the dry doughnut with bad coffee, it finally dawned on me how inconsiderate I'd been for eating in front of Storey. She loved food. She belonged to "The Mills Clean Plate Club." Hayden and I were the thin, picky eaters. I exhaled, dropped my shoulders, tossed the remaining doughnut in the trash, wiped my mouth, and smiled at Storey.

A week later Dr. Swoboda, John and I visited with the PICU doctor on duty. Storey was almost done with her third round of strong antibiotics. They studied Storey's chart and directed us to a private room. Behind the first door, the mother of the daughter waiting for a heart sat alone and wept. Behind the second door, a parent was sleeping in a chair. Behind the third door, four chairs and a table waited for us. I pulled out an old chair and wondered how many life-altering conversations had taken place in this stale, windowless room.

Dr. Swoboda began. "You know at this point it's likely will NOT find out what is wrong with Storey. Unfortunately, many kids in similar situations remain undiagnosed; some live short lives, some long. Genetics are advancing quickly but not as fast as I'd like. There is hope in the future to find a diagnosis and perhaps a treatment for kids with rare diseases. But we have come to a dangerous crossroads with Storey. She has been intubated for three weeks. Her throat is swollen; her lungs and brain have grown to depend on the machine to breathe for her."

My right temple and eye pounded. I dropped my face into my hands. John wiped his tears and tapped his fingers together.

"Let's do a few more breathing trials and see how long she can go without added oxygen. However, we can almost certainly say Storey has a progressive neurodegenerative disease. I know that is not what you want to hear. Rarely do patients come out of these situations and go home without a tracheotomy. And when these kids do go home, they are back in the PICU at every illness."

I couldn't see across the room. Both my eyes were burning.

A few minutes later I said, "John and I don't want to put in a trach or feeding tube. I know in my heart she will not survive a tracheotomy and/or an esophagogastroduodenoscopy surgery. We don't want her to die on the operating table or without us."

Dr. Swoboda heard me through my semi-hyperventilating breath. John reached for my hand and squeezed. He shook his head in agreement. He couldn't speak.

"Deep down I know that Storey has a progressive disease. If her life depends on a breathing tube and feeding tube, when does it end? When doesn't it end? We'd never do that to an animal. John and I know Storey wouldn't choose that. Neither of us would choose that.

Who would choose that?" I said, looking down at my fingers tearing at my shirt hem, then I looked up at Dr. Swoboda.

John and I fought about parking spaces and how to make a bed, but fortunately we agreed on this. We looked at each other through a veil of tears. I just wanted to go back to Storey's room and lie next to her.

"Let's just see how she does through this week with the rest of the antibiotics and do a couple more breathing trials," I said.

"Okay, we will take an X-ray toward the end of the week," the PICU doctor glancing at Dr. Swoboda.

I mumbled thanks. John and I knew that this conversation was inevitable. We left holding hands.

When we entered Storey's room, I listened to a message on my phone from my dad. They had made it back to our house. Dad had turned right around and headed back to us to meet Valerie at the airport the next day.

All I wanted to do was curl up next to Storey in her bed, wrap my arms around her and fall asleep. I didn't want: anyone around, new advice, beeping machines, smart doctors, drool suctions, diarrhea, decisions, alternative medicine, or sad faces. I just wanted to fall asleep next to Storey forever.

Chapter 57

The next day the respiratory therapist let me stay in bed with Storey during her treatment—a horrific event, that after weeks had begun to seem normal. I wrapped the room with light and whispered, *"Hush Little Baby..."* The therapist mentioned that he had hoped by now Storey's lungs didn't need to be cleared as often. John sat in the chair next to us reading his newspaper; sad, helpless.

Grandjack returned with Valerie the next day. Storey woke and gave a courageous smile when they entered her room. We updated them on the antibiotic plans for the rest of the week. My dad cleared his throat and did what always made him feel comfortable: he gave us a brief history on antibiotics. I half smiled. *Yeah, yeah, whatever,* I wanted to say. *I just want the goddamn antibiotics to work, I don't care about how far science has come. As far as I'm concerned, it hasn't come far enough.* Valerie read to Storey. Without a design, I slipped beads on strings and glanced up at a grandmother reading to her grandchild. I knew I'd never see that moment again.

"Storey just had a little trauma. Two people came and took ten milliliters of blood that Dr. Swoboda had ordered to bank for genetic research. They drew the blood from the inside of her leg because they couldn't find a vein in her arms," John told us when my dad and Valerie and I returned after dinner.

"What?" My throat tightened; I shrank to her bed. "I wouldn't have left her side had I known they were going to do that."

"She's okay. I held her hand and talked to her. It went fast," John said.

I was helpless. My world spun. Storey didn't look like she was getting any better after almost four weeks in the PICU. Her skin began to turn translucent, and she slept most of the day.

She smiled less.

The next morning, I got up early and called Kristin. She said she would ask our yoga friends to send healing energy from class. I wished I could be there; I needed relief. My shoulders were knots, my naturally flexible body was tight, my muscles ached, and my head and throat never stopped hurting. I felt like I had the flu.

Over the next few days, I called for a miracle. A miracle to walk through the door like a man on a white horse. I did everything I could to help Storey feel relaxed. I kept New Age and classical music playing on the TV. I wrapped the room and everyone who walked in with white light. I silently prayed. And I tried to replace fear and frustration with presence and love. I still believed; not believing meant I had given up. Doctors never used the word "miracle" because it meant they believed in something other than science. A couple nurses I befriended talked about miracles they had witnessed over the years. Yet I saw the look in their eyes when they looked at Storey—they, too, silently wished. I knew hope and love were the same thing. I wouldn't let that go. It was all I had left.

The night before Dad and Valerie left, they wanted to take me to Park City where I first rode K2 skis with numb toes in shiny red boots with laces and two buckles. The drive was another nostalgic outing with my dad. More than thirty-five years had passed since I walked Park City streets with him. That warm January day looked promising. The day before, Storey had gone seven hours without needing added oxygen, which meant there was a possibility to transition her from intubation to a BiPAP machine. By the time dad parallel-parked on Main Street in Park City, I felt panicky. I didn't want to be there. Thirty-three miles away from Storey felt like three hundred, and I knew how long my father could spend in art galleries. We walked past shops, in and out of galleries, and stuck our heads into the Old Saloon.

Restless and trying to hide my anxiety, I said, "Dad, we need to go. It looks like it is going to snow any minute, and I want to get back."

He cleared his throat. "What, already? There are more galleries to visit," he said with a chuckle.

My phone read 4:30 p.m., and I knew the ski traffic would slow the drive. I looked up at the large snowflakes falling from thick clouds. I felt sick. I wrapped the car in light as we drove through heavy, slushy snow. Storey never left my thoughts. The wipers were at full speed. I knew they weren't going to fail thanks to Dad's road trip protocol of keeping everything in tip-top shape. By mile marker 25, I relaxed knowing I'd be kissing Storey's beautiful face before the 7:00 p.m., nurse shift change.

I walked past the girl with the long blonde braid on my way to Storey's room.

"Hi, Sweetheart, I'm sorry I was gone so long," I said, kissing her forehead.

I looked up and noticed John's long and swollen eyes.

"What's wrong!?"

"They just did another lung X-ray. One of her lungs is collapsed," he said.

"What? What? How did that happen, she did so well yesterday! HOW DOES THIS HAPPEN?"

"It means the antibiotics aren't working… she isn't going to ever recover," John whispered, facing away from Storey.

"But she did well in the breathing trial, she was basically breathing on her own for eight hours," I said, shaking.

I wanted to shake the nurse and ask why this happened. I put on my clown smile and faced Storey. I noticed she struggled to breathe even with the machines. I took my shoes off and slid my body into bed next her. I weaved my fingers around her left hand and pulled the blankets to our chins. John sat in the chair next to us. He reached for my hand.

"She can't live like this. No one should have to," I whispered.

In five years, there were only a couple times it truly looked as though Storey was going to recover from whatever was going on. We both knew her body was failing her. And I'm sure she knew it too.

I closed my eyes. My body shook. I let denial drop away and allowed the truth to surface. She really *did* have a progressive neurodegenerative disease.

John didn't have to say anything. An hour later I slid out of the bed so we could talk in the hall. We asked the nurse to call in the counselor in residence. She arrived within fifteen minutes. The counselor's young face was familiar; in the last few weeks she had visited Storey's room a few times.

"In your experience, we're wondering if it's best for the siblings to be part of this dying process in the long run?" I asked her.

WOW! I said it. Dying… Storey is going to die. Startled by my own words, I buried my face in my hands.

"We have found it is best to include the siblings if you're willing," the young counselor said.

The counselor said more, but that was all I remembered. That was all I needed to know.

"Okay, that's what we want, we haven't hidden anything from Hayden so far. I know you have probably seen this many times. We just needed a little affirmation. Thank you," John said.

John and I wanted Hayden there. This was and would always be part of his life story. At

9½, Hayden had already experienced more than any of his friends, and he was still happy. He and Storey were old souls who always shared their light, even in sadness.

> *Storey,*
>
> I can't write anymore. My body feels beat up, like I have the flu, but I don't.
>
> *Mom*

> *Mom,*
>
> I'm right here on your left side sending love to your heart. You can do this.
>
> I love you further than hummingbirds can fly,
>
> *Storey*

Storey,

I have always depended on you for strength. How much more can I take from you?

Mom

Mom,

My supply—the supply—is infinite. Remember our love is forever.

Storey

P.S. Ask Hayden, he gets it.

Chapter 58

You're doing the right thing for your daughter. I wish more parents had your courage. We see kids with degenerative diseases suffer with little quality of life spending their last days, sometimes years, in the hospital because parents don't agree—or they can't let go," the doctor said through tears.

My eyes felt like rust; I couldn't open my right eye. I squinted at John, then at Storey. Over the last five days, she had awakened very little. When I touched her body, it felt stagnant. Her light had dimmed. Her energy had slowly dissipated like sage smoke. I realized I couldn't remember the last time her beautiful blue eyes had glanced into mine. My head felt like it was being clamped. Memories of Storey spun. I reached out to grab pieces of our life with Storey, but the time had slipped through my fingers like rice.

"John, is she going to wake up before they take out the tube? I want to see her eyes. Her smile. I know once they place the BiPAP over her nose and mouth she will close her eyes forever. What happened to the last seven and a half years? A monstrous disease slowly took our princess, and it doesn't even have a fucking name."

"I don't know," John sighed.

Storey's neurodegenerative disease was evidently rare, yet for years we feared and denied the words. Then we were forced to embrace them.

I squinted and looked out the window. It was dark. Fat snow-flakes falling under the parking lot lights looked like a scene from a horror movie. I turned and looked at the clock I had grown to hate. It read 7:00 p.m.

Nurse Maria's shift began, and she stood in the door frame, speechless.

I slid into bed next to Storey's sleeping, warm body. I gently rested my hand on her right hand which held her IV. John tucked pillows around us.

"Sweetheart, the doctors are going to take the tube out for good. Then they will put the BiPAP over your nose and mouth one last time to test if your lungs are strong enough to function with it. Hayden and Meredith will be back. I will not leave your side," I whispered, squinting at the bouncing lights on Storey's Christmas tree.

I looked at Storey as the tube was being pulled out of her throat. She took a labored breath. Her eyes slightly opened. The respiratory therapist softly placed the BiPAP mask on her swollen face, trying to avoid the red marks the tape holding the breathing tube had made.

"Sweetheart, it is going to be okay. Mommy is here."

Storey closed her eyes for the last time.

I lied. Nothing about this was okay.

The machines beeped. Maria turned down the volume, but their noises echoed in my head. As anticipated, Storey's oxygen level imme-diately dropped. Maria adjusted the BiPAP.

John sat awkwardly next to Storey, rubbing her leg, then mine. Maria knew we were waiting for Meredith and Hayden to arrive the next day.

"Tomorrow is going to be an exhausting day. I suggest you both get some sleep in one of the parent bunkrooms," Maria said.

I looked at her like she was out of her mind.

"There is no fucking way I'm leaving Storey's side on the last night she is going to be on this earth," I said, looking at the tree.

I knew Maria was only trying to help. But I didn't care how tired I'd be. I had the rest of my life to sleep without Storey. My arms snuggled Storey's life like a mother otter floating nowhere.

Around 10:00 p.m., John closed his eyes and tried to sleep in the uncomfortable chair next to the bed. Eventually he went to a bunkroom. One of us needed to function the next day. The machine sounds ping-ponged between my ears. I could hear Maria's footsteps between us and the boy with Down syndrome. There were no more horrific experiments, no more blood draws, no more tests.

No more hope.

This was our first quiet night in the hospital in three and a half weeks. I kissed Storey's cheek over and over. I tried to turn the BiPAP machine noise into a pleasant white-noise sound. I imagined we were watching the Yellowstone Falls and Storey was sitting in my lap.

Storey drifted in and out of her body. She grew pale. I studied the little ornaments hanging above her bed. When I closed my eyes, images and sounds bounced around: beeping, faces, white coats, sounds of inflating balloons, intercom announcements, running feet. Every half hour I opened my eyes to delete the images and touch Storey's face just to make sure she was still there.

She knew I was.

Linda, our favorite nurse, returned in the morning. She smiled; she thought we'd be gone. I was grateful when the morning light snuck in through the blinds. It made our nightmares seem a pinch better.

John and I knew we had made the right choice. And, in my heart, I knew Storey thanked us. Storey was a beautiful star. Doctors, nurses and visitors liked to loiter in her room. They felt her love. Perhaps her love energy was so brilliant, it was too hot for the DNA of her physical body. In just seven years, Storey shared a lifetime of love. I knew her love wouldn't die with her body. Her job was done here; mine was not. I was still trying, learning her teachings—how to love.

In dark moments I doubted myself. I imagined Storey living longer, hooked to machines like so many children whose parents couldn't let go. Storey could possibly live like that for years until she caught the flu. When would it end? If she could breathe on her own, we would have had a gastrostomy performed. If she could have swallowed, we would have had a tracheotomy performed.

The morning of January 10th, 2006, John slid in next to Storey and I slid out. On the way to the bathroom, I glanced over at Storey's roommate sleeping, his mother steadfast in the chair next to him.

"Is there anything I can do?" she asked.

We hugged and she handed me a wooden block with the word *FAITH*. "I want you to have this." We had become friends; our wordless fears had woven together.

I tried to keep my composure when I called Meredith in Bozeman. "Storey is not going to make it. Her lungs are collapsing. Last night we authorized the doctors to take out the breathing tube and put her on the BiPAP machine to see if she could survive, but it isn't enough, it won't work. We want you and Hayden to be with us."

Meredith had an innate talent for knowing what needed to be done. I didn't have the strength to do anything more than lie in bed with Storey and tell the nurses what to do.

Meredith called back quickly. "We got a flight in the afternoon landing in Salt Lake around six o'clock and we'll taxi to the hospital. Hayden keeps asking me, why are we going back? It is just breaking my heart. I don't know what to say," she said.

"Just tell him we want him here with us."

"It's so hard. I'm soooo sorry!" Meredith cried. "I'll drop Chisel off at the Careys on my way to the airport, and Libby will check on the cats and horses. I love you."

I remained in bed with Storey all day. Staff on duty stopped by to give us a hug, including Dr. Swoboda. All of us knew the BiPAP machine wasn't enough, and that we had chosen to listen to our guts and take no more extreme measures to keep Storey's broken body alive. They all respected our choice.

Around seven o'clock, Hayden and Meredith walked into Storey's room. I got out of bed and ran to Hayden. I didn't want to let him go. He wiggled out of my embrace.

"What is going on?" he asked, looking at John then Meredith, sobbing. "Why didn't you tell me? Why didn't you tell me?"

John and I knelt and held his hands. He was wearing his favorite oversized blue sweater with an embroidered black airplane on the front.

"Hayden, we had to take the tube out of Storey because it wasn't helping her get better. They put this machine over her nose and mouth so she could breathe until you arrived. She can't live like this anymore. You were such a good brother to her. She loves you very much, always remember that." I squeezed his hands, sat on the back of my calves and feet, and pulled him into my lap.

"I don't want her to die. I was mean to her when she was little," Hayden cried.

"You were not mean to her at all; you were a nice big brother. You let her play with your cars and trucks. She knows you love her, and she loves you very much. The love between you and Storey is forever."

John sat down on the edge of the bed and Hayden climbed into his lap. Hayden wiped his runny nose with the sleeve of his blue sweater. I slid back into bed next to Storey, folded her stiff fingers around my thumb, and rested my hand over hers. She was fading.

Hospital murmurs floated in and out of the room. I asked Linda to raise the back of the bed to forty-five degrees and stuff pillows behind my back to hold Storey comfortably in my arms. The PA on duty, who we had only met once, paced in the hall. It was 7:20 p.m.

Linda must have seen the looks in our eyes because she immediately said, "I'll stay."

I nodded my head. I wondered how many times these nurses had witnessed families, especially mothers, explode into a million pieces while their child's soul left them. Left this world.

"Hayden, now that you are here, we are going to take the BiPAP machine off Storey's face. She will take her last breath," I said.

Hayden didn't say anything. His swollen eyes grew big.

"You are a wonderful brother to Storey. She loves you so, so very much. Let's share fun stories of the time we had together," John said as he hugged Hayden. "Remember all the times you and Storey threw rocks in the rivers? You piled rocks next to Storey for her to toss. Remember lining up your cars and trucks in the living room and you asked her, 'Storey do you like trucks?'"

"'Yes,' she'd say. And I'd say, 'No Storey, you like busses,'" Hayden replied, wiggling his fingers.

"Remember all the fun walks on our road and Licorice would ride in Storey's lap? Remember watching *Toy Story, Clifford, Seinfeld,* and going to Dairy Queen?" John continued.

I was speechless. I was uncomfortable in the bed as Storey's body grew heavy. I moved to the big chair and John handed Storey back to me as though she was my newborn baby. John picked up her quilt and wrapped it around us, and tucked pillows under my arms and back. Storey's head rested on my left shoulder and her legs draped over the side of the right armrest. I couldn't keep my burning eyes off her.

John and Hayden continued to tell stories to distract all of us. But we all watched as Linda slowly walked toward the beeping machines. She pushed a couple buttons, then moved to another machine and touched the screen what seemed like fifty times. The noise in the room—which had kept us all on alert for almost four weeks—dissipated, like a rollercoaster shutting off. A last beep… and then came an eerie quiet. None of us said anything.

Linda and another nurse carefully lifted the BiPAP mask from Storey's face like she was redressing a war wound. A red mark on Storey's forehead appeared where the mask was too tight. *She must have felt like she was drowning.* In the darkness, Storey gasped for air. Her eyes rolled back. Her torso flexed. Her head and body went heavy. A rush of energy filled me. *Is this the miracle, like in the movies where someone miraculously takes a deep breath then opens their eyes and smiles, and everyone cheers?* But Storey's eyes didn't open, and she gasped again, and again, and again…

"What is happening? Why is Storey gasping? We don't want her to suffer any longer!" I shouted in Linda's direction.

We assumed she would peacefully stop breathing. No one warned us this would happen.

"It's her body's neurological response to breathe. Sometimes this happens," Linda whispered.

"Can't you give her something to help her? Morphine? Anything?" I asked. "How long does this go on?"

"Probably about twenty minutes. I'll call the PA on duty and see if we can give her a little morphine. I'll also call the clergy on duty if you'd like."

I half nodded. My head throbbed with each of Storey's half heart-beats. Hayden stayed in John's lap. John wiped his face. Meredith gave us some space.

Storey's big front teeth were uneven, and her left tooth was shorter from the tube pushing against it. Her lips were swollen and cracked. A few minutes later Linda arrived with a syringe.

"The PA on duty approved a small amount of morphine, just enough for Storey to relax a little, but not too much."

"Too much to do what? I asked.

Storey continued to gasp. The morphine did nothing.

My "keep your shit together" resources were almost used up. I wanted to be present and remember every detail. I wanted to witness Storey's spirit float out of her body like a breeze. I wanted to see her wings. To see her smile. To see her wave goodbye.

But… Storey kept gasping for air.

"It's okay, Storey, you can leave now, you don't have to feel this pain anymore, we will be okay. You can let go," John and I said, over and over.

But every few seconds, another gasp. Her body got heavier. The clergywoman on duty arrived and introduced herself. I hardly looked up. Fifteen minutes later John asked her to leave—it wasn't our style.

I looked up at the clock on the wall. Two hours had gone by. Hayden hadn't had anything to eat besides a soda since he got on the flight in Bozeman. I, too, was starving; hunger and stress pains shot through my stomach. Not only did I feel like I was leaving my body; I wanted to. I wanted to go with Storey. I needed food, sugar, or to barf.

"Hayden, why don't you and Meredith go to the cafeteria and get some snacks. But I want you to know that Storey might take her last breath while you're gone. It's okay, you can leave. I know you are hungry."

Hayden lit up a bit. This experience was horrific. We always told him the truth; we felt any mystery around Storey's illness and death would leave greater psychological scars. We felt in the long run that this would be a healthier way to process the experience.

"Hayden, I want you to give Storey one last kiss on her forehead so we can take your picture," I whispered.

Hayden lowered his head and kissed Storey's forehead for one last time. John took several pictures with my small digital camera.

"She loves you very much," I repeated, telling myself to freeze-frame the image of Hayden and Storey's last tender moments. Then Hayden wrapped his right arm around my neck.

"Okay, we will hurry. I'll get some good snacks, and peanuts for you, Mom," he said.

"Can Storey have more morphine?" I asked Linda.

I looked over at Linda, then noticed the PA (who we didn't know) on duty standing back, peeking around Storey's door. *What a coward. I'm the one with a dying child in my arms and you won't introduce yourself or offer more morphine. What are you afraid of, a lawsuit?* But I didn't have the energy to fight.

We hoped each of Storey's long, labored breaths would be her last.

"You can let go now, we'll be okay," John and I kept saying.

Storey had already suffered enough; there was no turning back. If we suddenly changed our minds and insisted on a tracheotomy, she would live with severe brain damage.

As a loving society, most of us would never let our dogs, cats, or horses suffer like this because it's "inhumane." But we keep people alive; we watch people suffer; we watch people die slow, painful deaths. We, selfishly, give them just enough food to keep their broken bodies alive on a frayed string of hope because we can't let them go. Because we *don't* want to grieve.

"WHERE'S THE GODDAMN MORPHINE?" I yelled.

Chapter 59

Breathing is the first and last physical act of our body's intelligence. It gives us life and takes it away.

Storey's death rattle continued for two and a half hours. We knew Storey was offered less than the legal maximum amount of morphine because the legal amount might have "killed" her. And it infuriated us.

I kept my right hand on Storey's chest and summoned the energy and strength of White Buffalo Calf Woman.

"It's okay, Storey, you can let go now…"

Death stories swam in my mind. I had flashbacks of my sick childhood dogs that I kissed before my mom took them to the vet, never to return. Most recent was our last guinea pig, whose body was dug up by the neighbor's dog. I thought about my grandparents who died of "old age" when I was young. For a month in grade school my friends and I walked around the chalk outline of a 9-year-old neighborhood boy who was hit by a car on his way to school. I remembered how sidelined I was in college when a guy I had dated and loved, died of cancer.

And now, it only seemed like last month when Storey returned to the hospital with fever and diarrhea at 2 weeks old. Where did the last hard seven and a half years go? I spent so much time trying to heal her, I lost time. Time together.

If only I could read her one more book on the couch, to watch her look up and giggle as she pointed to something funny on a colorful page.

Each one of Storey's labored breaths sounded to me like she was being tortured. It was brutal. I wanted Storey free. John and I, and most certainly Hayden, weren't prepared to watch our princess gasp— much less degenerate for five and a half years. The only thing that comforted me was that I could feel her spirit outside her body, hanging around and waiting for her last disconnect breath.

With the little vision I had from swollen, red eyes, I noticed my red shirt. I had unconsciously chosen to wear red: the color of blood, heat, power. I wanted Storey to see me wearing her favorite color, pink. I wanted her to remember me as a mother who was still colorful and smiled on her worst days.

Then I reminded myself that Storey would forgive me for being human, for doing the best I could with the resources and personality I brought with me when I arrived on this earth. We were in this together. We had a contract to become better people. I was her mother, but she was and would continue to be my teacher and guru—showing me how to love like a golden retriever. But I knew it would take me ninety-plus years to learn what Storey learned in fifteen minutes, sharing her toys in the pool when she was 2 years old.

A few different mystics and healers said Storey was a Bodhisattva, a term originated from Buddhism. There are many definitions: One worthy of nirvana but postpones it to help others; someone who has an abundance of compassion and offers light by their own sacrifice and presence. When Storey was 3 years old, she said to me, "Mom, give Hayden a hug," when I was upset with him for being messy.

Hayden and Meredith returned at 9:39 p.m., with a tray of snacks. Hayden smiled at me, then all of us looked at Storey a second later. She hadn't taken a gasp breath in about fifteen seconds. Then she gasped differently, and the corners of her lips turned up.

"She smiled!" John said. The room filled with cold silence. I looked up and waved, hoping to see her spirit rise like an angelic cloud. But I knew she had made the journey out of her body little by little, until there was just a thin stream of her spirit that finally broke with her last smile at 9:40.

"Hayden, I think she waited for you to return. I'm so glad you are here. Storey, I love you forever," I whispered, waving up to the ceiling.

"I love you, Storey," Hayden repeated.

John wiped his tears. "I love you, Princess."

"I love you, Storey," Meredith said.

My body cramped under Storey's weight. John lifted her back onto the bed and I closed her eyes completely and crawled in next to her. I expected someone to enter and say, "Time of death…" but the nurses gave us space. Hayden watched every move I made. My throat locked up. I didn't know what to do next. I wanted to lie next to Storey forever and read her books. Hayden touched Storey's limp hand with one finger.

"Storey, we will never forget you and we will always love you," John said again.

A few minutes later, a nurse asked if we wanted to donate her organs. In unison, John and I said "yes." There was no question Storey would want to help others.

My body felt like a punching bag and a pincushion, and I knew if I didn't get something to eat, I'd have severe stomach cramps and a week-long migraine. I forced myself to eat. Each bite of a yogurt pretzel gagged my dry mouth. And in the horror of the situation, I heard the words, "these pretzels are making me thirsty," a *Seinfeld* line. My knees buckled. I crumbled to the floor my eyes were swollen and burning, and I couldn't get up.

Meredith took all the cards and posters off the wall and unhooked the streamers from above Storey's bed. For the last time I slid a comb through Storey's beautiful hair and nuzzled my nose around her neck. Slowly I braided her silky hair and cut off the braid. *She's not going to be as pretty for the person doing the autopsy,* I thought.

Then John laid with Storey and closed his eyes. Our little princess was gone, and we still didn't know why.

Thinking about an autopsy on our child made John and I feel ill, but we were still hoping to find a name for this fucking disease and ultimately a closure.

Dr. Swoboda visited around midnight. She apologized for the PA's lack of assistance and assured us that our banked blood would be studied and analyzed as the science of genetics progressed. She was more than hopeful the autopsy would provide some answers.

I was amazed by how well John kept his composure for more than an hour while talking to the Salt Lake City organ donation bank. The Moran Eye Center concluded that Storey's eyes would make perfect cornea donations for two older folks. Because of Storey's undiagnosed disease, her major organs didn't qualify for donation. I had hoped that one of the children in the PICU waiting for a heart would receive hers. Months later I learned that a 5-year-old girl did receive Storey's heart valve.

With some food in my stomach, I was almost able to dodge a massive headache. I couldn't believe how much stuff had accumulated in

Storey's room. I tossed Storey's kneepads and leg braces in the trash without thinking they could be passed onto another child. We donated her wheelchair. A cart held Storey's Christmas tree on the mounds of stuff we had collected. When we were done, we stood around, wondering what was next. It was 1:00 a.m. Storey's body was white and still, her head was to the side, her closed fists rested near her face. For a second, I thought she was sleeping. I expected someone to arrive, to tell me she was alive and they would safely buckle her in her car seat. I wanted someone to tell me I was hallucinating. I cuddled every feathery detail. I looked at John and Meredith. I hugged Hayden. He was tired and speechless. Unknowingly, he had just stepped into an adult role; to be steadfast with courage and humility, and to be the smiling glue for his parents in their new world of horrific grief.

Gently, I cupped Storey's beautiful face in my hands and gave her one last triangle kiss. "I'll love you forever, and please send me pink signs you're with me because I will be noticing."

My eyes felt as though I had been in the desert during a windstorm. I had no more tears. My brain had shrunk under pressure and a softball of emotions was still stuck in my throat. My weighted feet shuffled across the floor.

Storey was free to fly, run, ride horses, swim; to be a spirit of her choosing. She went back to a place we weren't invited. I felt a blanket of Storey's love drape around us. Her last gift. A gift to be shared. We took turns kissing her forehead. I softly opened my hand until just the tips of our fingers touched.

I had to let go…

I had to let her… go.

She was free from a broken body. Long dark eyelashes softly framed her eyes that would give eyesight to two others. She was our precious daughter for a second in a lifetime. She was not ours to keep in this world.

My feet dragged away from her room. I sank into my heavy body, and then turned back for one last look. She wondered if she was just sleeping. I felt her love follow me down the hall, no disease could take our love away.

> Dearest Pumpkin, Beauty Queen, Artichoke Lover, Sweetheart, Princess *Storey*,
>
> In the dark, grieving hour of 3:00 a.m., my soul was pulled to a sliver of light. There I saw a holograph of your beautiful face and heard your giggle. My arms grew to you like "Elastigirl"; our souls puzzled together. We have bodies, and we don't. Our love is a love only a mother and daughter can feel.
>
> Illuminated by your light, I saw you are an avatar and through the essences of time you ripple love to heal lost souls. I saw you with your star friends who also lived short childhoods, and their light shines brighter too. I know you and your friends don't want your parents to be sad. Your star friends send messages to their grieving mothers and fathers that they are healed and happy, and in a twinkle of time, they will all be reunited.
>
> All those nights I kneeled by your bed and prayed to whomever was listening, all those times I searched to heal your body, to keep you with me in this life... now I understand. Your body was perfect all along. Our life was perfect.

Wishing I could have stayed forever next to you in your bed, you smiled at me. Perhaps my prayers were answered. Perhaps the gods listened and healed you and you ascended into a perfect bliss.

It's time for me to return to my darkness... to let you go again.

I love you, forever in a world,

Mom

Dear Mom, *Mommy*,

I didn't want to let go either. When our hands separated for the last time, an angel reached for mine. She held me, and we watched all of you walk out of the hospital room. I want you to know I was never in much pain and when I took that last breath, I felt an indescribable wave of lightness and love. But I saw a part of your soul break off when my physical body died. I know you're a "tough cookie" (as Grandma Pat would say), but I didn't want you to be sad for very long. I want you to know that I went to a beautiful place—a place where we're all together, a place that humans can't know. Many angels sent you extra love during your grief and meditations, and eventually your broken soul returned to you.

Sometimes I miss being human. You made life fun with colors, nature, our animals, walks, and watching the "funny guys" on TV. And of course, I miss eating and licking Dairy Queen ice cream.

Mom, it warmed my heart when you still smiled at me on your toughest days. Know that when you're having a bad day I'll whisper, "Mom, I love you. I love you."

Before I chose you as my mom, I hung around other families, but I chose you because I already loved you and I knew you would be okay.

In this world I can be omnipresent. It's fun. That first night after I left, I visited you and Dad, and Hayden and Meredith at the same time even though they were in a different room. I watched you clench my quilt. At 4:00 a.m., I gave you the biggest hug and filled the room with love because you were having a nightmare of beeping machines and respiratory treatments. I'm sorry I woke you, but I wanted to erase your terrifying dream.

Most of my energy was with you and Dad for about a week after I reached for the angel's hand. Then I folded through the veil that separates humans from the heavens. Then I learned how to come and go.

Always feel my love and look for signs. Our love is forever, never forget,

Storey

Afterword

The day after Storey's fingertips and mine broke apart, I curled into a fetal position in the passenger's seat of our van and hugged her quilt and stuffed moose while John drove home through a snowstorm. I wondered how I would find joy again, and then I turned my head to the back seat and looked at Hayden, his innocent sparkle intact— a sparkle I lost years ago. My breath deepened. With him and John by my side, I knew I would make it. We would all somehow make it.

The sun dropped behind the mountains at five o'clock. The darkness of winter cut through my frail nerves until I walked into our house. It felt unfamiliar and smelled like a candy store. Dozens of pink flowers dressed each room. In the last few minutes with Storey, I remembered asking her to send me pink flowers.

I searched for Storey and called for Chisel. A smoothie-stained shirt rested in the hamper; a small sock was on the floor of Storey and Hayden's room; her favorite book was next to her bunk bed. A wave of dizziness hit me. I didn't want to forget our *before*. I ran outside and stroked Spirit's lightning bolt. I buried my face in Angel's neck and ran my hand over their hearts, then collapsed at their hooves. Sleeping without Chisel next to my side of the bed was unacceptable. I drove to the Careys' house and listened for Chisel's "I've missed you" squeal.

CHISEL

I heard Mom's footsteps. I was living at a different house for what seemed like forever. It wasn't bad because two cute messy little girls lived there, and I got lots of hugs and extra treats.

"Chisel, where are you? I need you," I heard Mom say.

I didn't move because I was having a staring contest with a string of dried noodles the girls were making.

"Chisel?"

I wanted Mom to run her fingers through my wrinkles, but a crunchy noodle was about to pass by my nose.

Mom sounded different, like night. I wondered if that had something to do with why I was with these girls who made noodle necklaces. You see, she loved me so much I rarely stayed away for long.

Mom sat next to me. I rested my face and feet on her shoulders, and she cried. We were one again. She rolled her hands over my wrinkles and wiped dried dirt from my eyes. All the way home she played with my ears. I sniffed the seat where Storey always sat. I'll miss spooning with her.

Our first morning home, John was up early. He talked about getting a suit. I was paralyzed in bed listening for Storey's giggles. Hayden came bouncing into my room. The landline phone rang. He answered it and said hello a couple of times.

"No one was there, maybe it was a fax," Hayden said, smiling and facing his palm up.

I glanced at the clock. It read 9:40 a.m. Storey took her last breath at 9:40 p.m. I froze. Hayden ran off to make pancakes. I tried to roll out of bed. I knew Storey was with me, and I wanted the tingling of her connection to last forever. The other part of my body felt like it had been beaten up.

The next day our friends and Meredith planned Storey's celebration of life. On January 23rd, 2006, more than 400 people arrived wearing pink. From the podium they looked like a giant, pink flower bouquet. John and I both spoke. In the background Eva Cassidy sang "Somewhere Over the Rainbow." People reached for pink tissue boxes that dotted every table. Afterword, the guests released balloons into a pearlescent pink sunset that hovered over town. I felt Storey's presence and love.

She was happy.

Later when people asked how I was doing I said: "Well at least Storey is having a lot more fun than I am." I didn't know what else to say, and I didn't want to talk.

Eight weeks after we walked out of Primary Children's Hospital, a diagnosis arrived. Our five-and-a-half-year nightmare ended with five words: Neuronal Intranuclear Hyaline Inclusion Disease (NIID). We finally had a fucking name, and as I had known in my gut all along, a muscle biopsy would not have given us those words. The pathologist performing her autopsy recognized the disease. He was from Johns Hopkins University, while there he had seen NIID only once.

The fatal storage disease is diagnosed by the presence of eosinophilic hyaline intranuclear inclusions in neuronal and glial cells (neurons/nerve fibers) and neuronal loss by testing rectal tissue. In simplistic terms—NIID is a protein stored (storage disease) in nerve fibers, which causes havoc. Any part of the nervous system can be affected including central, peripheral, and autonomic systems. This disease comes in all shapes and sizes: infantile, juvenile, and adult. At 2 years old, Storey had the infantile form, the most aggressive. Adult onset can last years and is often misdiagnosed as dementia. This disease is both sporadic—targeting random victims—or familial, which runs in families. The complicated disease was so rare at the time of Storey's death that only thirty people—thirty people in the world—yes, you read that correctly—had been given a NIID diagnosis. There is no treatment, no cure, and presently no hope.

In layman's terms, NIID is a massive rare multisystem neurodegenerative nightmare. It's like an uninvited fucked-up party goer on meth, steroids, and alcohol crashes your party and invites all his toxic friends. They lock everyone inside and destroy all your prized possessions, and burns down your house with everyone in it that you love.

Unfortunately, the list of storage diseases Storey had been tested for at the time wasn't scientifically advanced enough to detect NIID. Except for Dr. Swoboda, the rest of the neurologists I contacted after receiving this news had never heard of NIID.

Four months after Storey passed, Zuzana's daughter, Sara, passed away near her ninth birthday from Batten Disease, a disease similar in presentation to Storey's. It hit close to home. Because of my vulnerability at the time, I didn't attend Sara's service, and that I have regretted.

Six months after Storey died, we bought Hayden a golden retriever. He named her Chauncie in honor of his ball-fetching next-door golden retriever companion, Chauncy, who had moved away.

John's stone business survived the recession and he was able to keep his dedicated employees. The first time I went back to Bikram yoga, a week after we got home, I felt supported and held, like I was in the arms of a large and nurturing grandmother. I have continued with hot yoga to this day.

As a mother who lost a daughter, I survived as best as I could. I got out of bed, fed my family and animals, and was grateful that we had the courage and the legal right as Storey's parents to make the choice to not prolong her suffering (this was a year of scrutiny after the Terri Schiavo political and right-to-life appeals). Had Storey exhibited static symptoms instead of multi-neurodegenerative ones, we would have had to explore other horrific options. Today we might not have as many rights.

A year after Storey passed, I contacted one of the two men who received her corneas. We exchanged letters for years. The recipient always apologized for wanting sight, knowing that a child had to die because only a young cornea could be used. I reassured him that Storey danced from wherever she was, knowing she had given him sight. Her heart valve helped a small child. I dreamed that her heart could have gone to the girl with the rope braid, or to any other child whose parents prayed in the corners of the PICU for a heart. Years later we found Storey's name on the Heart-to-Heart glass donation wall at the Salt Lake City library.

My committed time at my computer to write this book led me to occasionally Google NIID. I cautiously researched, hoping a cause and perhaps a miracle treatment had been found. Research taught me that most diseases are genetically rooted. In semi-simplistic terms, humans have somewhere between 20,000-25,0000 genes, each with sixty-four codons attached. Exchange one codon in a gene with a wrong codon—or missing one—and a mutation is born. Sometimes it is a positive mutation, but when it's a negative mutation it's like those uninvited party goers who lock the doors and starts drinking shots.

When my mother passed away from dementia in 2019, I ordered an autopsy and donated her brain to the Mayo Clinic in Florida, because I wanted to know if she was our familial NIID genetic link. The Mayo Clinic discovered she did not have NIID. But they identified four different types of dementia (another extremely rare combination, and Alzheimer's was not one of them). I know my mom is happy helping science. I wished we could have had John's mother, who lived with Alzheimer's for years, tested for NIID. I fantasized that Storey's disease would lead to discoveries that could help others with NIID or similar neurodegenerative diseases. I created a NIID page on my Facebook account. Fortunately, in eighteen years I only heard from two people diagnosed with NIID. Because of the extreme rarity and no funding for NIID, it won't be researched unless cases become a household name like ALS, and no one wants that to happen.

Unless CRISPR technology becomes as common as chemotherapy, which might take a lifetime, I had to finally let go of the idea that in my life there would be a treatment for NIID or other ultra-rare childhood storage diseases. Medical breakthroughs are never fast enough when your loved one is suffering.

Nine years after Storey passed, Dr. Swoboda and her genetics research team ran Storey's and our banked blood through extensive exome genetic sequencing using the latest technology. The geneticists hoped to identify a pathogenic mutation and/or the gene responsible. Once again, the sequencing failed to identify a specific gene in our familial codes.

Fourteen years after Storey died, once again I Googled NIID and learned other researchers had found a candidate gene (NOTCH2NLC) possibility responsible for NIID. By then Dr. Swoboda was researching other rare diseases and lacked the funding to do it all (she would if she could).

My grief and suffering came in different forms. I had debilitating migraines. It wasn't the smells in the hospital that stuck with me—it was the noises. And when it was time to put Chisel down a few months after she turned twelve, I swore to John I'd never be happy again. But he was right... I am.

Sometimes I have dreams: Storey walks over to me, hugs me and says, "I'm happy." In those dreams I tell everyone she was still alive, that it was all a mistake and that she hadn't really died. Those mornings I felt Storey's presence, and all I wanted to do was put the covers over my head and chase down that dream.

Day after day I got up. I went to yoga. I tossed the ball for our Chauncie. I listened for the red-breasted robins in March, and hummingbirds in May. I joined a writing group and a women's equine therapy group. Chisel, before she died, and Chanucie became therapy dogs. I quilted. I became a certified energy healer. I prayed for Storey's soul and mine at the famous Chimayo Church, New Mexico, where

I left her picture and gathered holy dirt from a pit in the church's dirt floor. I took pictures of horses and had a few photo exhibits. I volunteered at Eagle Mount with the equine and ski program and helped Storey's friends ride and ski. When I sat with my pain at my medicine wheel on my hill, I called White Buffalo Calf Woman for strength and intuition—she always delivered. Hayden and I ate a lot of Dairy Queen and watched *Seinfeld* most nights.

John, Hayden and I traveled. We continued with our summer birthday parties. We talked about Storey often and reminded Hayden what a great brother he was and how much she loved him. On Storey's birthday, July 1st, and anniversary January 10th,— I'd still rather skip—traditionally we took Hayden out of school to go skiing in January, and made Storey's favorite meal: tenderloin, artichokes, and pink cake on both anniversaries. Every Mother's Day—I still hate that day too—we visited Pumice Point in Yellowstone and wrote Storey's name in the lake's crushed obsidian beach sand. And I never stopped looking for signs from her: a single Easter egg floating in the swimming pool months after Easter (she played with those eggs year-round); a random white feather; a hummingbird landing on my finger; every pink and orange sunset.

During meditation the night before Storey's first anniversary, I asked her to show me a sign that she still visits; something obvious, like something breaking. That morning, I woke to the sound of glass shattering in the kitchen. A vase with pink flowers had fallen off the counter. Her sweet love hugged and healed my shattered heart, and I heard her giggle.

And still every single second, I think of Storey.

People told us the first year would be the hardest. It wasn't. John and I agreed that the second year was the hardest because we thought it was going to be easier. I thought people had forgotten Storey and it made me angry. Then, a few months after Chisel died, Storey's horse Angel passed away at 30 years old with me and Spirit by her side. Spirit stayed calm instead of pacing and whinnying for days like the way she did when they were separated. Spirit understood. It's us humans who get side-lined by grief.

Our cats Licorice and Big Dark Cloud eventually passed, as did the remaining guinea pig. Coincidentally, Chauncie started to show physical signs not unlike Storey's movements in the beginning of her decline. I hoped the vet could help, but they didn't know what was wrong with her. Naturally I got back on the healing rollercoaster. Chauncie received acupuncture, then energy healing. She, too, died at 7 years old.

Even though I still research alternative medicine and tried it on my dog, I can feel my body get triggered when I hear someone talking about some new diet that will change their life, or an unorthodox healing method that's going to help them with whatever is going on, because I can see long road ahead. Or I want to laugh when someone says: "Have you ever been to a naturopathic doctor?" (I went to a few after Storey died and I never found a good one.) Or: "Do you know what muscle testing is." Or something like that. I'll carefully give my opinion if asked, but I don't want to crush their hope, I don't want to tell them it's way more complicated, that they have a journey coming.

My fingers began to type weeks after Storey passed. I thought I could write and hold my memoir in my hands in ~~three, ten, fifteen,~~ nineteen years later I was still processing, writing, editing, more editing, and *more* editing. In 2018 I got serious and committed to a book plan. But of course, life happened. I flew to California often to help my ailing mother. In the fall of 2019, I moved her to Bozeman. Three months later, she passed. Then Covid hit (as a germaphobe I'll leave you to imagine how I fared with all that). In November 2021 my father, my cheerleader, and whom I mostly resemble, passed away in Davis, California. I showed up for my parents like they always had for me. Four months later, John's father passed. His mother moved into memory care and later died at ninety. Burying your parents is a painful, expected part of life. Burying your child is not.

Any grieving parent abhors the expression: "Time will heal." We know it's true, but I felt like pulling my hair out whenever I heard it. The truth is, we don't want to live through time. We want to live in the time *before*. Time *after* means we'll have to change, grow, become better people. It's exhausting, it's been done to death. Yet we know the alternative means digging our own grave.

John and I are now forever "Angel Parents." We experience time differently: the before and the after. We are in a club no one wants to join.

"Angel Parents" don't want to buy benches with our kids' names attached. We don't want to write books. We just want our children back. Grieving parents want friends to remember our children and to share favorite memories. We want our friends to let us cry without feeling embarrassed. We don't want to be avoided. We want people to feel the love we miss. Yes, time does heal, because it offers us a door in space to find a new normal, to find ourselves again, to create new memories, to remember the special times of how our loved ones lived, their gifts to us and to the world, not the last sad weeks, days, they were here. Time gives us an opportunity to be present and for us to realize that we have some control over our choices and our future.

Storey often visits me at night. She crawls into my lap and tells me she is okay, that she's happy. In a different dream I'm with Storey, she's about 5 years old and I tell people that she didn't really die, it was all a mistake. I wake and remember the last time we were together; a dull ache follows me around the rest of the day. We know our dead loved ones want us to keep living. We know they want us to be happy. They send us reminders in many forms.

After Storey's celebration of life, her kindergarten teacher sent us a card every year for fifteen years on Storey's anniversary. Those cards meant more to me than all the cards put together the first year. And each Christmas Grandjack and Grandma Valerie bought an angel ornament for Storey's tree (the same tree that was in her hospital room). It warms my heart. However, time never replaces our yearning. We never forget. We never, ever stop thinking about them.

Storey would have turned 26 in 2024. I'm picturing her gorgeous, with long, black wavy hair framing John's blue eyes. She's beyond mature, frighteningly independent with wings that leave a trail to the secrets of unconditional love.

Hayden's years of occupational therapy, neurofeedback, and math tutoring with one of the best teachers, who became a mentor and a friend, Mike P.—thank you, you're a gift. Hayden learned how to channel his ADHD like it's a secret power by solidifying information and numbers through his unique memory bank. And he learned to play the piano well by ear. He gathered unusual facts, like what we ate and wore on a particular day and memorized every line in every *Seinfeld* episode. In collage Hayden started in Algebra 1 his freshman year and chose to retake math classes when he got a C and/or didn't understand the material to his standards. He graduated in the spring of 2023 from Montana State University, with a degree in Math and a minor in Physics. His years of perseverance, passion, and pizza paid off. He still chooses happiness, empathy, and gratefulness despite the loss of his sister at 9 years old.

Meredith's bother Zack, moved to Bozeman in the spring of 2006, and four years later she joined us, then their brother Taylor. And years later, their mother, my sister Cindy, moved here. We have celebrated the turning of seasons, new beginnings and holidays. Meredith and her husband Nate now have three daughters: Mabel, Hadley, and Eloise. As hard as it is for me to not grieve Storey's lost childhood, I treasure watching Meredith's girls show me how their dresses spin in the golden light—there is nothing more precious. The seasons of life continue even though, at times, we thought they had stopped… forever.

On a warm spring day in 2024 I take a break from editing to sit on the steps of our deck to admire Mount Ellis. I hear Storey: "Someday I'm going to climb that mountain," like she said many times. She knows where my favorite white bark pine tree is at the highest point of Mount Ellis. A photo of her is nestled in its roots.

I look away from Mount Ellis to study Spirit and her pasture mate Dun, a retired therapy horse from Eagle Mount. They are lying down, half asleep in the mud, their warm noses rub against the earth. Spirit arrived by some miracle twenty years ago. Her presence lightens my being when loss creeps in. Her short thoroughbred white face looking my direction reminds me of the yin and yang of life. She's eye candy for my soul until it's her time.

MoonPie, my golden retriever puppy, sits next to me on the steps. I wrap my right arm around her. A second later she nibbles my ear then runs off to chase the cat. She's our third golden retriever. She joined us in the middle of a windy Montana winter when I was ready to drink the antidote of puppy breath and to surrender to fresh moments of a changing seasons after the sudden loss of my second golden retriever, CherryPie. That winter I saw more moose on our hill than I had in thirty years. In late spring 2024, a moose ran down our hill followed by her newborn calf—a sight I had never seen out my window. At the beginning of summer an extremely rare white buffalo calf was born in Yellowstone National Park, two hours south of us, for me it was a sigh to share Storey with the world. One door has closes, another opens: the dance of life, the dance of seasons.

MoonPie ignores my call to quit eating fresh horse poop. I climb on Spirit, whose half awake and lie back to look at the clouds. The sun warms my face, I close my eyes and I see Storey smiling.

I'm sorry, *Storey*…

I couldn't save you…

Mom…

you did save me…

I'm still…

here…

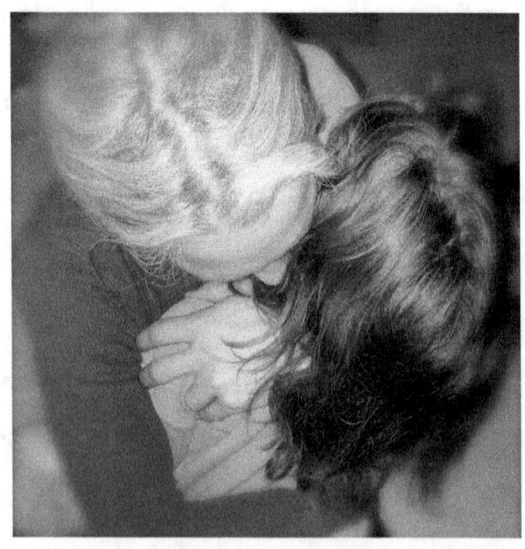

Photo: Hayden.

Acknowledgements

My mother, Pat, needs to be mentioned first. If it wasn't for her overall high IQ and superfluous vocabulary who always corrected my, my sister's grammar, and anyone else's within ear shot, I'd never know the proper way to answer a landline phone: "this is she," when someone asked for me—or the many tenses of lay and lie. Thanks mom, now when I hear someone say, "me and her went…" my nerves jump and I itch to correct them. You always wanted to write a book, it's ironic that I, your dyslexic daughter wrote one. I just wish you could have helped me edit this huge project. It just took me too long. Thanks for introducing me to a world of alternative therapies, I know it helped Storey live longer.

And next my father, who also wrote a book, and whom I inherited dyslexia, and taught me the importance of being organized and to work hard at anything I decided to do. Your and Mom's ceaseless encouragement that I work in Yellowstone during my collage summers, changed my life—of course you were both right! You were my cheerleader during this project. I hope you and Mom have read this book wherever you are. I can sense that both of you are proud of me.

My book team began with a weekly writing group that Karen O, facilitated years ago. Karen, even though I rarely see you now, your encouragement sustained me all these years. I knew during our group readings when I crumbled to tears, that my story definitely needed to be shared with the world. I found a local writing coach, Anika H., who complemented my ability to create a scene well even though I was new to writing, and who inspired me to keep at it, thank you! Cathy C., who helped with developmental editing and pointed out that I needed to revise most of the book. And a deep appreciation to Carter W., your knowledge and suggestions and sincere encouragement to keep with it, did just that. Our Montana-business-handshake is hard to come by these days but it worked for us. Thank you for the many drafts of marked up hard copies with coffee rings. To the online editing/writing business: Reedsy, whose YouTube videos, blogs and classes became my go to for writing information. This is where I found Miles M., a kind, experienced proof editor, and a creative book designer Steve H., who put up with my many changes. I give Reedsy 5-stars plus and recommend them to anyone crazy enough to write a book like this. Reedsy.com, is a must.

My husband John who has supported me and through all my messy hobbies from horses to beekeeping to quilting, etc.. I love you. If I had to go to a job every day I wouldn't have completed this book, because of you I have fulfilled one of my life's most important works. I feel so fortunate that I was able to stay at home with our children. I know that this book is too hard for you to read, I understand. After all the edits, I still have a hard time reading it. John, thanks for putting up with my animals, I know you wouldn't have it any other way. I treasure our lifestyle that you worked hard for and gives us the opportunity to recreate in nature and have animals and allows you to ski powder days.

And of course our Hayden, who always makes me laugh in the hardest of times, you taught me perseverance and how to have a close child/parent relationship. You learned early the gift of a positive outlook on life. It took me years to figure that one out. You were our glue, like you told many people, a big responsibility for someone so young. Hayden phone home, Tai-chicken and *Seinfeld* is on at 6:00.

To our extended families who loved and worried about Storey. And to Valerie who still sends an angel gift for Storey's Christmas tree every year. And my never-ending gratefulness to my niece, Meredith who carried us through the dreadful time in the hospital. Hayden got through that stronger because of your support. You are an amazing, successful, working mother. Busy with this project I've fallen short helping you with your beautiful girls, and I'm sorry. They are too growing fast.

And to my friends, especially Libby, my road walking buddy who read and corrected one of my many drafts and listened to all my nutty ideas. Each step of your loving reassurance helped me more than I can calculate. I love that you came up with the perfect name of this book: Seasons with Storey. To Kathy C., who got me out to hike, bike and ski for the last thirty-eight years. Let's keep at it, time is moving faster. P. S. Chisel loved staying at your house while Storey was in the hospital. To Julie (Dr. Hansen) who became a good friend after Storey died, edited my medical terms, and got me back on my Spirit more than once and showed me how a real Montana cowgirl rides. You helped me expand my stiff comfort zone. How did you know I needed that? I hope our sons remain best friends for life. Of course to Kristin Z., who was with me every step of the way and who was responsible for my purchase of Angel, who birthed Spirit (yes, we got a shelter that fall). I relax every time I see Spirit run down the hill coming home. Who needs a therapist when you have a horse and friends like these?

And to Eagle Mount and all their volunteers who loved Storey and gave her so much, you are my second family. You offered me a purpose during my hard times: helping others in Storey's honor. That taught me to be grateful for every minute and gave me understanding of what I came here to do. A 100% of the proceeds from this book will be donated to Eagle Mount whose mission provides recreation to kids and adults with unique needs and to kids with cancer.

I'm indebted to all my extended friends and yoga family who help me in the years of the *before* and in the *after*. My life is rich knowing you're here when I need any of you even though I have become a recluse these last years working on this project. I'm sure you're all tired of my answer when you ask what I've been doing lately. To a special memory of my dear friend Richard B., who was also writing a book, he encouraged me to keep at it during our rides up the ski lift volunteering with Eagle Mount, and hiking, but who was taken from us too soon by cancer. I miss you! After 19 years (+/-), "it's time to put this book on the shelf," Richard said before he died.

Disinterest, or ADHA comes to mind when I think of all the hobbies I've tried and got bored with, but this one I persevered. I had to do it for you and for me.

To all the doctors, nurses, alternative, and integrative healers I called to help Storey, I'm indebted to all of you knowing you tried your best with your known specialties. Thanks for loving and caring for Storey. You saved me day by day and every one of you helped Storey in your own way. And to all the strangers who stopped me to tell me they were praying for my daughter. Of course I need to acknowledge the show Seinfeld that came to my rescue in a funny way. And to the talented artist and writer, Sylvia Long, who wrote the book: *Hush little baby, don't say a word, Mama's going to show you a hummingbird.* Your book saved us.

I hope this book brought you some laughter through Chisel and gives parents' permission to be proactive and to trust their intuition. This book is also to encourage a parent whose personality is a little more passive to step up and insist on finding out what is needed to support their child. All these crazy things I tried didn't save Storey, but I think they extend her life, and made her spirit want to stay a little longer.

After Storey died a friend said: "Well at least you can skip the guilty stage of grief." But of course I thought of more things I could have tried, more that I could have done, which sounds ridiculous; but that's what a mother's love does.

Storey 5, tossing rocks on the Gallatin River, Chisel keeping guard.
Photo: Grandjack.

Addendum

STOREY'S RX AND SUPPLEMENTAL LIST 2004-2005
(Guided by Dr. Grabe & Dr. Marc)

Morning:

- 250mg Depakote
- 2 teaspoons L-carnitine/Acetyl carnitine
- .3cc of liquid Sinemet (L-dopa/Carbidopa)
- 1 t. MiraLAX
- 125 mcg B-12
- 250mg Vit C
- 1 child's chewable multi-Vit (with 300 mcg Folic Acid)
- 3 drops CELLFOOD

Lunch:

- 250mg Depakote
- .3cc liquid Sinemet
- 50 Co-Q 10 chewable
- 250 mg Vit C
- 500 mcg Biotin chewable
- 1 t. Carnitine
- 4 drops CELLFOOD

Evening:

- 250 mg Depakote
- .3cc Sinemet
- 200 mg Vit-E
- 200 mg calcium
- 100 mg Magnesium Carbonate
- 240 mg Vit-C
- ½ t. fish oil
- 50mg Alpha Lipoic Acid
- 200 mg N-Acetyl Cysteine
- 1 t. Soy Lecithin
- 1 superfood chewable
- 1 chewable probiotic blend
- 1 t. Flax seed oil
- ¼ t. turmeric

DISEASES TESTED ON STOREY
(a few missing)

Hypo-or hyperthyroidism (thyroid function test)

Hypobetalipoproteinemia (lipid panel)

Abetalipoproteinemia (lipid)

Ataxia-Telangiectasia (alpha-fetoprotein, immunoglobulin profile done several times)

Friedreich's ataxia (DNA test, Nerve conduction)

Biotinidase deficiency (biotin level, blood)

Acanthocytosis (lipid panel, Complete cell count)

Hartnup disease and other aminoaciduria's (urine and serum amino acids)

Glutaric aciduria and other organic acidurias (urine)

Refsum's disease (phytanic acid level)

Ataxia with Vitamin E deficiency (Vit E level)

Epstein-Barr Virus infection (mono) (EBV titers)

Prophyria (metabolic urine screen)

Mucopolysaccharidoses (Hurler, Hunter, and Schein syndrome— metabolic urine screen)

Opsoclonus-Myoclonus (due to neuroblastoma) and other paraneoplastic syndromes (urine

HVA and VMA levels and NeoComplete screen for paraneoplastic antibodies)

GM-1 gangliosidosis (cell enzyme screen)

Beta-mannosidosis (cell enzyme screen)

Tay Sachs disease and variants (cell enzyme screen)

Metachromatic leukodystrophy (cell enzyme screen)

Krabbe disease (cell enzyme screen)

Sensory ataxias (Electromyography/Nerve conduction velocity)

Chromosomal abnormalities (chromosome test)

Chronic meningitis/encephalitis (spinal tap)

MELAS (mitochondrial encephalopathy with lactic acidosis and
stroke-like events)

(DNA tests, spinal fluid and arterial lactate levels)

MERRF (myoclonic epilepsy with ragged red fibers) (same as above)

NARP (neuropathy, ataxia, and retinitis pigmentosa) (same as above)

Other mitochondrial disorders (same as above)

Celiac disease (Gluten free diet, not symptomatic)

Batten disease (blood, urine)

Rett syndrome (observation)

Spinal Muscular Atrophy (SMA) and other genetic diseases ruled
out through,

Chorionic Villus Sampling (CVS) genetic tests at 17 weeks of
pregnancy.

Lennox-Gastaut syndrome (EEG and MRI)

Niemann Pick type C (blood test)

IN 2003, WHEN WE WERE RESEARCHING PEDIATRIC NEUROTRANSMITTER DISEASES THEY WERE:

- Tyrosine Hydroxylase Deficiency (TH)
- Aromatic L-Amino Acid Decarboxylase Deficiency (AADC)
- Guanosine Triphosphate Cyclohydrolase I Deficiency (GCH 1 ("Segawa"), GTP Cyclohydrolase, GTPCH)
- Sepiapterin Reductase Deficiency (SR)
- Dopamine Transporter Deficiency (DTDS)
- Succinic Semialdehyde Dehydrogenase (SSADH)
- Dopa Responsive Dystonia (DRD—a treatable disease if that's all that's going on)

     (it's unknown how many there really are as of now)

OTHER DISHEARTENING FACTS ABOUT RARE DISEASES THAT I RECENTLY FOUND GOOGLING.

- There are roughly 10,000 rare diseases, roughly 1 in 10 people in the United States has a rare disease, or 30 million people.
- Each rare disease affects fewer than 200,000 in the United States.
- Rare diseases can be genetic, caused by an infection or allergy, a rare mutation, or the result of some cancers.
- They are often difficult to diagnose and treat than more common diseases.
- On average, it takes 5 years for a rare disease patient to get a diagnosis.
- 95% of rare diseases lack an FDA approved treatment.

SOME RARE DISEASE SITES

Pediatric Neurotransmitter Disease Association (PND)
28 Prescott Place
Old Bethpage, NY 11804
(603)-733-8409
www.pndassociation.org

Dystonia Medical Research Foundation
1 East Wacker Drive, suite 2810
Chicago, IL 60601-1905
(312)755-0198 | (800)-377-3978
www.dystonia-foundation.org

Genetic and Rare Diseases (GARD)
PO Box 8126
Gaithersburg, MD 20898-8126
(301) 251-4925 | (888) 205-2311
www.rarediseases.info.nih.gov/GARD

National Organization for Rare Disorders (NORD)
1900 Crown Colony Dr.
Quincy, MA 02169
(617) 249-7300
www.rarediseases.org

Every Life Foundation for Rare Diseases
1012 14th Street, NW, Suite 500
Washington, DC 20005
(202) 697-RARE (7273)
www.everylifefoundation.org

Things that Kept me Sane

(during and a bit after)

Wrote affirmations on recipe
cards and hid them

Hot yoga

Qigong

Hayden, Storey and I bellowed
"Ommmmmm" from our hill

Meditations: visualized Storey healed

DNA adjustment

Hot springs

Tuesday vanilla lattes

"Doing Candle" before bed

Essential oils

Training Spirit

Read Thich Nhat Hanh

Beaded like a mad woman

Talked to flowers, animals, and trees

Rescue Remedy

Psychics 1, 2, 3, 4, 5…

Sunsets

Scooping horse manure

Neurologists 1, 2, 3, 4, 5, 6, 7, 8…

Dr. Feist

A few cigarettes

School aides: Serena and Melissa

Moose

Ron from the Education Co-op

Summer birthday parties

Big Sky with family

Prayer

Massages

Friends

Energy of White Buffalo Calf Woman

Skied, Hiked, Biked, Ran

Screamed

Read authors from Hay
House Publishing

Weekend workshops

Hot tub

Ate gross green stuff

Girls weekends

Nightly meditations with
Storey visualizing healing
light from the heavens

Seinfeld

Movies: *Toy Story, Spirit,*
Fantasia 2000

PBS kids

Hummingbirds

Chocolate

Walks up the road

Journaling

Sugar

Supplements

Friday night pizza

Eagle Mount

Sitting by the river

Visiting Yellowstone National Park

Thursday's advanced hot yoga

Ran ½ marathon

Volunteering

Watched *The Medium* Monday
    nights while folding laundry

Walks on our hill

Learning energy healing

Not going to the Mayo Clinic

Energy healers 1, 2, 3, 4, 5…

Sessions with Tara

Wine

Smelling horses' noses

Learned Reconnective healing

Creative hobbies

Petting Chisel's wrinkles

Feeding guinea pigs

Memorizing Hayden and
    Storey's smile

Eating dinner together

Family

Local and PND friends

Dairy Queen smiles

The change of seasons

Storey saying: I love you.

Things I Tried to Help Storey

(not in order, and not everything)

Color therapy

Castor oil treatments

Naturopathic medicine

Had key lines adjusted
    on our property

Slept with her head facing north

Sisters of the Light DNA adjustment

Used stander

Swimming at the hot springs
    and with Eagle Mount

"Doing Candle" before bed

Essential oil defused

Walking holding hands

Psychic surgery

Flower essences

Psychics 1, 2, 3, 4, 5…

Watched pink, orange, red sunsets

Neurologists 1, 2, 3, 4, 5, 6, 7, 8…

Blood tests

Played cars with Hayden

School aides Serena and Melissa

Watching wildlife

Gallatin Valley Educational Co-op

Botox in mouth to decrease saliva

Summer birthday parties

Dairy Queen

Prayers

Weeks of antibiotics

Painting watercolors

Hot tub therapy

Medical tests

Eating gross green stuff

PT & OT

Network Chiropractic

Craniosacral therapists 1, 2, 3, 4…

No acupuncture

Muscle testing people with herbs

Lasers

Our nightly meditation
    visualizing healing light
    coming into Storey's body

Seinfeld, Toy Story, Spirit, Fantasia
    and Friday night movies

PBS kids

Horseback riding with Eagle
    Mount and at home

Play-Doh with mom

Gluten free diet

Frozen peas for snack

Compression leggings and gloves

Dairy-free diet

Walking up the road to visit Classy

Low sugar diet

Supplements and medication

Swinging with Hayden

Detox food baths and patches

Eagle Mount therapy

Tossed rocks in the river

Picnics with family

Watched buffalo in Yellowstone
  National Park

Energy healers 1, 2, 3, 4, 5…

No Mayo Clinic

Primary Children's hospital

HANDLE Therapy

Family pets

Sessions with Tara

No Hyperbaric Oxygen Therapy

Ate dinners together

Read favorite books

Walk-about

Dark Cloud looked out for Storey

Spooning with Chisel

Bouncy on ball to music with Mom

Home exercises

Watched hummingbirds with Hayden

Big Sky with family

I love yous, and hugs

Extra Photos

(Just becasue)

John playing with the kids after a summer day.

Storey wearing her AFO's. Photo: John

Walking 15 months.

Storey 18 months, Hayden 3½.
Riding a bus Grandpa made for them.

Storey 2, Hayden 4 on our front porch

Storey 3, Hayden 5

Dagwood. Thanksgiving 2003

Dagwood. Photo: John

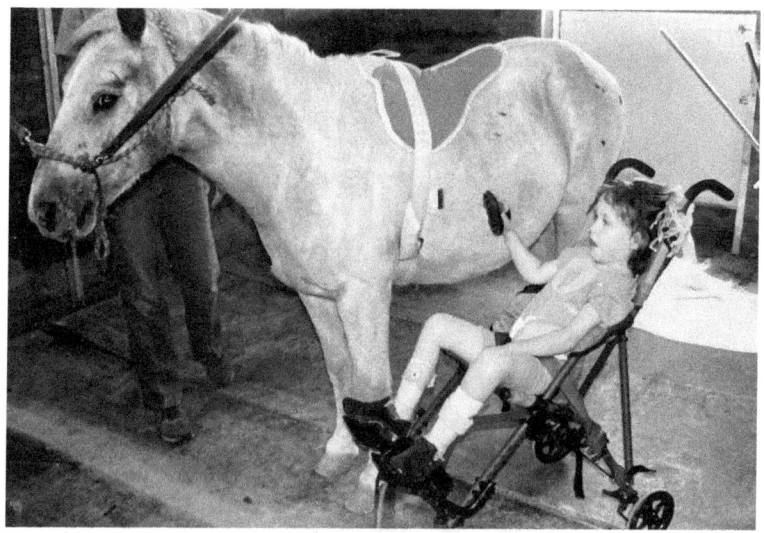

Storey 7, brushing a horse at Eagle Mount
after a ride in her glorified stroller.

On Angel. Photo: John

Back row: Grandjack, Grandpa John, Hayden
Grandma Valerie & Grandma Joan's holding Storey.
Summer of 2000, Storey 2, when she began walking slower.

Grandma Pat, Storey 2 years. Thanksgiving a few
months after we began our healing journey.

Meredith's family: Eloise Wilki, Meredith, Hadley Storey, Nate, Mabel Anne. At one point the girls were all under 3. (10/2024) And the circle of life goes on...

Hayden 9 years old, Chauncy the Golden from
next door visited often. Chisel got used to it.

Pumice point, Yellowstone. We visit this same spot (where the cover
photo of this book was taken) annually on Mother's day. This is the first
Mother's Day without Storey. Photo: John

Julie and I rode our paint horses to see Storey.
Photo: Julie Hansen 6/2014

Grief never ends…but it changes. It's a passage, not a place to stay.
*Grief is not a sign of weakness, nor a lack of faith… **It is the price of Love.***

–AUTHOR UNKNOWN–

Storey Anne Mills

July 1st, 1998–January 10th, 2006

Spirit 20 years, 10/2024.

www.ingramcontent.com/pod-product-compliance
Lightning Source LLC
Chambersburg PA
CBHW061547120626
46550CB00004B/1398